Frank "Home Run" Baker

Frank "Home Run" Baker

Hall of Famer and World Series Hero

BARRY SPARKS

McFarland & Company, Inc., Publishers
Jefferson, North Carolina, and London

Otherwise unattributed photographs in this book are from the author's collection.

LIBRARY OF CONGRESS CATALOGUING-IN-PUBLICATION DATA

Sparks, Barry, 1949–
    Frank "Home Run" Baker : Hall of Famer and World Series hero / Barry Sparks.
        p.   cm.
    Includes bibliographical references and index.

    ISBN 0-7864-2381-1 (softcover : 50# alkaline paper) ∞

    1. Baker, John Franklin, 1886–1963.   2. Baseball players — Biography.
3. Baseball — History.   I. Title.
GV865.B255S63   2006
796.357092 — dc22   2005027666

British Library cataloguing data are available

On the cover: Frank Baker with his 52-ounce black bat (*National Baseball Hall of Fame Library, Cooperstown, N.Y.*)

Manufactured in the United States of America

McFarland & Company, Inc., Publishers
  Box 611, Jefferson, North Carolina 28640
    www.mcfarlandpub.com

To my wife, Ann, a patient listener who
provides constant encouragement

Contents

Preface

Having been born in Cambridge, Maryland, and grown up a baseball fan on the Eastern Shore, I was always aware of Frank "Home Run" Baker, who was born in Trappe, seven miles north of my hometown.

I met Baker in 1960 at a Seaford, Delaware, Little League banquet when I was 11 years old. The 74-year-old Hall of Famer shared the podium with Philadelphia Phillies pitcher Chris Short. They both autographed a baseball for me, and it held a treasured spot on our mantel until one summer day when the neighborhood baseball team lost the ball we were playing with in the field across from my house. The Baker-Short ball extended our afternoon of fun.

I maintained my interest in Baker while attending Towson University. In 1970, as a college junior, I requested an interview with Mrs. Baker to talk about her late husband. She graciously accepted and shared a few stories with me one afternoon. That summer, I had an article published in *Baseball Digest* about the declining popularity of the triple. As a result, Bill Mowbray, sports editor of the *Cambridge Daily Banner*, offered me an opportunity to write a regular column, "Spotlighting the Past." My first column was about Frank "Home Run" Baker.

Over the years, I occasionally thought about writing a book about Baker. The idea was like a burr under my saddle for years, causing discomfort and frustration from time to time. Joining the Society for American Baseball Research (SABR) in 1994 renewed my interest in the Maryland star. Then in 1996, my wife, Ann, gave me a biography of Honus Wagner as a Father's Day present. Reading about the Hall of Fame Pittsburgh Pirates shortstop and the Dead Ball Era rekindled my book idea. But I didn't think I would have time to research and write a book. Sensing my frustration,

1

Ann made it easy for me. She said, "Just do it." Within two months, I was headed to the Reading, Pennsylvania, Library to begin my research.

Writing about a player from the Dead Ball Era (1900–1919) has its challenges. Fans followed their teams and favorite players through daily newspapers because there was no radio or television coverage. Reporters of that era covered the game on the field and seldom strayed from that focus. Player quotes and features were infrequent. I have tried, however, to let the players and managers of the time tell as much of the story as possible by using their quotes whenever available.

Baker, never a colorful player, was shy and felt uncomfortable giving interviews, particularly early in his career. In 1914, the *Easton Star-Democrat* wrote that he was one of the toughest people to interview because "he didn't like to talk about himself and he never said anything bad about anyone." He didn't change over the next 50 years.

While writing this book I have been fortunate in having a computer, access to the Internet, the assistance of a network of extremely knowledgeable SABR members, and a supportive wife.

It's impossible to write a book without some frustrations. But the frustrations I had writing the book pale in comparison to those I had not writing it. There were days, however, when I thought a long magazine article would suffice.

A number of people have helped me along the way. I owe a debt of gratitude to Bill Mowbray, my mentor and role model; Steve Steinberg, Marty Payne and Mark Millikin, three SABR members who took a great interest in my project; Bobby Layton, who helped open the doors to the Baseball Hall of Fame for Baker; the late John Steadman, the late Crawford Foxwell, Bill Tanton, Donnie Davidson, Joe Harring, David Voigt, Alden Mead, Dave Trautman, John Martinsky, John Schoon, Joe Dittmar, Tom Kerrigan, Cyril Morong, Rev. Jerome Romanowski, Kyle Barrett, Arthur Levine, Dave Smith and the volunteers at Retrosheet (www.retrosheet.org), SABR, staff members at Martin Memorial Library in York, York College of Pennsylvania Library, Talbot County Library and the Maryland Room, Delaware County Historical Society, the National Baseball Hall of Fame Library, the Pennsylvania State Library, and Towson University's Albert S. Cook Library.

I have used the seventh edition of *Total Baseball* as the source for statistics and spellings of players' names. When newspaper game accounts differed, I tried to stick with the version reported by the majority of papers.

Whatever shortcomings this book may have, I am glad to have played a role in giving one of baseball's greatest players his due.

Barry Sparks
Fall 2005, York, Pennsylvania

ONE

From Trappe to Philadelphia

From the age of 10, Frank Baker dreamed of being a professional baseball player. As he worked on his father's farm in Trappe on the Eastern Shore of Maryland, he envisioned wearing a uniform and playing before large crowds of cheering fans. He dreamed of being a hero.[1]

It wasn't that he disliked farm life. He enjoyed his chores, feeding chickens, tending livestock and helping to harvest wheat and other crops. Farming was hard work, but it was rewarding. Farming was in his blood. His relatives had farmed land in Talbot County since before the Revolutionary War, and he would carry on the tradition.

Farming, however, wasn't as exciting as baseball. There was nothing quite like attending a Trappe baseball game on Saturday. Most of the town's 300 residents looked forward to it. They talked about the game for days before it happened and for days afterward. Many of them attended to root for family members or neighbors as they battled teams from other nearby towns such as Oxford, St. Michaels and Easton. A town's pride was reflected in its baseball team. Having a good baseball team was important and the best players were greatly admired.

Competition among town teams on the Eastern Shore was so intense they often recruited semiprofessional players. Washington College in Chestertown, founded in 1782 and located approximately 40 miles northeast of Trappe, was a hotbed of baseball. It attracted some of the most talented players from Maryland and Delaware. Many of those players joined town teams after the college season ended. Other players from metropolitan areas such as Baltimore, Philadelphia and Wilmington supplemented their income by playing for town teams. Independent teams in larger cities had long been paying their players and town teams on the Eastern Shore were often willing to do the same.

In the late 1890s, baseball's popularity on the Eastern Shore was booming due to a thriving economy and a much improved transportation system. By this time, most of the towns in the region were connected by the Pennsylvania Railroad, and steamships served the towns along the Chesapeake Bay. Eastern Shore teams from Trappe, Easton, St. Michaels, and Chestertown regularly employed existing railroad lines, or hired tugs with a sloop of hundreds of their fans in tow. Teams and their fans arrived from Baltimore on charters. Because a trip to a neighboring town was long and costly, the visiting club was usually treated to at least one meal, a tour of the town, speeches, a parade, or entertained privately in the homes of their hosts.

Playing for a town team was a logical starting point for any young man hoping to be a professional baseball player. Competition was so intense that many teams required aspiring players to submit resumes. By 1908, Cambridge was receiving hundreds of applications a year for less than 15 positions. Eastern Shore teams also attracted former major league players, who even though they were past their prime were much sought after and well paid for their services. The area was well known for its high-quality baseball. Major league teams from Washington, Baltimore, New York and Philadelphia were keenly aware of the baseball talent on the peninsula. From 1892 to 1921, approximately 50 major leaguers played on Eastern Shore teams.

Attendance at games among Eastern Shore teams often matched or surpassed the host town's population. Baseball fervor was deeply rooted on the Eastern Shore. Baseball, played by soldiers in the Civil War, was introduced to Talbot County in 1866 and one year later Trappe, Easton and St. Michaels had organized teams. According to a local newspaper account in 1887, "carpenters dropped their tools, merchants left their counters, and professional men forsook their office for the baseball field."[2]

In 1896, 10-year-old Frank Baker had undoubtedly heard adults talk about the exploits of the Baltimore Orioles, who won their third consecutive National League pennant that year. The exciting play of John McGraw, Wee Willie Keeler, Steve Brodie, Joe Kelley, and Hughie Jennings captured the attention of baseball fans. Baker's inspiration, however, came from watching town teams play. When he got a break from his farm chores, Frank and his brother Norman, who was five years older, played baseball wherever they could. They played together for Trappe on an old farm outside of town. Even in the winter when snow was on the ground, Frank, his brother and his father would be out playing baseball. The father would field, Norman would pitch and Frank would hit.

Trappe resident W.W. Seymour recalled Frank's "unbelievable running catches" as an outfielder and Helen Berry, a Baker classmate, mentioned a home run he once hit which went "so far into the cornfield that nobody found it that day."[3]

But it was Norman, nicknamed Patsy, who attracted the most attention. As a pitcher, he overpowered hitters with an impressive fastball and fooled them with a curve ball. Some fans thought he was good enough to play in the major leagues, but it isn't clear whether this was the case. He did travel to Philadelphia for a tryout with the Athletics, but his dislike of the city discouraged him from pursuing a baseball career. He preferred life on the farm and in a small town.

Baker attended a one-room school next to the Methodist church in Trappe, which was incorporated in 1856. The town derived its name from a band of Trappist monks who established a monastery in a farmhouse just beyond the town. They had come from LaTrappe, France, and were part of a colony of Trappists who had come to Maryland through the nearby seaport town of Oxford.

Classmate Helen Berry recalled Baker: "He came in the fall after the farm work was finished. He was a rather clumsy boy ... so dark he seemed almost sun-baked, with thick black lashes and dirty hands." What she remembered best, however, was the "typical Baker grin, so good natured and sympathetic that it was consoling. Frank was always the one to sharpen the slate pencils, turn the jumping rope, climb the mulberry tree and throw down the mulberries to the girls who couldn't climb; very quiet and easy going, but a great borrower when it came to slate rags and sponges."[4]

One of the students' favorite pastimes was playing baseball on the school grounds. Berry recalled that Frank was always willing to help the girls, showing them how to hit the ball and assisting them in their swings. They used a home-made ball consisting of a dozen kinds of string covered with a roughly fitted leather jacket.

John Franklin Baker was born on March 13, 1886, to John Adams Baker and Mary Catherine Fitzhugh on the family farm just south of Trappe, Maryland, where his father, grandfather and great grandfather had lived. He was the sixth generation of Bakers to live in Trappe. A large English family, some of the early Bakers went to Virginia, others settled in Baltimore and one in Texas. But most of the Bakers settled in Maryland. Catherine Fitzhugh's family was Scottish and came from Virginia. They were said to be related to Robert E. Lee.

The Eastern Shore appealed to the English, Scots, and Welsh for a number of reasons. The land is flat and its low shoreline provides countless creeks, coves, and tidal rivers. The land was easy to clear and cultivate and its many waterways and moderate tides allowed English vessels to sail within a few hundred feet of plantation wharves. Loading and unloading of ships was a simple process. With easily available water transportation, a farming economy thrived.

The tidal water which virtually surrounds Talbot County played a significant role in its development. Talbot County is 477 square miles, 269 square miles of land and 208 square miles of water. It has 602 miles of tidal shoreline, supposedly more than any other county in America. Nowhere else in America does earth and salt water meet in so small an area over so many miles of tidal shoreline. The Wye River and its branches on the north, the Miles and Tred Avon bisecting the center, and the Choptank and Tuckahoe on the south and east come close to making Talbot County an island, so that no place within its borders is more than three miles from the tidewater.[5]

Captain William Mitchell was Talbot County's first recorded landowner in 1649. To Mitchell and the rest of the seventeenth century settlers, tobacco was king. It was the only crop they could produce and sell for cash. The success of their crop was paramount for they counted on it to buy whatever goods they needed from Britain. Growing tobacco was hard work for every member of the family and it quickly depleted the soil.

Tobacco farmers, however, seldom had to worry about putting food on the table because the Eastern Shore and Talbot County offered an abundance of wildlife. White-tail deer, wild turkeys, wild pigeons and waterfowl were plentiful. In the 1640s, Robert Evelyn wrote of seeing a flock of ducks which covered a mile in flight.[6]

Nearly 200 miles long, the Chesapeake Bay has provided a bountiful harvest of clams, crabs, and oysters for hundreds of years. The bay dominates the Eastern Shore. It runs almost to the northern border of Maryland and divides the region from the main part of the state. It is the nation's largest estuary, a place where salt water from the ocean meets fresh water from rivers. It is fed by 48 major rivers and drains a 64,000-square-mile basin.

Native Americans hunted Eastern Shore wildlife and harvested seafood from the Chesapeake Bay, which was created at the end of the Ice Age some 12,000 to 18,000 years ago, long before the arrival of European settlers. They built their villages along shores were oysters were plentiful, counted on snapping turtles and diamond back terrapins for both food and their shells, and enjoyed crabbing. They had great respect for the

Chesapeake Bay, calling it Great Waters, Mother of Waters, and Great Shellfish Bay at various times.

The Chesapeake Bay and tidal water have long influenced the lives of those in the region. Baker was a quintessential Eastern Shoreman, proud of his heritage and shaped by the environment. He grew up on a farm and developed a strong work ethic, physical strength, and an appreciation for nature. He also developed a lifelong love for the outdoors, particularly hunting and fishing. He became known as one of the best duck hunters on the Eastern Shore.

James Michener, author of *Chesapeake*, wrote that the golden age of the Eastern Shore occurred from 1880 to 1920 "when the rest of the nation allowed the marshy counties to sleep undisturbed."[7]

After he stopped attending school, Baker clerked in a combination grocery store and butcher shop, owned by several family members. He always looked forward to Saturday nights because that's when just about everybody in the Trappe area came into the store. Trappe was the shopping hub for local farmers who were well known for their peaches and cantaloupes. On Saturday nights the town was so crowded it was difficult to walk down the streets, which were paved with oyster shells. Trappe provided almost anything a farmer and his family needed. There was a farm machinery outlet, a general merchandise store, three drug stores, a butcher shop and grocery, a jeweler, a stove and tin shop, a millinery store, bicycle and clock shops, and a sawmill. The town's six churches hosted social activities such as suppers, strawberry festivals, fairs, and sewing bees.

Baker followed in his older brother's footsteps and pitched for Trappe's high school team. Preston Day, owner of the local sawmill, was impressed with the youngster and alerted 20-year-old Charles "Buck" Herzog, manager of the team in Ridgely that wanted to make a name for itself. Ridgely was a small Caroline County railroad and food processing town of less than 1,000 people 20 miles northeast of Trappe. Day was the brother of Herzog's father-in-law. In 1905, Herzog signed the 19-year-old for $5 a week plus board. Baker arrived in Ridgely, carrying his clothes in an old telescope valise, and introduced himself to Herzog, who was sitting on the veranda of the Kranz Hotel, the town's only hotel. Although he could pitch and play the outfield, Herzog didn't need another pitcher or outfielder. He was most interested in Baker's hitting ability. Early in the season, the team's starting third baseman was injured and the shortstop left the team. Herzog moved Baker to third base, where he played the rest of the season.

Years later, Herzog recalled, "Baker couldn't pitch and he couldn't

The 1905 Pocomoke, Maryland, Baseball Club dressed up for this formal photograph. Baker, 19, right in the front row, played for both Pocomoke and Ridgely in 1905 as did Simon Nicholls, second from left, second row.

play outfield. So I brought him to play third base and I played shortstop. Baker wasn't an ideal infielder at any point for Ridgely, but he could everlasting hit."[8]

Baker spent the summer living at a boarding house, playing baseball, and doing odd jobs to earn more money. Herzog once dragged Baker and his teammates to his future father-in-law's farm to pick strawberries before sunrise. They picked until it was time to return to Ridgely to play a doubleheader on Memorial Day.

Baker was forever indebted to Herzog, who was one of his biggest fans and boosters, and they became lifelong friends. After reaching the major leagues, Baker said, "What I am in baseball I owe in large part to Charlie Herzog, who helped me through my early career. Although he isn't much older than I am, he was always fatherly in his attitude toward me. I must have been a pretty poor player when I got that job with the Ridgely team in 1905, but Charlie was patient with me. Instead of panning me for my blunders, he spent much of his time working with me. Charlie always plugged for me as a player and his plugging finally landed me in the big show."[9]

A native of Baltimore, Herzog toured the Eastern Shore with the Baltimore Atlantics, a semiprofessional team, and was offered a contract for $75 a month to manage and play for Ridgely. He put together an impressive team. Ridgely's 1905 team was one of the best on the Eastern Shore. It was so rich with talent that the entire infield went on to play in the major leagues. The infield featured 19-year-old Bill Kellogg at first base, Herzog at second, 23-year-old Simon Nicholls at shortstop and Baker at third. Nicholls, a teammate of Herzog's at Maryland State College, which later became the University of Maryland, followed him to Ridgely. Later in the season, Nicholls and Baker also played for the Pocomoke, Maryland, team.

Nicholls, who had appeared in two games with the 1903 Detroit Tigers, played 12 games with the Philadelphia Athletics in 1906. The following year, he hit .302 in 124 games, playing mostly at shortstop. His future with the club dimmed in 1908 as his average dropped to .216. In 1909, he was limited to 21 games, hitting .211. His major league career ended in 1910 with Cleveland, where he played three games before signing with Jack Dunn to captain the Baltimore Orioles in the Eastern League. He died the following year at age 29 from typhoid fever. Kellogg finally made the major leagues when he was 30 years old. He played 71 games, mainly at first base, for the 1914 Cincinnati Reds, managed by Herzog.

It was Herzog and Baker, however, who made names for themselves in the major leagues. Both played 13 seasons. Herzog played in 1,493 games, spanning from 1908 to 1920, and four World Series, while Baker appeared in 1,575 games and six World Series.

Their baseball careers intersected a number of times after 1905. They both played for Sparrows Point in Baltimore in 1906 before Baker returned to the Eastern Shore to play for Cambridge, seven miles south of Trappe, later in the season. In 1907, Herzog played with the Pennsylvania cities York and Reading in the Tri-State League. Baker continued to play for Cambridge against small town teams such as Delmar, Easton, East New Market, Hurlock and St. Michaels. Details of the games are sketchy, few names are mentioned in the Cambridge *Daily Banner* game accounts and there's rarely a box score. A box score from August 10, however, showed Baker playing third base and batting cleanup. Cambridge had a talented team as evidenced by its sweep of a doubleheader from Sparrows Point, considered the strongest amateur team in Baltimore, to end the season. On September 5, Cambridge, without Baker, played B & O Railroad

The 1907 Cambridge, Maryland, Baseball Club was considered one of the most talented teams in the state. Baker, standing fourth from the left, was a 21-year-old third baseman on the team. While playing for Cambridge, he dated 19-year-old Ottilie Tschantre, a Swiss jeweler's daughter whom he later married.

from Baltimore for the unofficial state championship and split a double-header.

While playing for Cambridge, Baker dated a Swiss jeweler's daughter, 19-year-old Ottilie Tschantre. During their courtship, he frequently went to Kirby's Wharf and rowed across the two-mile wide Choptank River to visit her in Dorchester County. She later moved to California and he kept in touch with her. They were married on November 12, 1909, after his second season in the major leagues.

In mid–September, Baker received a tryout with the Baltimore Orioles in the Eastern League after attracting the attention of one of the scouts for New York Giants manager John McGraw while playing for Sparrows Point. He made his Eastern League debut as a pinch hitter in the ninth inning of the second game of a doubleheader between Baltimore and Rochester at Oriole Park on September 14. He failed to hit safely as the Orioles lost 3–2. Jack Dunn, in his first year at manager of the Baltimore club, started Baker at third base against Buffalo on September 16. Undoubtedly nervous, he failed to get a hit in three at bats, made four assists and committed one error. He still impressed the *Baltimore Sun* reporter covering the game who wrote that Baker's appearance was the feature of the game. He concluded that Baker's showing was "as a whole favorable to the judges of a young ball player."[10]

Baker did not play the following day, but started in left field on September 18 against Buffalo. Although he hadn't played outfield in a long time, he was credited with saving the game with a magnificent catch of a long fly in the sixth inning with two outs and a runner on second. The catch was the highlight of the game and the crowd gave him an ovation. Baker also collected a hit. His performance led the Baltimore reporter to write, "Baker has the makings of a good player and manager Dunn says he will make good."[11]

Baker played left field in both games of the September 20 double-header against Buffalo. He registered one hit in seven trips, made four putouts, one assist, and one error. In five games with the Orioles, Baker made one appearance as a pinch hitter and played one game at third base and three games in left field. He batted .133, going 2-for-15 in the brief tryout.

Dunn made one of his biggest errors in judgment when he failed to sign Baker, saying he was clumsy, awkward and couldn't hit. Although many people described him as awkward in the field, few ever said he couldn't hit. It was one of the few times that Dunn, who later discovered Babe Ruth and led the Orioles to seven consecutive International League pennants, ever misjudged talent. Baker, who seemingly impressed the

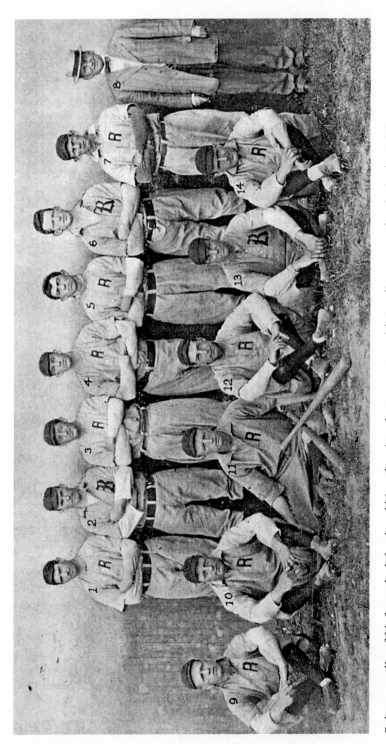

Baker, standing fifth from the left, played his only minor league season with Reading, Pennsylvania, in the Tri-State League in 1908. He finished the season batting .299, mainly as a leadoff hitter. Connie Mack of the Athletics purchased him for $500 at the end of the season. COURTESY OF JOE HARRING.

Baltimore reporters covering the team, said he didn't sign with the Orioles because he and Dunn couldn't agree on contract terms. He later turned down an offer to play in the Texas League.

His big break came after the 1907 season, when Herzog, who had played third base for Reading in the Tri-State League, recommended him as a replacement. Dan Brouthers, a former teammate of New York Giants manager John McGraw, had noticed Herzog while he was playing for the York team in 1907 before the club transferred to Reading. The Giants invited Herzog to a tryout and he made the roster as a utility player in 1908.

Baker, 22, showed he was serious about making baseball a career by moving to Reading. He had never played baseball so far from his home. He reported in early April to Reading manager Tom "Red" Owens, who had played second base briefly in the National League. It didn't take long for Baker, who was referred to as "Freddie" instead of "Frank" for the entire season by his teammates and the *Reading Eagle*, to make an impression on fans and sportswriters.

In an April exhibition game against the Philadelphia Giants, a Negro team, he leaped into the air and snared a line drive that looked like a sure single. It led the *Reading Eagle* to write, "Baker promises to be a capable successor to Herzog."[12] He had another great day in the field the following game, despite two errors. He cut off several base hits and both of his misplays were difficult chances. In a 7–0 exhibition win over Wilkes-Barre, Baker hit one of the longest home runs seen in Reading.

Baker had already created a buzz by the time the season opened on April 24. He collected nine hits during the first week and was considered the "find" of the Tri-State League. His fast start, however, didn't translate into wins for Reading. On May 9, the club was 3–8 and in last place in the eight-team league.

By the end of June, Baker was clearly a star in the Tri-State League and had attracted the attention of several major league clubs. Cincinnati scout Lewis Hellbrunner and Ralph "Socks" Seybold, a veteran outfielder in his last season with the Athletics, traveled to Reading to watch Baker and were impressed. In its glowing late June assessment of the third baseman the *Reading Eagle* wrote, "There are few faster base runners in the league.... The big fellow [Baker stood five-foot-eleven and weighed about 165 pounds, but he was muscular, strong and one of the best built players in the league] is a virtual ground eater at third. There are few drives that get past him. As a bunter, he has few equals. All in all, he has the qualifications to go toward making him a successful major leaguer. It would be no surprise to see him with a big league club next year."[13]

Baker was one of the youngest and most popular players in the league. His good looks and rugged physique made him a favorite with female fans as well as the males. He always sported a deep, pecan-colored tan which accented his fine crop of black hair and dark, bushy eyebrows which nearly connected. His smooth, boyish face was framed by a pair of larger than average ears. His powerful forearms and broad shoulders were evident every time he swung a bat. His hands were large and as strong as vises. With wide hips, heavy thighs and thick calves, Baker carried most of his weight below his waist. His pear-shaped body and bowed legs made him look slower and less athletic than he was. One writer once described him as "walking like a soft-shell crab."[14]

He was quiet, shy, gentlemanly and polite. Modest and backward like the storybook version of the farm boy he was, he appeared embarrassed when interviewed. He didn't like to talk about himself, didn't gossip about others, and never said anything bad about anyone. He didn't smoke, drink, or curse. He didn't smile much, but when he did, it could light up a room.

Although Reading had gotten off to a slow start and struggled, it continued to make roster moves throughout the summer, upgrading its talent. While Reading's fortunes were improving by the beginning of August, Connie Mack's Athletics were clearly out of the American League race. The club was 12 games behind first-place Detroit at the end of July. Mack decided to experiment with younger players the remainder of the season with an eye toward developing a stronger team for 1909. In late September, Mack sent little-used left fielder Frank Shaughnessy to Reading. Part of the deal with Reading's owner/manager Jacob Weitzel, who had replaced Owens at the helm, was that Mack could purchase Baker at the end of the season for $500. Shaughnessy roomed with Baker for the remainder of the season and later became president of the International League. He played an instrumental role in Baker's life nearly 50 years later.

From mid–July to the end of August, Reading moved from seventh place to fourth. With newfound confidence, the club issued a challenge that it could beat any other team in the Tri-State League in the best-of-three, five- or eight-game series. Reading owner Weitzel offered to put up $500. Reading finished the season in mid–September in fourth place behind Williamsport, Harrisburg and Lancaster. Reading's confidence was boosted because it had won the season series against Williamsport and Harrisburg and split the series against Lancaster.

Lancaster was the first team to accept Reading's challenge. They agreed to play a five-game series, two in Lancaster and three in Reading. Each team posted a $500 forfeit fee with E.J. Coyle, sports editor of the *Reading Eagle*. The winners would earn 60 percent of the receipts and the losers 40 percent. The winners would also split $1,000 wagered by the owners of the teams.

Mack had notified Baker to report to the Athletics at the conclusion of the Tri-State season but Baker wanted to stay with Reading until after the Lancaster series. He asked Harry Barton, who was handling the affairs of the Reading team, to write Mack and request permission for him to delay reporting to the Athletics. Mack sent a telegram to Barton, reading: "Baker can remain with your team until after the series with Lancaster. Want him to report to me September 23 in Detroit. Wish you luck in the series."[15]

Baker finished his first minor league season hitting .299, mainly as the lead-off batter. One of only seven players to play the entire season with Reading, he had distinguished himself in every category and had earned a trip to the major leagues.

The Lancaster-Reading postseason series generated tremendous interest in both towns, located only 25 miles apart. There was heavy betting and record crowds were expected. The rivalry was so intense that Harry Coveleski, Lancaster's best pitcher, requested and received permission from Philadelphia Phillies manager Billy Murray to stay with the club until the end of the series. The six-foot southpaw hailed from the Pennsylvania coal-mining town of Shamokin and was the older brother of future Hall of Fame pitcher Stanley Coveleski. He got the nod to start the series on September 14. Coveleski, who had appeared in four games for the Phillies in 1907, dominated Reading as he tossed a two-hitter en route to a 3–1 win before approximately 2,000 fans. Lancaster scored two runs in the first inning and that's all it needed. Coveleski flashed the form that earned him the nickname of "The Giant Killer" later in the month when he joined the Phillies' staff. He beat the pennant-seeking New York Giants three times in five days, including Christy Mathewson once. The Giants finished one game behind the first-place Chicago Cubs.

Reading won Game 2 10–5, behind pitcher Jack Emerson. Baker batted lead-off and recorded a single, but committed two errors. With the series even, Reading reversed the outcome on Coveleski in Game 3, beating him 3–1 while collecting nine hits. The series moved to Reading with a doubleheader scheduled on Saturday. Lancaster forced a fifth and deciding game with a 12–2 romp in the opener as Reading committed nine errors.

In the series-deciding Game 5, the score was tied 2–2 in the bottom of the tenth. Reading's George Boice flied out to start the inning. As Baker picked up his bat, captain and second baseman Curt Weigand said, "See how far you can drive the ball, Fred." Baker smiled and walked confidently to the batter's box as the crowd of 3,000 fans cheered wildly. It was getting dark and it looked as if the game might be called for darkness at the end of the inning. The crowd yelled, "Hit it out, Fred." "Smack a three-base hit." "End the game, Fred."[16]

Baker didn't waste any time. He slugged the first pitch from former Phillies right-hander Walter Moser between right and center field. It was a terrific smash that sent the Lancaster outfielders chasing after the ball as fast as they could. The speedy Baker was approaching third base before they touched the ball. It was obvious they had no chance to catch him at the plate. Enthusiastic fans rushed onto the field and half the Reading players ran with Baker from third base to home. After he crossed the plate, he was mobbed by excited fans, many of whom had won big bets on the game. They carried him off the field on their shoulders. It was a fantastic finish to his first minor league season.

After the series, Baker boarded the train and reported to the Athletics in Chicago on September 20. He went to the Lexington Hotel where the A's were staying and inquired where he could find Connie Mack. Upon finding him in the dining room, he said, "Well, here I am." Mack looked at him and replied, "I see you are."[17]

Baker stepped into "one of the most tumultuous, fascinating, controversial and exciting baseball seasons ever."[18] The season was coming down to a situation where every game was critical. Only one game separated Cleveland, Detroit, and Chicago in the standings in what would be one of the tightest pennant races in baseball history.

His timing to become Mack's next regular third baseman was perfect. Athletics third baseman, 38-year-old Jimmy Collins, was nearing the end of his career. Mack had acquired the aging veteran, who was considered to be the game's greatest third baseman during his playing days, from the Boston Red Sox in July 1907. Collins had revolutionized how to play third base by rushing in to scoop up bunts and dribblers barehanded and firing to first in a single motion. He was also the first third baseman to chase short flies down the left field line. His best days, however, were clearly behind him. After hitting .278 in 1907, he fell to .217 in 1908. He was the first third baseman inducted into the Baseball Hall of Fame, gaining membership in 1945.

Baker's conversion to a third baseman by Buck Herzog at Ridgley was a stroke of luck for the Trappe star. Although he had played the outfield and pitched before playing for Ridgely, he didn't like either of those two positions. He felt there wasn't enough action in the outfield and the pitcher received too much criticism when a team lost. He believed third base was the best position to play for several reasons. "It may not be the hardest or the most important position, but it certainly gives you a chance to keep in the thick of the fight. A third baseman has to be on his toes all the time. That is one of the main reasons why I like to play there. You never know what to expect from one moment to another. It is this uncertainty that appeals to me," he said.[19]

When Baker joined the Athletics, he was reunited with Ridgely teammate Simon Nicholls, who was Mack's starting shortstop. He entered the lineup batting third on September 21. The first pitcher he faced was Chicago's Big Ed Walsh, a six-foot-one, right-handed spitballer and future Hall of Famer, en route to an astounding 40–15 record. Baker was excited about playing in the major leagues, but less enthused about having to break in against the most dominating pitcher in the American League. Walsh held the Athletics hitless for six innings as he posted a 2–0 win. In the ninth, a nervous Baker laced a single to right field off of Walsh for his first major league hit. He had always heard that getting your first major league hit was the hardest and he was happy to have it under his belt. In the field, he recorded two putouts and four assists.

The following day, he singled home a run-off starter Frank Smith in the first inning before the game was called in the bottom of the inning. Smith got the call the following day and the White Sox beat the Athletics, 3–2, in 10 innings. Baker went 2-for-4, delivering doubles in the sixth and eighth innings. He also scored a run and drove in a run.

Although the Athletics were hopelessly out of the pennant race, every game was important for their opponents. Consequently, a playoff atmosphere existed when the team arrived in Detroit for five games. He singled in the first inning as the Tigers and A's tied 4–4 after 10 innings and the game was called for darkness. His three-game hit streak was snapped the following day as the Tigers swept a doubleheader. Eddie Summers pitched both games for Detroit, surrendering six hits in the opener and only two in the second game. Baker went hitless in the opener, but collected one of the Athletics' two hits in the second game.

The A's were the worst hitting team in the American League and their offensive futility showed down the stretch. On September 26, the Tigers' Wild Bill Donovan held Mack's men to just three hits in the first eight innings before forging a 3–2 victory. The following day, Detroit regained the lead in the pennant race with a 5–2 win before more than 12,500 fans at Bennett Park, the largest crowd Baker had ever played before. On September 28, Detroit, Cleveland, and Chicago were still separated by less than one game.

The A's moved on to Cleveland where they played the third team that was immersed in the thick of the pennant race. Just as in Chicago and

Detroit, the Athletics offered little resistance. Unable to play the spoiler, the A's lost a doubleheader to Cleveland and again the following day, stretching their losing streak to nine games. The Athletics finished September with a 7–23 record. Baker watched the Cleveland series from the bench as Mack played 25-year-old Frank Manush at third. Manush offered little competition to Baker as he hit .156 in his 23-game tryout.

Baker was back in the lineup when the A's traveled to Boston. Although the Athletics lost, he went 2-for-4 and hit a double that almost went over the Huntington Avenue Baseball Grounds fence. The following day, October 1, the Red Sox beat the Athletics again. Baker started the game at third and went hitless in one at bat before he was replaced by Manush. Baker's late-season tryout was over. In nine games, he collected nine hits in 31 at bats, hitting .290

Philadelphia ended the season in sixth place, 22 games behind first-place Detroit. The Tigers finished one-half game ahead of Cleveland and one and a half games ahead of Chicago. Baker had impressed Mack in his brief tryout and set the stage for spring training when he would try to earn a starting position.

TWO

Rookie Season

The winter of 1908 was unlike any Frank Baker had experienced. He was now a major league baseball player and family members, friends and fans in the many small Eastern Shore towns where he had played were interested in knowing about his experiences. He had traveled to Chicago, Detroit, Cleveland and Boston, cities where most Eastern Shoremen had never been. He had batted against Ed Walsh, Wild Bill Donovan, and Eddie Cicotte, pitchers most fans had only read about but never seen. He had played against batting champions Ty Cobb of Detroit and Nap Lajoie of Cleveland and had been a teammate of Eddie Plank, Chief Bender, and Harry Davis, participants in the 1905 World Series. He had taken the field in front of 12,500 screaming fans in Detroit's Bennett Park.

Despite the interest of others, Baker was uncomfortable talking about his experiences. He never discussed them, unless he was asked. And then, he would politely give a brief answer and modestly downplay his achievements. People noticed that playing for the Athletics hadn't changed him. He was still the same Frank Baker they knew when he was trying to help the Trappe baseball team win games and they liked that.

While he was proud of his brief stint with the Athletics, Baker knew it didn't guarantee him a position with the club in 1909. He was counting on his hitting ability to earn a spot on Mack's roster. Pitchers dominated the game and solid hitters were at a premium. Both leagues combined for a .239 average during the 1908 season, a mark of futility that stood until 1968. The American League earned run average was 2.39. Hitting a soft, sometimes lopsided and discolored ball was challenging. Every run was important as scores were typically 1–0, 2–1, or 3–2. Hitters choked up on

Baker's good looks and rugged physique made him popular with female as well as male fans. He always sported a deep, pecan-colored tan. He grew up on a farm and considered himself a farmer first and a baseball player second. He developed a strong work ethic, physical strength, and an appreciation of nature. Baker was quiet, shy, gentlemanly and polite. He didn't smoke, drink or curse.

NATIONAL BASEBALL HALL OF FAME LIBRARY, COOPERSTOWN, NY.

their bats and tried to knock the ball on the ground through the infield or poke it on a line drive over the infielders' heads. Hitters focused on bat control and making contact. "Wee Willie" Keeler, a diminutive star outfielder for the National League Baltimore Orioles in the late 1890s and a future Hall of Famer, summed up the approach with his "hit 'em where they ain't" philosophy. Advancing runners by bunting, employing the hit-and-run, daring base running and stealing bases were the keys to scoring runs. These methods were part of what was known as "inside baseball." Although conditions would change somewhat over the next 10 years or so, the era prior to 1920 was known as the Dead Ball Era.

Baker hadn't made much money in his two weeks with Philadelphia, but the potential existed for him to significantly improve his finances. The average major league player in 1909 earned slightly less than $2,500, while rookies drew from $1,500 to $2,500. Honus Wagner of the Pittsburgh Pirates was the highest paid player with a salary of $12,000. Nap Lajoie of Cleveland topped the American League players with a salary of $7,500. The average major league player earned far more than the regular working man. The average steelworker made $700 a year, a typical worker in manufacturing made $650 and a cotton mill employee made $250.[1]

While the young Trappe slugger was envied by many of his friends and former teammates, not everyone was enthused about his pursuit of a baseball career. Unlike today, baseball wasn't a respectable sport. The game was often associated with gambling, drinking and rowdy fans. Early professional players were often roughnecks, poorly educated, and ill-mannered.

Sam Crawford, a Hall of Fame outfielder who broke in with Cincinnati in 1899, said, "Baseball players were considered pretty crude. We couldn't get into the best hotels. And when we did get into a good hotel, they wouldn't boast about having us. They would shove us way back in the corner of the dining room so we wouldn't be so conspicuous."[2]

Rube Marquard, a Hall of Fame pitcher who debuted with the New York Giants in 1908, became a major league baseball player despite his father's strong objections. His father, who wanted him to go to college, told him, "Baseball players are no good and they never will be."[3]

Davy Jones, an outfielder who broke in with Milwaukee in the American Association in 1901 and played in the Detroit outfield with Ty Cobb from 1906 to 1912, recalled how the parents of a girl he was dating refused to let her see him after he became a professional baseball player. "In those days, a lot of people looked upon ballplayers as bums, too lazy to work for a living," he said.[4]

Players like Christy Mathewson of the New York Giants, however, helped to erase some of the negativity associated with baseball players. He had attended Bucknell College in Lewisburg, Pennsylvania, for three years, was well-spoken, mannerly and as handsome as a matinee idol. He was six-foot-one, 195 pounds and affectionately known as "Big Six" or "Matty." He was the best pitcher in baseball, having won 30 games three consecutive years from 1903 to 1905. His talent seems immeasurable as he hurled three shutouts in the 1905 World Series, almost singlehandedly defeating Mack's Athletics. In 1908, he won 37 games while posting a 1.43 earned run average. Men and women of all classes held Mathewson up as a role model for their children.

Baker was facing a career crossroads as he prepared to attend spring training in New Orleans in February of 1909. If he failed to make the Athletics, he knew he could always find a minor league job, or work on his father's farm in Trappe and play for a nearby town team. But he was determined to fulfill his dream of being a major league baseball player.

As he approached spring training, Athletics manager Connie Mack was coming off of his first losing season since arriving in Philadelphia in 1901. After losing to the New York Giants in the 1905 World Series, the A's had remained competitive the following two seasons, finishing fourth and second.

In 1906, Philadelphia led the league until August when they faltered as the Chicago White Sox, known as the "Hitless Wonders," put together a 19-game winning streak to finish 12 games ahead of Philadelphia.

The following year, the Athletics led the American League and the Detroit Tigers by three percentage points on September 27. The Tigers took over first place, however, as they won the first game of a crucial three-game series. A 17-inning game which ended in a 1–1 tie because of an umpire's controversial decision, and the second game of the doubleheader, which was never played, proved costly for Philadelphia. In those days, postponed games were not made up at the end of the season, even if they could affect the standings. The A's finished 88–57 and finished one and a half games behind the 92–58 Tigers.

Despite nearly winning the 1907 pennant, the Athletics needed to get younger and faster. They were the oldest team in the league with six regulars over the age of 30: Harry Davis, 34, first base; Danny Murphy, 31, outfield and second base; Jimmy Collins, 38, third base; Tully "Topsy" Hartsel, 33, outfield; Ossee Schreckengost, 32, and Mike Powers, 37, who split catching duties.

Ages and injuries caught up with the Athletics in 1908 as their offense and pitching declined significantly. They were the weakest hitting team in the league and failed to produce a 20-game winner for the first time since

Mack held the reins. Harry "Rube" Vickers, a 30-year-old right-hander, led the staff with an 18–19 record. Former ace George "Rube" Waddell, an eccentric southpaw, had been sold to the St. Louis Browns, and lefty Eddie Plank fell from 24 wins to 14. Charles "Chief" Bender and John "Jack" Coombs had sore arms and were ineffective.

Looking ahead, Mack added a number of young players to his roster during the 1908 season. They included infielders Baker, 22; Scotty Barr, 21; Jack Barry, 21; catcher Jack Lapp, 23; outfielders Joe Jackson, 19; and Amos Strunk, 19; and pitchers Harry Krause, 20; and Victor "Biff" Schlitzer, 23.

Eddie Collins had joined the team in 1906 as 19-year-old, playing six games under the pseudonym Eddie Sullivan to protect his amateur status at Columbia University. He played six games in 1907 and 102 games at three positions in 1908. His fine all-round play indicated he was ready to be a starter.

Mack and the Athletics left Philadelphia in early March for spring training in New Orleans. "I think I have the makings of a winning team,"[5] said Mack.

Of Mack's 40 players reporting to spring training, 12 had played baseball in college. No other 1909 major league team had more than six players with college experience. Mack had a fondness for college players and it served him well through the years. He liked college players for their intelligence and felt he could teach them the game better.

On March 17, Mack conducted an exhibition game between his collegians and non-collegians. The game was the result of a discussion between Rube Vickers and Jack Coombs on the merits of college players. The collegians consisted of Harry Davis, Girard College, first base; Eddie Collins, Columbia University, second base; Jack Barry, Holy Cross, shortstop; Simon Nicholls, Maryland Agricultural College, third base; Mike Powers, Notre Dame, catcher; Jack Coombs, Colby College, center field; Scotty Barr, University of North Carolina, left field; Heinie Heitmuller, Leland Stanford College of California, right field; Chief Bender, Dickinson College, pitcher; and Eddie Plank, Gettysburg College, pitcher.

The noncollegians, led by Baker at third base and Joe Jackson in center field, defeated the collegians, 5–2, as brawn won out over brains. While neither Baker nor Jackson had attended college or were accustomed to city life, Baker made the transition much better than Jackson. Breaking into a major league team wasn't easy because veteran players made it as difficult as possible. They saw young players as someone who potentially would take their job and their source of income. One trick veteran players employed was squeezing rookies out of batting practice by quickly jumping into the batter's box, causing the youngsters to miss their turn. Their goal was to make the newcomers feel unwelcome and harassment was a form of entertainment for some of the veterans. Jackson, from Greenville, South Carolina, was razzed unmercifully about his Southern accent and illiteracy. The quiet Baker didn't draw much attention to himself. He got along with his teammates, collegians and noncollegians, and became lifelong friends with Collins, Barry and other better educated players.

An intense and competitive atmosphere permeated spring training as several starting positions were up for grabs. Veteran first baseman Harry Davis was the only certainty in the infield. Danny Murphy had played second base for Mack's two championship teams. But he had been forced to split his time between second base and right field in 1908 as regular right fielder Socks Seybold, 37, was injured for most of the season. Murphy sprained his ankle in spring training and his absence from the lineup opened up the competition to the younger players.

Nicholls, Collins, Barry and Barr competed for second base and shortstop. The third base job seemed to be Baker's to lose. Nicholls, the most experienced infielder, was erratic in the field and declining in his hitting ability. His hitting, however, was better than his fielding as he committed 56 errors at shortstop in 1908. Collins played second base, shortstop and outfield in 1908. He was a natural ballplayer, intelligent, a fine defensive fielder, an excellent hitter, fast on the bases and a proficient base stealer. Barry covered a lot of ground, but made his share of errors. At times he could impress at the plate, but defense was his strength. Barr, who wasn't particularly strong at the plate, drew quick notice with two triples and three singles in an intrasquad game.

The Athletics' outfield looked shaky as Tully "Topsy" Hartsel in left field and Reuben "Rube" Oldring in center were coming off poor seasons. Although Murphy could play right field, Mack hoped rookie William "Heinie" Heitmuller could handle the duties. But Heitmuller was a defensive liability and had a problem hitting curve balls. Mack had acquired 28-year-old Ira Thomas from Detroit and 23-year-old Jack Lapp from the Hazleton, Pennsylvania, Atlantic League team to handle catching duties. Both were strong defensively and were expected to carry their weight at bat. The A's' strength was pitching. Veterans Eddie Plank, Chief Bender and Jimmy Dygert had proved steady performers while young pitchers Jack Coombs, Jimmy Vickers, and Biff Schlitzer showed promise.

Plank, 33, had five 20-win seasons under his belt, averaging 20 victories a year since joining the Athletics in 1901 as a 25-year-old. Mack had recruited the six-foot southpaw from the Gettysburg College campus. Quiet and shy, the side-arming Plank was known for his control, knowledge of the hitters, and the inordinate amount of time he took between pitches.

The six-foot-two Bender was 24 and already in his seventh year with the Athletics. One quarter Chippewa Indian, Bender had attended the Carlisle Indian School. After graduation, he played for a semipro team in Harrisburg, Pennsylvania, and came to Mack's attention after he pitched against the Chicago Cubs in a 1902 exhibition game. He won 17 games as a rookie in 1903 and averaged double-figure wins the next four seasons. Bender was always tough under pressure and Mack considered him his greatest clutch pitcher. Plank and Bender anchored Mack's pitching staff for more than 10 seasons.

Baker started at third base and batted third when the exhibition season opened on March 18 with a game against the New Orleans Pelicans of the Southern League. It didn't take him long to make an impression. On the first pitch in the first inning, he smashed a home run over the right field fence. The *Philadelphia Public Ledger* reported that the drive "carried fully 50 yards beyond the field."[6] Baker's homer accounted for all the runs in the Athletics' 2–1 win.

In addition to winning the game, Baker also made a sensational fielding play in the third inning to save the game. With bases loaded, he dove to his right to snare a hard line drive, held the ball as he fell to the ground, and tagged third base to complete a double play. He stunned the crowd with the quick action of his fielding.

Five days later, Baker turned in another impressive performance in a game against Mobile, another Southern League team. With the score tied 3–3, and two outs in the eighth inning, he walloped a home run, clearing the right field fence, "an extremely long drive" according to the *Public Ledger*.[6] Once again, he turned in a couple of outstanding fielding plays.

In the following game, Baker delivered another game-winning blast. In the seventh inning, with the score tied 3–3, he drove the ball over the right field fence to give the A's a 5–3 victory. In the first week of spring training, the muscular third baseman had clouted three game-winning home runs and turned in a handful of outstanding defensive plays. After leaving Mobile, the Athletics traveled to Atlanta for a three-game series with that city's Southern League team. Baker went 7-for-14, collecting three hits each in two of the games.

The Maryland rookie was virtually assured of being Mack's starting third baseman when the season opened as the Athletics headed back to Philadelphia for a seven-game preseason series against the Philadelphia Phillies. All the games were to be played at Baker Bowl, the Phillies' home park, since final touches were being made to Shibe Park, the A's new home.

On April 2, Baker batted third in the Athletics' lineup against the Phillies but went hitless before a crowd of 7,600 fans. In the second game, he came within a few feet of hitting a homer over the right field fence in the fifth inning. He had to settle for a long single, disappointing the fans who were hoping to see him display the power he had in spring training.

Phillies outfielder Sherry Magee collided with Baker while sliding into third base in the fourth inning of the third game. Baker, who had gone 1-for-11 in the series, severely strained a ligament in his left leg and had to be rushed to the hospital in an automobile. He was expected to be out of the lineup for two weeks.

The Athletics dropped five of six games against the Phillies and previously optimistic fans were concerned. Although the club had shown promise in spring training, there were still plenty of question marks, the biggest of which were second base and shortstop. Davis was a dependable fixture at first and Baker, although young and inexperienced, looked solid at third.

As Mack was trying to figure out his starting lineup, the A's were preparing to open Shibe Park, the first concrete-and-steel ballpark, located on a city block surrounded by Lehigh Avenue, 20th Street, Somerset Avenue, and 21st Street. Shibe Park, built at a cost of $500,000 was the finest major league ballpark at the time. The *Philadelphia Public Ledger* termed it "a palace for fans, the most beautiful and capacious baseball structure in the world."[7] It replaced Columbia Park, a wooden ballpark at 29th and Columbia. Shibe Park boasted a seating capacity of 20,500 and it was located on a trolley line and close to the railroad stations, making it easily accessible to fans.

The opening of Shibe Park on April 12 was one of the most momentous sports events in the history of Philadelphia. More than 30,000 fans attended Opening Day and another 15,000 were turned away, according to newspaper reports. The gates to Shibe Park were closed long before the game was scheduled to start. Frustrated fans who were unable to purchase tickets created a "howling mob of thousands"[8] that eventually forced open one of the gates, allowing hundreds of fans to stream into the ballpark without paying admission. An estimated 6,000 fans viewed the game from the field, ringed around the outfield behind a rope that ran from the left field seats to the right field bleachers. At some points, spectators were seven deep. Another estimated 3,000 fans viewed the game from the roofs, porches, and windows of the houses on 21st and Somerset streets. "It seemed as if all of Philadelphia was there," wrote the *Philadelphia Public Ledger*.[9]

After the Opening Day festivities, southpaw Eddie Plank limited the Boston Red Sox to six hits and one run as the A's scored an 8–1 victory. Danny Murphy, Simon Nicholls and Eddie Collins were the hitting stars. Murphy collected four hits and Nicholls, subbing for the injured Baker at third, had three hits. Collins added two hits and a pair of walks. The Athletics looked sharp, fueling speculation that they would be competitive with the defending American League champion Detroit Tigers, as well as the talented Cleveland Naps and the Chicago White Sox.

Immediately after the opening game, A's catcher Mike "Doc" Powers collapsed with a severe pain in his stomach. Powers, a physician who graduated from the Notre Dame College school of medicine, thought he had acute indigestion. He was taken to Northwest General Hospital in Philadelphia two days later, where he underwent surgery for an intestinal infection. The surgeon gave him a one-in-five chance of surviving. Powers, one of the most popular players on the team, died on April 25, at age 38.

By April 15, Baker was ready to return to the Athletics' lineup. But with Nicholls playing so well at third, Mack decided to give Baker another week to recuperate. Baker made his 1909 debut on April 21 in a 6–2 loss to the Red Sox in Boston. It was an embarrassing game for the Eastern Shoreman as he committed two throwing errors and went hitless in five trips at the plate. His throwing error with two outs in the third inning, allowed five unearned runs.

Baker redeemed himself three days later when he clouted a grand slam homer in the first inning against the Red Sox to lead the A's to a 4–1 win. In the top of the first inning, Hartsel singled to left off right-hander Frank Arellanes, Nicholls walked, and Collins sacrificed. Murphy also walked. Davis failed on a squeeze play as Jake Stahl grabbed his pop up near first base. That set the stage for Baker, who slammed six-foot right-hander's first pitch over the right field fence. Oddly, it turned out to be his only career grand slam.

Baker's homer created a buzz among the 13,000 fans in the stands and was the talk around the league for a week or so. It wasn't often that a player cleared the fence with a homer. In fact, according to the *Philadelphia Public Ledger*, no player had accomplished it in the Huntingdon Avenue Baseball Grounds in 1908.

When Baker recalled his grand slam in a 1955 interview with Frank Yeutter of the *Philadelphia Evening Bulletin*, he didn't get all the facts right, but he was close.

Baker told Yeutter, "We got men on second and third and the Boston pitcher, Frank Arellanes, walked Danny Murphy to get to me. When

Murphy got down to first base, he said to Jake Stahl, 'That was a mistake walking me. That kid can hit the ball outta the park.' And on the first pitch, I hit it over the right field fence. When I got back to the bench, Murphy said to me, 'Kid, you made Jake Stahl think I am the greatest prophet in baseball.' And then he told me what happened."[10]

Despite Baker's grand slam, he remained mired in an early-season slump. On May 8, he was hitting .105 with four hits in 37 at bats in 11 games. And to make matters worse, he had committed six errors.

On May 29, the new third baseman impressed more than 14,000 fans at Shibe Park with a feat many thought would never happen. In the first game against the Red Sox, he muscled the second pitch from second-year, right-handed pitcher Frank Arellanes, the victim of his grand slam homer in Boston, over the right field fence, 340 feet from home plate.

In its initial view of Shibe Park, the *Public Ledger* reported, "As to the extent of the outfield it is sufficient to say that the first slugger to put a ball over the fence will insure that his name will have a place in baseball history."[11]

Home runs were rarities in the Dead Ball Era (1900–1919). In 1909, there was one home run hit every 311 at bats, the second lowest frequency in baseball history. Only 1907 had a lower frequency with 329 at bats per home run. In contrast, major leaguers clouted a home run every 30 at bats in 1999. Of the 259 round-trippers recorded in 1909, many were of the inside-the-park variety. It was particularly unusual for a player to clear the fence and have the luxury of trotting around the bases on a home run. There were almost four times as many triples as home runs in the major leagues in 1909.

The combination of a dead ball and spacious ballparks discouraged hitters to swing up on the ball, producing a high fly, which usually resulted in an out. Shibe Park's original dimensions were 378 feet from home plate down the left field fence, 515 feet to center, and 340 down right field. By comparison, Camden Yards in Baltimore, which opened in 1992, measures 333 feet to left field, 400 feet to center, and 318 feet to right field.

A batter had a much better chance of reaching base by hitting the ball on the ground. Hitters used heavy bats (Baker swung a 52-ounce bat, one of the heaviest ever), shortened their strokes, and seldom swung from their heels. Striking out was frowned upon because it negated any chance of advancing a runner. Few players possessed the power to clear the fence or the strength to swing a bat as heavy as Baker's, which he handled with ease. The bat was about 20 ounces heavier than the average bat used by today's major leaguers. Jack McGrath of the Louisville Slugger Company said that Baker's bat was antiquated even in its time. It was short with a thick handle, almost as round as the barrel. There was no flex and it was almost like a piece of lead.

On June 12, Baker received the "Billy" Brady loving cup, filled with roses, prior to his first plate appearance in a game against the St. Louis Browns at Shibe Park. The cup was a gift for his grand slam in Boston two weeks earlier. Although Baker's homers were causing a stir, he was still struggling for consistency at the plate, hitting just .218.

The second-place A's took two out of three from the first-place Tigers, June 16–18, in Shibe Park and Baker started to heat up offensively. He slugged his third homer of the season on June 30 against Red Sox right-hander Charlie Chech. He enjoyed his biggest day of the season during a July 3 doubleheader against the Highlanders in New York. He went 5-for-8, collecting a pair of triples. Baker combined his batting power and better-than-average speed for a large number of triples in his early years in the majors.

On July 4, the Athletics trailed first-place Detroit by five games. Collins led the American League in average, hitting .381, and Baker had hiked his average up to .261, fourth best among Mack's regulars. Krause, a five-foot-ten lefty from California, had provided an unexpected spark on the mound, tossing six shutouts in his first eight decisions en route to an 8–0 record. He surrendered just one earned run in 71 innings.

The Athletics had played well as a team and become a contender more quickly than anyone anticipated. The *New York Sun* wrote, "Mack has not only developed Collins in a hurry, he has turned out two brilliant stars in Baker and Barry. He has made Thomas, one of the best catchers in the league."[12]

Philadelphia opened a western road trip on August 19 with Washington, Cleveland, Detroit, and St. Louis scheduled. The three-game series in Detroit turned out to be the showdown fans had hoped for. The Athletics arrived in Detroit with a slim one-game lead over the Tigers. Baker was now batting cleanup, where Mack had moved him about a month earlier.

In the opener, Detroit right-hander Ed Summers matched up with Harry Krause, who the Tigers had had trouble with all season, in the opener. When the Athletics jumped out to a 4–0 lead after two innings it appeared as if Mack's men would widen their league lead. But the Tigers, trailing 5–3, knocked Krause out in the seventh inning, scoring four runs and a 7–5 win.

The game created an intense controversy, one of the biggest of Ty Cobb's career. In the first inning, Cobb drew a walk from Krause and stole second base. While hard-hitting Sam Crawford was taking ball four, Cobb

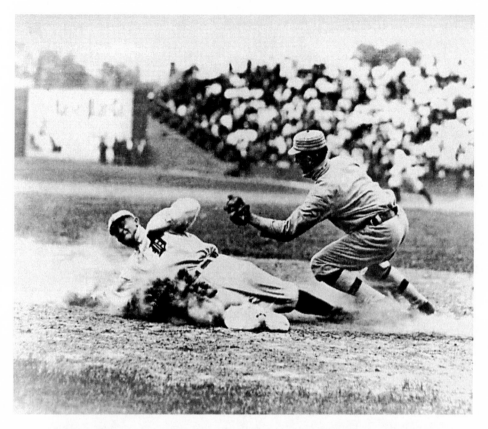

Detroit Tigers star Ty Cobb is shown sliding into third base as Frank Baker takes the throw. Cobb's spiking of Baker in August 1909 created an intense controversy. Baker and A's manager Connie Mack thought the spiking was intentional. Baker said if the gash on his right arm had been one-eighth of an inch deeper it would have ruined his career. Cobb denied that the spiking was deliberate. NATIONAL BASEBALL HALL OF FAME LIBRARY, COOPERSTOWN, NY.

took off for third. Patrick "Paddy" Livingston's throw to Baker at third base had him beaten easily. When Cobb hook-slid to Baker's left, Frank reached over the bag (toward the direction of the outfield) and tagged him with the ball in his bare right hand. Cobb's right foot grazed Baker's right forearm and opened a small cut. Baker and the rest of the Athletics were livid. They believed the spiking was deliberate and insisted Cobb be ejected from the game. The umpires turned a deaf ear to their pleas. The combative Tiger upset the A's even more in the seventh inning when he upended Collins, sliding into second base.

Baker said if the gash had been one-eighth of an inch deeper, it would have ruined his career because he would have been unable to throw the ball. "Cobb cut me deliberately," he declared. "I put the ball on his left leg and had him easily. When he saw he couldn't get to the bag, he made a scissors motion with his right leg, which came up like a meat cleaver and cut me on my throwing arm. I accused him of doing it on purpose and he invited me to go behind the stands and fight it out."[13]

Cobb's spiking of Baker infuriated Mack. He wanted American League President Ban Johnson to investigate the star's tactics. Mack added he knew Cobb had threatened to get Baker, Barry and Collins.

Cobb fired back at Mack's charges, "Mack knows I have never spiked a man deliberately. He also knows that the runner is entitled to the line and if the baseman gets in the way, he's taking his own chances. When I slid, I made for the bag."[14]

The hard-nosed outfielder didn't think he had done anything differently from the Athletics. He cited Barry and Collins barreling into Tigers' second baseman Herman "Germany" Schaefer while leading by seven runs in an earlier game in Philadelphia. Cobb said if the Tigers got hurt, they didn't complain. They just kept playing the game and the Athletics should follow suit.

Being charged with deliberately spiking Baker always stuck in Cobb's craw. In a letter to J. Taylor Spink, editor of *The Sporting News*, in 1955, he wrote, "Baker's spiking was in no way intentional and it was unavoidable. He did not lose one inning of play and I think records show he played in all the games for the rest of the season. I have always resented the unfair and untrue account of this matter."[15]

"If the A's weren't so high in the race, I would press charges against Cobb," declared Mack, who lost his composure for one of the few times in his career.[16] He said he wouldn't take action because it would seem that he was trying to win the pennant on a technicality.

Ban Johnson responded quickly, saying that Cobb had to stop his style of play or he would have to quit the game. But after viewing the photographs taken by the *Detroit News* photographer that showed Baker off the base and reaching across to tag Cobb, Johnson announced that Cobb had been within his rights.

Joe S. Jackson of the *Detroit Free Press* defended Cobb. He suggested that "soft-fleshed darlings" like Baker should follow the example of Norman "Kid" Elberfeld, a New York Highlander shortstop who blocked second base, took the spikes, grinned and bore the pain.[17]

Even D.L. Reeves of the *Philadelphia Public Ledger* sided with Cobb. He didn't think the Tiger star had spiked Baker intentionally. He wrote that if Baker had been spiked by any other Tiger, it would not have received passing notice. Reeves didn't believe Cobb would take the cowardly approach of deliberately spiking Baker, trying to hurt him.

The A's dropped the second game, 4–3, as the Tigers scored the winning run in the ninth inning off Eddie Plank. The Tigers convincingly completed the sweep as George Mullin posted a 6–0 shutout. The Athletics committed four errors and the Tigers roughed up starter Chief Bender, who lasted just three innings.

Philadelphia trailed the Tigers by two games and Mack remained optimistic. "Detroit's lead is only temporary," he said. "We'll overhaul them and win out. All the luck in the series was with Detroit."[18]

The Athletics returned to Shibe Park for their final home stand in the beginning of September, five games behind the Tigers in the loss column. The Athletics proceeded to take four straight from the hapless Washington Senators. All eyes were pointing toward a four-game series with the Tigers in mid–September.

Detroit held a four-game lead over the A's when they arrived in Philadelphia on September 15. Anti-Cobb feelings were still running high in the city. Cobb had received a dozen notes from Philadelphia fans, threatening to kill him upon his return to the city. There was plenty of tension as the crucial series opened. Hundreds of policemen were stationed in and around Shibe Park. They were in the stands, near the Tigers bench, and directly behind Cobb in right field. Although Cobb was a fierce competitor who was seldom distracted, he appeared jittery and nervous. The hostile crowd of 25,000 unmercifully booed him each time he came to bat or took the field.

He struck out in the first inning against Plank, bringing a loud cheer from the crowd. In the third inning, the Tigers loaded the bases with one out. Cobb came up to the plate, looking for redemption and a chance to quiet the boisterous crowd. Plank worked him to a full count before striking him out on a high fast ball. Reporter D.L. Reeves described the scene: "The cantilever stand and the concrete bleachers rocked with the crowd's volcanic roars. On all sides straw hats were shattered into shreds and tossed out onto the playing field."[19] Plank ended the inning by getting Sam Crawford to ground weakly to first. The A's managed to manufacture two runs on five singles in the 2–1 victory.

"That was the hardest game of the series and I'm glad we're through with it," said Mack afterwards. "The rest will not be so hard."[20]

After the game, Cobb left the Aldine Hotel for his customary dinner walk and cigar, only to be confronted by a crowd of angry Philadelphians. Refusing to be intimidated, Cobb walked into the crowd, which parted muttering and let him go through.

The next day, the Detroit star returned to his normal form as he collected a pair of bunt singles off Krause as the Tigers won 5–3. The Tigers used their speed in the victory, stealing seven bases, including three double steals. In the first inning, the left-handed batting Cobb bunted down the third base line, catching the Athletics' infield by surprise. He was past first before Baker picked up the bunt. He moved to second on Crawford's out and then stole third. After stealing third, Baker shook Cobb's hand, signaling there were no longer hard feelings between them.

Cobb turned in the best defensive play of the day as he snared a hard line drive to rob Harry Davis of a double in the fourth inning with the Tigers leading 3–1. He initially misplayed the ball, running in on it. But, he suddenly turned, ran back as fast as he could, and caught up with the liner with a spectacular one-handed catch over his head on the edge of the right field rope line, which held back the fans from the playing field. His momentum from running straight back carried him into the crowd beyond the rope. The following inning, he returned with five dollars for the man whose straw hat he crushed when making the catch. Cobb's gesture won him a few friends—when the game ended, a number of Philadelphia fans shook his hand and slapped him on the back.

On September 18, right-hander Chief Bender, on his way to 18 wins, blanked the Tigers, 2–0. The game attracted an estimated crowd of 35,000, the largest in baseball history at the time. Fans were everywhere inside and outside Shibe Park. They were atop the concrete outfield walls and on the roofs of row houses outside the park.

Another 30,000 fans turned out for the final game of the series, pushing the four-game total to nearly 120,000. Philadelphia defeated the Tigers, 4–3, behind Plank's six-hitter. Cobb spiked shortstop Jack Barry in the fourth inning, opening a three-inch gash between his ankle and knee. This time, however, there was no bad blood as everyone agreed it was unintentional. As Barry was limping off the field to receive medical attention, he signaled to the crowd that everything was okay.

The A's had taken three out of four games in the crucial series and trailed the Tigers by two games on September 20. Mack's youngsters chased the Tigers down the stretch, but couldn't overtake the more experienced club. Philadelphia was eliminated on October 1, dropping a doubleheader to the Chicago White Sox. Although the Tigers won by three and a half games, the Athletics had proven to everyone that they were a young team with enough talent to win it all.

Baker, Barry, and Collins had established themselves as Mack's infield of the future. Collins hit .346, rapped 198 hits, scored 104 runs and stole 67 bases. Baker finished the season hitting .305, placing him among the top 10 hitters in the league, and a league-leading 19 triples. He added 27 doubles, four homers, and a team-high 85 runs batted in, a category that didn't become an official major league statistic until 1920. Although Barry hit only .215, he made up for his lack of offense with his stellar defense and leadership qualities.

THREE

World Champions

When reporters asked Connie Mack what he thought about his team's chances for the 1910 season, he answered the question with a question. "If last season I took a green team and made all kinds of changes such as putting infielder Murphy in right field and taking chances with boys such as Collins, Barry and Baker, not one of them more than 22; if I was made the laughing stock of the baseball world for putting in a team of experiments as they were called, say, how do you suppose I feel this season?"[1]

Mack's experiments had, indeed, turned out far better than anyone could have imagined. Collins was the talk of the American League and Baker and Barry had established themselves as solid starters. With a full season of experience, they comprised one of the league's best infields—fast, strong defensively, reliable and productive offensively. Collins and Baker were two of the main reasons the Athletics raised their team batting average more than 30 points, scored 119 more runs, and went from last to first in slugging percentage.

The five-foot-nine Collins was at the beginning of a Hall of Fame career that spanned 25 years (1906–1930). He was extremely talented, excelling at bat, on the bases and in the field. The only thing he lacked was power. The right-handed hitter topped the .300 mark 18 times and finished his career with a lifetime average of .333. He won four stolen base titles and finished his career with 743, second only to Ty Cobb at the time. One of the smartest players in the history of the game, Collins earned the nickname "Cocky" for his aggressive play.

The five-foot-nine Barry, nicknamed "Black Jack," established a reputation as one of the league's top defensive players during his 11-year career.

Although he was a .243 lifetime hitter and never batted higher than .275, he delivered an amazing number of clutch hits. The Holy Cross product was highly respected by his teammates. In retirement, Baker advocated for Barry's induction into the Baseball Hall of Fame.

Baker, Collins and Barry all benefited from playing under the soft-spoken, gentlemanly and patient Mack, who was an excellent teacher. He never shouted at his players or criticized them in front of others. He preferred to say something to them quietly, perhaps at the end of the dugout or during batting practice the following day. Mack addressed his players as "Mister" and they always called him "Mr. Mack." The 47-year-old manager always wore a suit and a tie in the dugout and never cursed, smoke, or drank. Nicknamed "The Tall Tactician" because of his six-foot-one, 150 pound frame and reputation as a brilliant strategist, he was a master at developing young players.

Years later, Baker recalled, "It was a real treat to play for Mr. Mack. He taught me more about baseball than any other man. He taught me more baseball than I had ever known. He developed me as a baseball player in almost every respect. Always patient, Connie was like a father to all of his players. We took all our troubles to him."[2] Baker said Mack had a number of suggestions for how he could improve his hitting, but he never insisted that he change his stance or how he played.

The A's had earned the respect of the veteran Tigers' team and the rest of the American League. If Mack's club hadn't gotten off to a slow start, it's conceivable they could have ended the Tigers' reign as American League champions. Mack planned to rectify that. "There will be no bad start this season," he proclaimed. "We will go right out from the jump. Now, if we can finish second with a team of experiments, why can't we win with a seasoned team?"[3]

Mack's assessment was shared by his rival managers. Detroit's Hughie Jennings said, "Mack's men are to be feared. The Tigers consider them formidable rivals for pennant honors. They are a scrappy lot of clever ball players." Washington's manager James McAleer added, "Mack has one sweet group of players. Detroit and Boston should be close, but the Athletics should capture the flag by a good margin."[4]

In addition to a potent offense and tight defense, the A's were well-armed. They were the only team in 1909 to produce five pitchers with double-digit wins. Eddie Plank led the way with 19 wins, while Chief Bender and Harry Krause added 18 each. Cy Morgan chalked up 16 wins and Jack Coombs had 12.

Washington Senators pitcher Walter Johnson apparently didn't pay much attention to the preseason assessment of the Athletics. The 22-year-old right hander shut out the Athletics, 3–0, on one hit on Opening Day, April 14, in Washington. President William Howard Taft attended the game and threw out the first ball, becoming the first President to do so.

A dose of bad luck kept Johnson from registering a no-hitter before a crowd of 14,000 at Griffith Stadium. In the seventh inning, Baker lifted a routine fly to right field. Harry "Doc" Gessler drifted back to make the catch, but tripped over a fan, who was among the thousands of spectators sitting on the field behind a rope. The ball fell into the crowd and was recorded as a ground-rule double. Johnson faltered slightly in the ninth when he surrendered a pair of walks following an error to load the bases. He proceeded, however, to fan the next two batters and forced Baker to fly to left field for the final out.

Despite wanting to avoid a slow start, the Athletics struggled until the end of the month, posting a 5–4 record. Baker was off to another slow start, hitting .162 after nine games.

On April 30, Chief Bender defeated the Highlanders 4–2, in 11 innings in New York to start a 13-game winning streak. During the streak the A's displayed dominating pitching and a powerful offense. They outscored their opponents 71–25 and allowed more than three runs in a game just once. It didn't seem to matter who Mack sent out to the mound: Bender tossed a six-hitter, a no-hitter, and a four-hit shutout; Krause pitched a two-hit shutout; Coombs recorded a two-hitter, and Morgan followed Bender's no-hitter by holding the Naps hitless until there were two outs in the eighth inning.

The red-hot Athletics were 18–4 and held a comfortable lead over the Highlanders when their streak came to a crashing halt on May 19. The Tigers pounded Krause and Jimmy Dygert for 19 hits to forge a 4–2 victory. The Athletics rebounded by taking the next two games from the Tigers, giving them 15 wins in 16 games. Pitching had carried the team and it would continue to do so throughout the season. In addition to dominating pitching, Mack's club provided plenty of offense. Philadelphia had four of the league's top 10 hitters on July 1— Danny Murphy (.309), Rube Oldring (.304), Jack Barry (.302) and Baker (.300).

By August 9, Mack's men had built a commanding 10½ game lead over second-place Boston. The Athletics virtually wrapped up on the pennant, winning three out of four in Detroit in mid–August.

Baker was part of a bit of home run history in the August 12 game against Detroit at Bennett Park when he, Thomas and Oldring homered. It marked the first time three homers had been hit in a game at the Tigers' ballpark. The feat corresponded with the limited introduction of a livelier ball with a cork center rather than a rubber center.

Philadelphia "Athletics" Champions
1910

Baker, shown here in action, was a dead-pull, right-field hitter. He was patient, always making the pitcher throw him the pitch he wanted. *New York Tribune* writer Grantland Rice called him one of the greatest natural hitters in baseball. BROWN BROTHERS.

On August 21, the Athletics were 76–34 for a winning percentage of .690 and led second-place Boston by 13 games. It was the largest margin any American League team had enjoyed in 10 years. By the end of the month, both Bender and Coombs had notched 20 victories. Coombs, a six-foot, 185-pound right-hander from Colby College, was starting to blossom in his fifth season. In 1908, Coombs had played 47 games in the outfield while pitching in 26 games. He had never won more than 12 games

Opposite: The 1910 Philadelphia Athletics ended the Detroit Tigers' three-year reign as American League champions and defeated the heavily favored Chicago Cubs in the World Series. Baker, second from left, back row, batted .283 in his sophomore season, but .409 in the World Series. The A's pitching staff compiled an ERA of 1.79, the lowest in baseball history.

prior to 1910, but he had worked with A's coach Monte Cross to develop an impressive overhand curve ball that baffled hitters. The 27-year-old Coombs put together 53 consecutive scoreless innings in September en route to a 31–9 record, one of the best pitching seasons ever. He erased White Sox hurler Ed Walsh's previous American League mark of 38⅓ consecutive scoreless innings. Coombs completed 35 of 38 games, hurled 353 innings and tossed 13 shutouts, still an American League record.

Because Philadelphia had led the American League by such a wide margin for so long, clinching the pennant on September 24 in Chicago was almost anticlimactic. The anticipation of the World Series, however, fired up the Athletics and their fans. For Baker, Collins, Barry and other teammates who weren't on Mack's previous championship teams, it was an unbelievable experience. The club put an exclamation mark on its season when it won its 100th game on October 1, defeating Boston to become the first American League club to reach that plateau. The Athletics finished with 102 wins, 14½ games in front of second-place New York.

Mack said, "I do not feel as if we have achieved any great triumph. For sure, we have won the pennant but this season it has been such a runaway race that it has not seemed hard. No other team in the league was in the same class as us."[5]

The Athletics paced the league in batting average, doubles, triples and slugging average. Collins led the team with a .324 average, 81 stolen bases and 81 RBI. Baker ended up hitting .283 with 15 triples, two home runs and 74 RBI. Baker's sophomore season was less productive than his rookie season, partially because of his wife's illness. The third baseman missed a handful of games to go home to Trappe to be with his pregnant wife, who was in poor health.Returning to the lineup, it was difficult for him to focus and it affected his play, both at bat and in the field.

The Philadelphia pitching staff had a combined earned run average of 1.79, the lowest in baseball history. Mack's hurlers combined for 24 shutouts, including 13 by Coombs. Three pitchers compiled ERA's under 1.60: Coombs (1.30); Morgan (1.55) and Bender (1.58). Bender posted a 23–5 record, the league's best winning percentage. Morgan added 18 victories and Plank, bothered by a sore arm, chipped in with 16.

Since the American League season ended earlier than the National League season, the A's played five games against an all-star team in Philadelphia and Washington, DC, to prepare for the World Series. Having lost the last three World Series, the American League had an incentive to have their representative well prepared. The All-Stars, managed by James McAleer of Washington included Ty Cobb of the Tigers, Tris Speaker and Jake Stahl of the Red Sox, Clyde Milan and Walter Johnson of the

Senators, Ed Walsh and Doc White of the White Sox. The All-Stars defeated the A's in four of the five games.

Although the Athletics had won the American League pennant in impressive fashion, the World Series was expected to be much more difficult. Mack's men were under pressure to prove that they were as good as their record.

The Cubs, under manager Frank Chance, compiled a 104–50 record, beating the New York Giants by 13 games. Chicago had averaged more than 100 wins a year since 1906, won four league championships and two World Series. The staff had two 20-game winners in Mordecai "Three Finger" Brown (25–14) and rookie Leonard "King" Cole (20–4). The Cubs' leading hitters were Arthur "Solly" Hofman at .325 and Frank "Wildfire" Schulte at .301 and a league-leading 10 homers.

The 1910 World Series was the first to feature two teams with 100 wins during the regular season. It pitted a veteran Cubs team against a mix of youngsters and veterans who had been developed by Mack over two years. Only five of the Athletics had played in the 1905 World Series against the Giants: Davis, Hartsel, Plank, Bender, and Murphy. Meanwhile, Chicago's lineup and pitching rotation had remained intact since 1906 when the club won a record 116 games.

The Cubs had built a dynasty through intelligent play, excellent pitching, hard hitting, and a tight defense. Chicago's storied infield of (Joe) Tinker to (Johnny) Evers to (Frank) Chance double play combo along with Harry Steinfeldt at third base was much more experienced than the Athletics' infield.

Chicago was, however, weaker on the mound than in previous years. Ed Reulbach, a right-hander who had averaged 19 wins in his first five seasons, accounted for only 12 wins. Right-hander Orval Overall, a 20-game winner the previous year, produced 12 wins. Jack Pfiester, a southpaw who won 17 games in 1909 fell to 6–3. They all struggled during the year. Reulbach had diphtheria and was sidelined much of the spring. Overall's arm went bad in the middle of the season and he couldn't pitch for weeks. Pfiester was seriously injured twice, once with a broken hand that sidelined him for a month. Chance filled in by acquiring 31-year-old Harry McIntire from Brooklyn and 26-year-old Lew Richie from the Boston Braves. The duo combined for 34 victories.

In addition to patching up the pitching, Chance also had to juggle his lineup due to injuries. He credited utility players Henry "Heinie" Zimmerman, Jimmy Archer, Ginger Beaumont, and John Kane for admirable jobs. Zimmerman played five positions; Archer divided his time between catcher and first base; Beaumont played 56 games in the outfield; and Kane played four positions. They combined for 112 RBI.

"I'm prouder of the Cubs than I've ever been in my life," said Chance. "They have beaten all records for overcoming obstacles. Never in the history of baseball did a team win under such a heavy handicap of sickness and injuries."[6]

The Cubs received another bad break in early October when second baseman and team leader Johnny Evers broke his ankle sliding into second base against Cincinnati. A much less experienced Zimmerman replaced him. The Athletics also lost a starter prior to the World Series as center fielder Rube Oldring severely injured his knee. Twenty-one-year-old Amos Strunk got the starting nod.

Despite their 104 wins, the Cubs didn't overly impress their National League opponents. St. Louis first baseman Ed Konetchy declared the Athletics would beat the Cubs in the World Series, even though he gave the Cubs the edge in every category except pitching. "Mack owns the sweetest bunch of hurlers in baseball," he said.[7]

On the eve of the World Series, William Weart, baseball editor of the *Philadelphia Telegram*, wrote, "The Cubs have reached or passed their greatest development and I believe that passed is the most fitting word, while the Athletics are still coming and have not yet exhibited their greatest power, except in flashes."[8]

Game 1 of the 1910 World Series at Shibe Park on Monday, October 17, created more baseball excitement than Philadelphia had ever witnessed. More than 1,000 eager fans formed a line outside the park at 8 o'clock the night before. They spent the night standing, leaning, or sitting on stools or soap boxes. By 9 a.m., five hours before the game was scheduled to start, there were 5,000 impatient fans clamoring for admission. The crowd was elbow to elbow and there was no place to move on the street outside the park. The original plan was to open the gates at 11 a.m., but that plan was abandoned as 300 policemen could not maintain control of the crowd, which resembled a mob. The gates were opened early and the crowd stormed to the ticket windows to purchase the remaining 20,000 tickets. By 1 p.m., more than 25,000 fans were in the park, many of them jammed onto the field behind the ropes. Fans were still streaming in, assuring a larger than capacity crowd. The upper storied windows of houses on 20th Street were filled with people who had paid $1 to $3 for the privilege.

The *Philadelphia Evening Bulletin* described the scene at Shibe Park, shortly before the game started: "Every seat in the stands and bleachers was taken. Fans in solid masses were ranked behind ropes in the field.

Festoons of other fans were strung for awhile along the fences, but the police pulled them down. Roofs of the houses on 20th Street and the porch roofs below them, overlooking the grounds were black with people."[9]

The crowd, estimated conservatively at 35,000, was the largest ever to watch a baseball game in Philadelphia or any city, according to the *Evening Bulletin* (the official attendance was 26,891). The atmosphere was electric as fans armed with rattles, horns, and noisemakers showed their pleasure. When the A's came onto the field for practice, the crowd erupted with deafening noise.

The start of the game was delayed due to a prolonged argument as to whether camera operators could remain on the field with motion picture cameras. It was the first World Series to be recorded on celluloid. American League President Ban Johnson ended the tiff, instructing the umpires that the camera operators could stay on the field. That didn't placate Chance, who argued they shouldn't be allowed behind home plate.

Mack gave the ball to 23-game winner Chief Bender for the opening game while Chance surprisingly tapped 12-game winner Orval Overall, who announced his retirement from baseball before the end of the series. At 29, he had been plagued by a sore arm and didn't feel appreciated. He retired at the end of the Series, but returned for 11 games with the Cubs in 1913. Mack had faith in Bender and always considered him the best clutch pitcher he had. Winning the first game of the Series was extremely important. The team that won the first game had won five of the six previous World Series.

Mack believed the first game was so important that he rarely pitched Bender in September because he wanted him to prepare for the World Series opener. Mack told Bender that he was his own boss and left it entirely to his judgment how best to prepare for it.

"I knew it (the first game) would be a crucial one — in fact, it meant almost everything," Mack said.[10]

Bender and Baker were the stars of the game as the Athletics recorded an easy 4–1 win. Bender, mixing blazing fastballs and deceptive curves, limited the Cubs to three singles and two walks and was masterful through the first eight innings as only two Cubs reached base. At the end of every inning, the crowd cheered the big Indian as he walked off the field.

Baker figured in three of the four runs as he slammed a pair of doubles and a single in four at-bats. He led off the second inning with a sharp ground-rule double to left field. The ball rolled into the crowd, behind the ropes, denying him a possible triple. He scored the game's first run on Danny Murphy's single. Murphy stole second, advanced to third on an infield out and plated the second run on Bender's single. Lord opened the

The 1910 Chicago Cubs' infield, from left to right, of Harry Steinfeldt at third base, Joe Tinker at shortstop, Johnny Evers at second base, and Frank Chance at first base, was considered the best of its time. Evers fractured his ankle shortly before the World Series and did not play. The more experienced Cubs' infield, however, was overshadowed in the World Series by Mack's much younger infield of Frank Baker, Jack Barry, Eddie Collins and Harry Davis. NATIONAL BASEBALL HALL OF FAME LIBRARY, COOPERSTOWN, NY.

third with a double over Hofman's head into the crowd in right center. Collins bunted him to third. Baker followed with a line-drive single to left, scoring Lord.

The A's led 3–0 when Chance lifted Overall at the end of the third inning. Overall hadn't fooled the Athletics at all as his fastballs lacked zip and his curves didn't break. His pitches were consistently high in the strike zone, favoring Mack's high-ball hitters. Spitballer McIntire entered the game in the fourth inning. He kept the Athletics in check until the eighth inning when he walked Collins and made a wild throw to Chance at first base, trying to pick him off. The throw allowed Collins to advance to third base. Baker rocketed a ball over Schulte's head in right field and it appeared to have a chance to clear the high stone wall. The crowd was vastly disappointed, however, as it hit a foot from the top of the right field wall and rebounded into the crowd on the field, limiting Baker to a ground-rule double. The crowd gave him a standing ovation.

Already the offensive star, Baker distinguished himself in the field with two outstanding plays. With two outs in the seventh inning, Hofman smashed a hard grounder with an ugly bounce to him. Baker partly stopped the force of the drive with his body, juggled the ball momentarily, raised from a stooping position and made a riflelike throw to Davis at first, nipping Hofman by a step.

In the ninth, the Cubs had scored a run and were threatening with runners on first and second with two outs. The pressure to keep the rally alive fell to Hofman, the Cubs' leading hitter. Hofman drove a wicked line drive to Baker, who fielded it cleanly to end the game.

Baker's World Series debut was impressive. Only in his second full season, he looked like a veteran player. The Cubs' strategy was to keep the ball away from the left-handed swinging Baker, a dead-pull hitter who liked the ball inside. They preferred not to give him any good pitch, but instead make him go after borderline strikes. His opposite-field double in the second inning impressed Cap Anson, one of the best players of the 19th century, who was covering the game for the newspapers. "The ball was well away from him and he showed that he knew what to do with it," wrote Anson.[11]

Sidelined Cubs second baseman Johnny Evers was equally impressed by Baker's ability to adjust to outside pitching and be patient. In his newspaper column, he wrote, "Baker surprised me with his splendid hitting. He is entitled to all the credit he can get."[12]

Teammate Eddie Collins also praised Baker for his final at bat. He pointed out that McIntire was willing to walk Baker, rather than to throw him a strike. He threw inside pitches hoping to get him to swing, but Baker remained patient, refusing to bite. When the fourth pitch was slightly over the plate, the strong third baseman smacked it off the right field fence. Nine out of 10 hitters would have let that pitch go by, according to Collins.

Fielder Jones, former manager of the Chicago Americans, was surprised by the play of Philadelphia's youthful infield. Instead of showing signs of nervousness, they exhibited poise, spirit, and were perfect in the field. They were as steady as the more seasoned Cubs infield.

Philadelphia had won the opening game and the psychological battles were underway. Mack said, "The great Chicago machine showed us nothing."[13]

Cubs outfielder Solly Hofman refused to be ruffled by the loss. "That's about the least discouraging defeat we ever suffered. There isn't one of us who doesn't think we will take tomorrow's game and three after that."[14]

For Game 2 on Tuesday, October 18, in Philadelphia, the Athletics' 31-game winner Jack Coombs matched up against the Cubs' 25-game winner Mordecai Brown. The expected pitcher's duel, however, never materialized. Although Coombs threw 29 pitches in the first inning, the Cubs could only touch him for one run. The A's took the lead in the third inning on Collins' two-run double. Philadelphia opened its lead to 3–1 in the fifth, but the Cubs narrowed the margin to 3–2 in the top of the seventh.

The Athletics, however, turned a close game into a rout in the bottom of the seventh as they scored six runs. Collins led off with a walk and went to third on Baker's single. Davis doubled into the crowd, scoring Collins. Murphy doubled to left, scoring two runs. Barry sacrificed Murphy to third and Thomas singled him home. Strunk lined a double to right, scoring Thomas and Strunk scored the sixth run on an error.

The Cubs missed an excellent opportunity to even the series as Coombs struggled. He surrendered nine walks and eight hits, yet the Cubs lost 9–3 as the A's rapped 14 hits, including five hits in the six-run seventh inning. Coombs allowed 19 runners, but the Cubs stranded 14 men on base.

Collins was the star of the game with three hits, including two doubles, two steals, two runs scored, two RBIs, and 10 fielding chances without an error. He was involved in two double plays and turned in a pair of sensational defensive plays.

Fielder Jones observed, "Collins has done it all in the first two games. He has been the timeliest hitter, the most prominent fielder, and the best base runner of the series."[15]

In the first two games, the Athletics rather than the Cubs appeared to be the veteran team. They were disciplined and patient at the plate, forcing Overall and Brown to work hard. They didn't swing at borderline pitches and they frequently outguessed the Cubs' pitchers. The *New York Sun* noted that the Athletics had shown stability, team play, and confidence while the Cubs had appeared uncertain and rattled.

Cubs manager Frank Chance didn't spend any time looking for excuses after Game 2. "When we get nine walks off a pitcher and can't beat him, we ought not say a thing," he said.[16]

The series shifted to Chicago's West Side Grounds for Game 3 on Thursday, October 20. The Cubs needed a victory badly and they hoped that their home field loaded with friendly fans would give them an extra boost. Chance's men had shown no signs of a team that had won 104 games.

Their fate seemed to depend wholly on the pitching staff, which had been unimpressive.

The pitching matchups for Game 3 were critical. The Cubs could ill afford to be down three games to none. Mack gambled when he elected to come back with his "Iron Man" Jack Coombs, on two days rest, even though he had thrown 153 pitches in Game 2. A sore arm eliminated Plank as a possible starter. Coombs had earned his iron man status as a rookie when he and Boston's Joe Harris battled for 24 innings on September 1, 1906, before Philadelphia won the game, 4–1, with three runs in the top of the 24th inning. Chance had to choose among right-handers Reulbach, Cole or southpaw Pfiester. The Cubs' manager bypassed the rookie Cole in favor of the veteran Reulbach. This was an ill-advised move given Cole's regular season record, the need to give him pitching experience in the World Series and the availability of Reulbach to relieve Cole, if the rookie faltered.

It didn't take Chance long to realize he had made the wrong choice. Reulbach lasted just two innings as he gave up three runs on three hits and two walks. McIntire, who had baffled the Athletics in Game 2, relieved Reulbach but lasted just one-third of an inning. He surrendered two singles, a home run, a hit batsman and four runs.

The Athletics roughed up Cub pitchers for 15 hits en route to a 12–5 romp. Coombs was closer to his natural form as he gave up four walks and six hits. He also contributed two singles and double to drive in three runs.

The Athletics broke open a 3–3 game with a five-run third inning. With one out, Collins greeted McIntire with a single. He scored when Baker tripled to right field, the ball scooting past Schulte. Davis was hit by a pitch and Murphy followed with a controversial home run over the screen into the right-field bleachers.

During the regular season, any ball hit over the screen into the bleachers was a home run and that rule carried over to the World Series. Temporary stands had been erected in right field, which didn't have any screen to prevent balls from bouncing into them. If a ball bounced into them, it was a ground-rule double. Murphy didn't know how far the ball had traveled and stopped at second base, thinking it was a ground-rule double because it had gone into the crowd. Umpire Tom Connolly motioned Murphy home, ruling it was a home run.

Chance and the Cubs vehemently argued that under the ground rules, Murphy's hit should have been a double. Chance, however, was well aware that Murphy's hit should have been a homer because Tinker had hit a home run to the same area in the 1908 World Series. Umpire Connolly ejected Chance from the game and Archer replaced him at first base. It was the first time a player had been ejected from a World Series game. Pfiester replaced McIntire and Barry greeted him with a ground-rule double into the center field crowd. He scored when Thomas reached first safely as Tinker made a wild throw to first. The Athletics piled on four more runs in the seventh.

Again, the A's hitting impressed observers, including the Cubs. "As sluggers, they are marvels," commented Evers. "They hit the ball savagely and seldom fail to hit hard. Most of the infield grounders are hot smashes, extremely hard to handle. I knew they were good hitters, but they bat considerably harder than I anticipated. Thursday's game [Game 3] was the most remarkable exhibition of slugging I've ever seen."[17]

Evers marveled at the Athletics' ability to hit all kinds of pitches in any location. They had earned the reputation as high fastball hitters like the Detroit Tigers. He had expected them to wait on fastballs, but they didn't. Nearly every hit they got in the third game was off curve balls. They also hit McIntire's sidearm spitball and Pfeister's fadeaway (the modern-day version of the screwball). It didn't seem to matter whether the pitches were high or low, a strike or a ball. Evers said the Athletics even hit pitch outs. He cited Collins's single in the first game against Overall, who was trying to waste the pitch since catcher Johnny Kling had picked up the sign for a hit-and-run. But Collins reached out and smashed it down the line.

Evers felt much of Philadelphia's offensive success resulted from their ability to know what pitch was coming. *Washington Post* reporter Joe S. Jackson wrote that a story was circulating that the A's had been stealing the Cubs' signals. He pointed out that Bender was in the coach's box when not pitching and the Athletics had been teeing off on the first good ball with great frequency.

After three embarrassing efforts, the only question was "Could the Athletics sweep the Cubs?" Mack sent Bender to the mound for Game 4 on Saturday, October 22 in Chicago, figuring to put the nail in the Cubs' coffin. Chance, virtually out of options, went to Cole, his 24-year-old right hander. Although he had been the Cubs' most effective starter, Chance believed he lacked the experience expected of a World Series starter. The Cubs' leader answered the second-guessers of why he hadn't started Cole earlier by saying he wasn't convinced he was better than the three he did start. "I know now that he can't be any worse than they have been," he said.[18]

Bender and Cole hooked up in the best game of the series. The Cubs scored in the first inning and the Athletics tied it in the third. Philadelphia took a 3–1 lead in the fourth on Murphy's two-run double into the left field crowd. The Cubs cut the deficit to 3–2 in the bottom of the inning, but missed a chance to tie the game or take the lead as Bender escaped a jam. With one run already plated, the Cubs had runners on first and second with no outs and Zimmerman at the plate. Zimmerman, however, grounded into a costly double play.

The Athletics carried the 3–2 lead into the eighth inning when they missed a chance to put the game out of reach and perhaps sweep four straight. Baker led off with a sharp grounder to Chance playing deep at first base, but Cole didn't get off the mound quick enough to cover the bag and Baker was awarded an infield single. Flustered, Cole walked Davis on four pitches and Murphy sacrificed the runners up a base. Cole hit Barry in the back to load the bases with one out.

Catcher Ira Thomas was due up. Mack was tempted to pinch hit for the 30-year-old, who was one of his favorite players. Thomas was one of the few veterans on the team and Mack didn't have the heart to pinch hit for him with a win so close at hand. Mack considered sending up Topsy Hartsel to pinch hit. Although Hartsel had hit just .221 during the regular season as a substitute, the veteran manager felt the five-foot-five outfielder could work the unsettled Cole for a walk to force home a run. But Mack, who hadn't pinch hit in the series and had only used 10 men in four games, decided to let Thomas hit. The big catcher fouled off the first pitch and then hit a soft bounder back to Cole, who threw home to Archer to force Baker. Archer's relay to Chance at first completed the inning-ending double play.

Three-Finger Brown relieved Cole in the top of the ninth and held Philadelphia scoreless. When outfielder Frank Schulte, who had led the National League in home runs in 1910 with 10, stepped to the plate to lead off the bottom of the ninth, the entire crowd stood up. The Cubs were on the verge of becoming the first team to be swept four straight in the World Series. The fans looked to Schulte to get something started. The right fielder tagged Bender for a line-drive double that rolled to the right field. Hofman sacrificed Schulte to third, bringing up Chance. The roar from the crowd was ear-splitting. It was fitting that all their hopes rode on the shoulder of their "Peerless Leader." The first pitch nipped him on the finger and he headed for first, but umpire Tom Connolly ruled he had walked into it. Chance slammed the second pitch for a triple to deep center over Strunk's head to chase home Schulte with the tying run as the crowd of more than 26,000 unleashed its frustrations. With Chance standing on third as the potential winning run and Cub fans roaring and cheering for their batters, Bender dug down deep to retire Zimmerman and Steinfeldt to force extra innings. Baker's sensational fielding play robbed Steinfeldt of a chance to win the game. The Cubs' third baseman lifted a foul into the left field boxes. Baker ran over from third to the stands, leaped

up and leaned over the fence, reaching his hand above the fans to snare
the ball.

The A's threatened in the tenth, but failed to score. Bender was tir-
ing, but Mack was willing to take his chances with his ace, who had never
been knocked out of a World Series game. Tinker popped out to start the
bottom of the tenth. Archer, who hit .182 in the series, doubled into the
left field crowd. Brown was thrown out at first, bringing up lead-off batter Jimmy Sheckard with two outs. He responded to the pressure, slamming the first pitch over second base to score Archer with the winning run.
The partisan Chicago crowd erupted in jubilation. The Cubs had played
the way they were capable of and had maintained some dignity. Baker led
the losing offense with a double, two singles, and a walk.

Game 5 on Sunday, October 23 at Chicago pitted Coombs on two
days rest against Brown, who had relieved in Game 4. Philadelphia scored
a run in the first and Chicago matched it in the second. Coombs worked
out of a jam in the fourth inning, striking out Tinker and Archer with the
bases loaded. According to Collins, this seemed to crush the Cubs' hopes
and proved to be the game's turning point. The A's responded with a run
in the top of the fifth as Murphy reached on an error, was sacrificed to
second, and scored on Lapp's single.

Things came unraveled for the Cubs in the eighth inning after a ques-
tionable call by umpire Jack Sheridan. With a 2–1 lead, Coombs opened
with a single and Hartsel grounded to Tinker, forcing Coombs. Hartsel
attempted to steal second and was called safe on a close play as second baseman Zimmerman applied the tag. If Hartsel had been called out, Brown
would have had two outs and the bases empty. The Cubs argued to no
avail. The floodgates opened after that. Lord doubled into right, scoring
Hartsel. Collins doubled in a run and stole third, but was out at the plate
when Zimmerman fielded Baker's grounder and threw home. Brown's arm
was gone at this point and he walked Davis on four pitches. Murphy
smashed a hot one off Zimmerman's foot and it bounced into center field,
allowing Baker to score. Zimmerman received the ball on the relay play
and threw wildly toward the stands, sending Davis home. Brown, upset
by the rally, uncorked a wild pitch and Murphy tallied. He walked Barry
before fielding Lapp's grounder to throw him out to end the inning. The
Athletics had batted around and scored five runs.

Trailing 7–2 with two outs in the bottom of the ninth, Archer kept
Chicago's slim hopes alive with a single. Kling slapped one over second
base, but Barry picked it up and stepped on second to give Philadelphia
the championship. Thirty seconds after Barry tagged second, the players
of both teams were swallowed up by a mass of spectators who surged onto

the field as the Cubs dashed for their clubhouse and the Athletics started for their bus.

Coombs, although never displaying his best form, joined Christy Mathewson of the New York Giants and Babe Adams of the Pittsburgh Pirates as the only hurlers to win three games in the World Series.

The Athletics finished the Series hitting .316, a team record that stood for 50 years until the 1960 New York Yankees broke it with a .338 mark. Mack's club knocked out 56 hits in five games, scoring 35 runs. Collins led the winners with a .429 average, collecting nine hits in 21 at bats. Baker finished with a .409 average, notching nine hits in 22 at bats. The Athletics had outplayed the Cubs in every phase of the game.

Before the 1910 World Series, there were no questions about the quality of Mack's pitching staff. Many doubts existed, however, about how talented his infield was and the strength of his offense. Now, there were no doubts.

Reviewing the Athletics' performance, Evers said, "It was their batting that won it. They showed considerable speed. They field well and at times brilliantly. But it was the remarkable ability to hit all kinds of pitching that carried off the series. Collins is one of the greatest players I have ever seen. The left side of the infield, which I expected to be weak was strong."[19]

Fielder Jones said, "In Collins, Baker, and Barry, Mack has three aggressive infielders who are the best I have seen. The defense these youngsters put up against the Cubs was brilliant in every game."[20]

Mack, who admitted he felt his team would win the World Series a month after the season opened, said, "I guess I'm the happiest man in the world. I knew the boys would win it. I'm disappointed not to win in four straight. I think we proved we are the better team. I believe we would win the pennant in any league with the team we have."[21]

Overjoyed Philadelphians had snapped up more than 300,000 copies of the special Sunday World Series edition of the *Philadelphia Times* by the time the Athletics arrived in Philadelphia by train around 5 p.m., on Monday, October 24. The team was given a rousing reception by a crushing crowd of 50,000 fans, headed by Mayor John Reyburn. Although extra precautions had been taken to prevent the crowd from entering the Pennsylvania Railroad Station, Athletics rooters outsmarted officials. Huge gates had been erected at the entrance to the Broad Street station and no one was allowed to reach the train floor without a ticket. Not to be outdone by this strategy, hundreds of fans purchased tickets to nearby stations, crowding the station to overflowing. A hurried call was made to the police stations and soon 300 policemen were on the scene and kept the crowd back from the entrances. When the train pulled into the station, the players had to almost fight their way to the street. Twenty automobiles, the First Regiment Band of Philadelphia, and a crowd that stretched for a block in every direction awaited the baseball heroes. Headed by Mayor Reyburn, the players were escorted to the Bellevue-Stratford Hotel. The players were entertained at dinner until 8 p.m., when they were taken to the theater.

The Athletics each received $2,062 for winning the World Series, a record amount. More than 124,000 enthusiastic fans attended the five games. That was 7,000 more than the first five games of the Pittsburgh-Detroit series the previous year and 24,000 more than the 1906 World Series that featured the White Sox and the Cubs. Interest in the World Series was growing and now it seemed as if the capacity of the park was the principal limitation in regards to how large a crowd could be drawn.

Baker and his young teammates had played on the national stage and proven themselves. They had beaten a veteran club which had won 104 regular season games and made it look easy.

FOUR

Everlasting Fame

After the 1910 World Series victory over the Cubs, Mack took the Athletics to Cuba for a series of exhibition games. Baker, anxious to return to his family and farm in Trappe, declined to accompany his teammates. His wife, Ottilee, had delivered their first child, a girl also named Ottilee, in September.

Each winter, he hunted ducks and geese, worked on his farm, and enjoyed the time away from the spotlight. Reporters and friends knew the easiest way to start a conversation with Baker, a man of few words, was to ask him about hunting. Farming was another good conversation starter.

Because he worked on his farm instead of simply managing it and having other people do the work, he was always in outstanding physical condition. He earned a reputation as one of the best conditioned and strongest players in the league. He had incredibly strong hands, forearms, and legs. His strength helped him to hit the ball harder than most players, making his grounders and line drives especially difficult to handle.

Buck Herzog witnessed Baker's strength as a young man on several occasions. He recalled when he and Frank's brother, Norman, were arguing over the weight of a sack of phosphate used in fertilizing. Neither could lift it. But Frank had his brother sit on it, then carried both the phosphate and his brother across the barnyard with no trouble at all. On another occasion, Frank bet his brother and Herzog that he could throw a wagon axle further with one hand than they could with both. Norman and Herzog managed tosses of 10 to 12 feet. Frank, however, picked up the wagon axle with his right hand and gave it a flip, sending it more than 20 feet.

Mack's $100,000 infield, plus one. The Philadelphia Athletics' infield of Stuffy McInnis at first base (left), Baker at third base (center), Jack Barry at shortstop (second from right), and Eddie Collins at second base (right) was considered the greatest infield in baseball history. Danny Murphy (second from left) played second base before the arrival of Collins. NATIONAL BASEBALL HALL OF FAME LIBRARY, COOPERSTOWN, NY.

Baker's exploits in the World Series had made him well-known throughout the country. Although the shy idol avoided much of the attention by living in Trappe instead of Philadelphia, he was still sought after by many reporters. Even the townspeople of Trappe had to use some deception to honor him. One night not long after the 1910 World Series was over, Baker, a volunteer fireman, responded to the town's fire alarm. He helped the other volunteers haul the hose cart out of a shed and they ran to the hotel at top speed. When they arrived, Baker followed the rest of the firemen inside, looking for smoke and flames. What he found instead was a magnificent banquet prepared in his honor. He was ushered to the head table for a special night. At the conclusion of the evening, the towns-people presented him with a fine Winchester rifle.

Baker's wife and six-month-old daughter accompanied him to spring training in Savannah, Georgia, in early March of 1911. A *Philadelphia Evening Bulletin* reporter observed that Baker's wife and daughter attended practice daily. "The baby never whimpers. She pats her hands when 'Dada' goes to bat,"[1] he wrote. The star third baseman stirred up fans and reporters when he hit a mammoth homer over the center field fence on the first day he reported to training camp. He continued to impress reporters throughout spring training as he appeared to be in midseason form.

Baker took advantage of a short right field fence and some mediocre pitching to put on an impressive power display during a three-game exhibition series against the Charleston, South Carolina Sailors of the South Atlantic League, March 23–25, as the Athletics headed North for the beginning of the season. He homered twice over the right field fence and singled as the A's routed the Charleston team, 14–0, on March 23. He repeated the feat the following day as Philadelphia once again thumped the host club, this time, 14–1. On March 25, Baker homered and doubled as the A's won, 3–0. In three games, he slugged five home runs, two singles and a double.

Philadelphia was favored to repeat as American League champions. They had run away from the rest of the league in 1910 and returned virtually the same lineup. With the best pitching staff in baseball, Mack was looking to strengthen it with depth. Twenty-year-old Clarence "Lefty" Russell, purchased for $12,000, and 23-year-old right-hander Allan Collamore were possible additions. Mack hoped that Harry Krause's arm troubles were behind him and he could join Eddie Plank, Chief Bender, Cy Morgan and Jack Coombs in the rotation.

The infield was one of the best and Mack figured to carry the same three catchers as he had the previous year. In the outfield, plans were for Rube Oldring and Bris Lord to alternate in center while Danny Murphy patrolled right field. Left field was a question mark. Young Californian Bill Hogan was getting a long look in left because Amos Strunk continued to have knee problems. Topsy Hartsel was expected to be used as an extra outfielder.

There didn't appear to be any serious challengers to the well-balanced, pitching-rich Athletics. The Highlanders, armed with a wealth of pitching but not much offense, were considered dangerous by some observers. New York's staff featured Russ Ford, Hippo Vaughn, Jack Quinn, Jack Warhop, Ray Caldwell, and Ray Fisher, all in their 20s. Ford had posted a 26–6 record in 1910, his rookie season. Quinn and Warhop had won 18 and 14 games, respectively. The club battled internal strife in 1910 as manager George Stallings and first baseman Hal Chase wrestled for control of the team. Stallings was ousted near the end of the season and Chase took the reins.

The question remained if the Tigers were still of championship caliber. A weak bench and shaky pitching were compounded by Cobb's spats with his teammates. He had feuded with Davy Jones and wasn't speaking to Donie Bush or Sam Crawford. The Red Sox had finished fourth and were the disappointment of 1910. They didn't appear any stronger in 1911.

The A's, however, didn't resemble their 1910 club when they started 1–5 in early April. They surrendered 26 runs in two games against the Red Sox. The outburst was an indication of the pending offensive explosion. The introduction of the livelier ball in the latter months of the 1910 season had signaled a new era. Hitting and scoring jumped significantly as did team ERAs. Compared to 1910, Philadelphia scored 190 more runs in 1911, increased its batting average by 30 points, slugging average by 40 points, and pounded nearly twice as many homers (35 to 19). The team ERA rose from 1.78 to 3.01 while shutouts decreased from 24 to 13. The American League batting average jumped 30 points. The number of .300 hitters leaped from eight to 27 while the league ERA increased from 2.52 in 1910 to 3.34 in 1911.

On April 28, the Philadelphia third baseman cracked a home run that had American League players talking for a couple of weeks. Baker touched Washington right-hander Walter Johnson for the first of his five career homers against the ace. Johnson won the game 2–1, surrendering a solo shot to Baker in the bottom of the second inning. It was the first home run hit over the fence against Johnson since he debuted in 1907. He had started more than 120 games and hurled more than 1,038 innings and given up just two inside-the-park home runs before Baker's feat.

While the Athletics were struggling, the Tigers won their first eight games. Fueled by Cobb, Crawford, and rookie first baseman Del Gainor, Detroit won 25 of its first 30 games. Hughie Jennings' club looked like it was uncatchable as it forged a nine-game lead over second-place Boston in mid–May. Mack's men were 13–12 and in fourth place, nine and half games behind.

The A's broke out of their offensive slumber and regained their championship form from May 18 through May 27. They collected double-figure hits for nine consecutive games, averaging 15 a contest.

The next six weeks were incredible as the A's went 34–7, overtaking the Tigers for first place on July 4. Baker played a key role in the surge as he hiked his batting average from .253 to .349 on July 8. He batted at a .398 pace (76 hits in 191 at bats) and put together several impressive streaks. From May 22 through June 3, he blistered the ball at a .510 clip (24 for 47).

The third baseman went 11-for-19 as the Athletics swept the Naps in a four-game series in Cleveland in late May. On May 24, he collected five hits—two doubles and three singles—in five at bats against Cleveland hurlers. When the Naps visited Shibe Park in early June, Baker continued his assault as Mack's men swept a three-game series. He batted 8-for-14, slugging a pair of homers, two doubles, and four singles. Still, the Athletics trailed Detroit by five and a half games when the Tigers visited Shibe Park for the first time in the season, June 7–9.

Philadelphia won the first game of the series, 4–3. The next day, Cobb had to be escorted off the field, following an incident with Baker that occurred in the Tigers' 8–3 win in front of nearly 18,000 fans. In the sixth inning, Cobb singled and stole second. He attempted to steal third but was easily thrown out by Ira Thomas. After being called out, Cobb's left leg became entangled with Baker. In the eighth inning, Cobb was on third and took a considerable lead against the southpaw Plank, who threw over to third three times to keep him close. On the third time, the Detroit outfielder slid into third and his spikes came dangerously close to Baker's nose as he bent down to get the throw. As both players straightened up, they jostled each other, grabbing and pushing. They were quickly surrounded by other players, who didn't want the situation to escalate.

When the Athletics made the final out of the game, a number of fans jumped out of the bleachers, surrounded Cobb and began to abuse him, pelting him with paper and lemons. The Detroit star was quickly whisked away by the Philadelphia police and several players into an automobile outside Shibe Park. Mack's club captured the series the following day with a 5–3 victory.

The Athletics continued their hot play through June, winning series against the St. Louis, Chicago, Washington and Boston teams. In the final game of the series against Washington on July 1, Baker and the Athletics roughed up Walter Johnson in a 13–8 victory. While other batters struggled against Washington's hard-throwing right-hander, Baker made it a habit of hitting Johnson well, particularly early in his career. On this afternoon, he enjoyed one of his best performances against the Senators' ace as he singled, doubled, and scored on an inside-the-park homer.

Baker, hovering around the .340 mark, continued his torrid hitting as the Athletics, one game behind the Tigers, arrived in New York for back-to-back doubleheaders. Philadelphia won the first game in 12 innings as

Baker collected a pair of singles. In the second game, the A's slugger battered right-hander Jack Warhop for a single, double, triple, and homer, completing the cycle. He finished the day 6-for-11.

Baker celebrated the 4th of July with another outstanding performance as the Athletics swept a doubleheader from the Yankees to move ahead of the Tigers into first place. After singling in the opener, Baker collected two singles, a double, and a triple in the second game. In back-to-back doubleheaders, he was 11-for-21.

The Tigers moved back into first place on July 5 and held a one and a half game lead over the Athletics when Mack's men invaded Detroit for a four-game series, July 11 through 14. The Tigers and Cobb sent a message, sweeping the series. In the opener, the Athletics were winning 8–7 going into the bottom of the eighth. The Tigers, however, scored seven runs in the inning, knocking out Coombs and reaching Plank for three walks, four hits, and a sacrifice fly.

Cobb stole the show on July 12 as Wild Bill Donovan blanked the Athletics, 6–0. In the first inning, Cobb reached on a fielder's choice against Krause, stole second and then proceeded to steal third. He completed the circuit by stealing home. In the seventh, he walked with a runner on first base and Crawford beat out a bunt to load the bases. Jim Delahanty sent a long fly to Murphy in right field scoring one run easily. Cobb, however, surprised everyone by scoring from second. He had done the same thing the previous game.

Cobb was the difference again on July 13 as he scored the winning run in an 8–7 victory by scoring from first base on a single in the bottom of the ninth. Cobb singled over short with one out and Delahanty smashed a hit to deep right field. Cobb started for second as fast as he could. Rounding second, he disregarded Hughie Jennings's effort to stop him at third and went into the plate on a fadeaway slide. Thomas tried to put the tag on him, but the umpire ruled Cobb safe and the game over. This ruling unleashed complaints from the Athletics, who declared to no avail that Thomas had applied the tag in time. The Tigers wrapped up the series with an easy 6–1 win. Cobb was relatively quiet, collecting a pair of singles and scoring a run. The Detroit star was putting together the best season of his career. In 1911, Cobb led the American League in hits (248), runs (147) runs batted in (127), doubles (47), triples (24), slugging average (.621) and batting average (.420).

The Athletics had played their worst series of the season and the Tigers had stretched their lead to five games. But Mack wasn't discouraged. "We simply played bad baseball and they played good baseball," he said. "So we must get started all over again if we are to repeat our 1910 feat."[2]

Frank Baker (second from left, back row) was among the American League stars who participated in a benefit game for Addie Joss's widow on July 24, 1911. Joss, a popular Cleveland pitcher, had died of tubercular meningitis on April 13 at the age of 31. Joss won 160 games in a brief nine-year career, including a perfect game on October 2, 1908. Other members of the all-star team are (back row, left to right) Bobby Wallace, Baker, Smoky Joe Wood, Walter Johnson, Hal Chase, Clyde Milan, Russ Ford and Eddie Collins; (front row, left to right) Germany Schaefer, Tris Speaker, Sam Crawford, manager Jimmy McAleer, Ty Cobb (in a Cleveland uniform), Gabby Street and Paddy Livingston. NATIONAL BASE-BALL HALL OF FAME LIBRARY, COOPERSTOWN, NY.

On July 24, Baker along with teammates Eddie Collins and Paddy Livingston played alongside a group of American League all-stars in an exhibition game against Cleveland to raise money for the widow of Addie Joss, a popular Cleveland pitcher who had died of tubercular meningitis on April 14 at the age of 31. Joss had won 160 games in a brief nine-year career, including a perfect game on October 2, 1908.

Baker's selection to play in the exhibition game was another indica-

tion that he was a star. The American League all-stars included Sam Crawford and Ty Cobb of the Tigers, Joe Wood and Tris Speaker of the Red
Sox, Walter Johnson, Clyde Milan, and Gabby Street of the Senators,
and Hal Chase and Russ Ford of the Highlanders. More than 15,000
fans attended the game, which raised well over $13,000 for Joss's widow,
Lillian.

When the Tigers invaded Shibe Park for a four-game series on July
29, Baker carried a 16-game hitting streak and the A's trailed the Tigers by
three and a half games. As so many times in the past, the Tigers-Athletics
series aroused passions of baseball fans. It seemed that whenever the bitter rivals met there was a lot at stake. The July 29 doubleheader had
Philadelphia fans in a frenzy. More than 35,000 fans packed Shibe Park and
thousands of others were turned away.

The *Philadelphia Public Ledger* reported the "never was the excitement so intense, the crowd so mob-like, the eagerness to purchase tickets
so pronounced and the vise-like jam to gain admittance so crushing. Altogether, it was the most remarkable and largest gathering that Shibe Park,
with its steel girders and concrete foundations, ever has held."[3]

Chief Bender and Ed Summers hooked up in a 0–0 pitching duel
through 10 innings in the opener. Summers, who had surrendered only two
hits in 10 innings, walked Bender to open the eleventh inning. Bender
moved to second on a sacrifice and Collins singled to right with two outs,
pushing home the winning run. That unleashed a wild celebration by the
capacity crowd. In the second game, the Athletics nipped the Tigers 6–5,
as left fielder Davy Jones dropped Jack Lapp's easy fly ball in the bottom
of the eighth inning, allowing two runs to score. The A's coasted to an 11–3
win behind Eddie Plank the following day before 28,000 fans, cutting the
Tigers' lead to one-half game. Detroit bounced back, however, taking the
next two games.

After leaving Philadelphia, the Tigers lost a doubleheader to the Red
Sox while the Athletics blanked the Browns. The A's took over first place
on August 4, sweeping a doubleheader from the Browns while the Tigers
dropped another game to the Red Sox. The Athletics held the lead for the
final two months of the season. Mack's team picked up steam down the
stretch, winning 38 of 54 games for a .703 winning percentage while the
Tigers faltered, winning just 26 of 55 for a .472 winning percentage. The
Tigers' pitching, suspect at the start of the season, finished with the second highest ERA in the league.

Philadelphia officially clinched the pennant with an 11–5 win over
Detroit on September 26. Baker celebrated the occasion by becoming the
first player to slug two home runs in a game at Shibe Park. In the second

inning, he blasted a two-run shot over the right field wall off right-hander Ed Willett and in the eighth inning he duplicated the feat off another right-hander Ralph Works. Baker also doubled in the third and ninth innings. Despite trailing the Tigers by 9.5 games in mid–May, the Athletics finished 13.5 games in front of the second-place Tigers.

Baker finished the season with 11 home runs, tops in the American League. He drove in 115 runs, tied for second with Detroit's Sam Crawford. He also finished with a .334 batting average, 198 hits and 38 stolen bases. Baker had improved in every offensive category, except triples, from the 1910 season.

While Connie Mack was guiding the Athletics to their second consecutive American League pennant, archrival John McGraw coaxed the New York Giants to the National League title by besting the once powerful Chicago Cubs. Fueled by the addition of Buck Herzog to play third base and the move of Artie Fletcher to shortstop, the Giants mounted a late-season drive to overtake the Cubs on August 24. The Giants won 20 of 24 games down the stretch to finish 7.5 games in front of Frank Chance's club.

The 1911 World Series featured a rematch of the 1905 World Series. The Giants won that series in five games as Christy Mathewson tossed three shutouts. McGraw, who had refused to play the 1904 American League champion Boston Pilgrims, terming them "bush leaguers," had wanted to humiliate the Athletics and he gloated after capturing the series. Mack and McGraw were contrasts in managing styles. Mack was quiet and appeared laid-back, but he was forceful and left no doubt that he was in charge. McGraw was often described as hot-headed, pugnacious, and intimidating. He would do anything to win. The 1911 World Series would be a grudge match between Mack and McGraw.

The Giants relied on pitching and speed as Mathewson and Rube Marquard presented a formidable righty-lefty combination. Mathewson, 31, one of the top pitchers in the game, posted a 26–13 record with a league-leading 1.99 ERA. The six-foot-three, 24-year-old Marquard, purchased by McGraw for $11,000 in 1908, had finally shed his "lemon" label by winning 24 games and losing only 7. Twenty-three-year-old James "Doc" Crandall, a relief specialist, went 15–5, giving the Giants a tough trio.

Offensively, the Giants utilized their speed to manufacture lots of runs. The club set a record with 347 stolen bases as five players swiped more than 35 bases. The outfield of Josh Devore (61), Fred Snodgrass (58) and John "Red" Murray (48), combined for more than 160 stolen bases. First baseman Fred Merkle led the team in RBIs with 84. Second baseman Larry Doyle paced the club with 13 homers and 25 triples while Merkle added 12 homers. Although the Giants led the National League in hitting, their team batting average of .279 was nearly 20 points lower than the Athletics' .296.

Like the Athletics, the Giants were a young team. No infield regular was older than 26 and in the outfield, Snodgrass and Devore were both 23 and Murray was 27. Catcher John "Chief" Meyers, 31, was the oldest starter.

Both the Athletics and the Giants had strong supporters who argued that they were the best teams ever. Former Athletic Monte Cross, perhaps a bit prejudice, touted the Philadelphia club. "I think Mack has the best team ever. The A's have the greatest pitching staff ever pulled together. Perhaps the strongest thing about the A's is that infield of Baker, Barry, Collins and (John "Stuffy") McInnis."[4] Mack had switched the 21-year-old McInnis from his backup shortstop position to first base in June to replace 38-year-old Harry Davis. The move paid off handsomely as McInnis was brilliant defensively and batted .321. Many people thought the Massachusetts native, who was a shade over five-foot-nine, was too short to play first base. But he was agile, quick and covered a lot of ground. He went on to set a number of fielding records for first basemen and always contributed with his bat.

McInnis was on the sidelines for the 1911 World Series, however, due to a broken right hand he suffered as the result of being hit by Detroit's George Mullin in the last week of the regular season.

McGraw put it succinctly: "I think I have the best ball club in the world."[5]

The odds on the series were evenly split with sentiments falling along league lines. *Washington Post* writer Joe S. Jackson was convinced the A's were the better team. "There can be no argument on this point," he wrote. "The Athletics are a better hitting team, have superior infield and outfield and are strong in pitchers."[6] He maintained if the two teams were in the same league, the Athletics would beat the Giants because the Giants couldn't rely on just two pitchers (Mathewson and Marquard), which had been the Tigers' downfall. Jackson thought the Giants' biggest threat was being able to pitch Matty in back-to-back games, aided perhaps by a rain-out to give him more rest.

Although much was made about the Giants speed on the bases, Ty Cobb, the best base stealer in either league, said it wouldn't be a factor in the World Series. "Base running doesn't count in a short series," he said. "It never has and it never will. Each single game is of too much importance. Each time you try to steal a base, you give your opponent an opportunity to put you out. Unless you are winning, like the A's were last year against the Cubs, you cannot afford to take the risk. You must play the

Baker is shown being taken care of by the Athletics' trainer after being spiked by New York Giants' Fred Snodgrass in the 1911 World Series. Snodgrass spiked Baker in the first and third games of the World Series. Snodgrass was booed for 10 minutes by the hometown Polo Grounds crowd after he spiked Baker for a second time. NATIONAL BASEBALL HALL OF FAME LIBRARY, COOPERSTOWN, NY.

game reasonably safe and depend on your pitching and hitting because the loss of any one game could mean the loss of the series."[7]

Cobb also was confident the aggressive Philadelphia hitters would be able to beat the highly regarded Mathewson. "Batters who wait and let Matty get the first strike on them don't stand a chance. Batters who swing on the first good pitch, are the batters who hit him."[8]

The combination of the rematch of the two teams, the proximity of the cities, the growing popularity of the World Series, and the fact both teams were arguably the best ever, created more interest in the 1911 World Series than any previous one. Record crowds were expected and more than 300 baseball writers from across the United States applied for press credentials. Only the presidential nominating conventions received more coverage.

Game 1 of the 1911 World Series on Saturday, October 14, at the

Polo Grounds in New York was perhaps the most anticipated game in baseball history. Reserved tickets were at a premium as demand exceeded supply by 10-fold. Those who were lucky enough to obtain tickets treasured them like precious jewels. Thousands of fans were disappointed and rumors circulated that speculators had acquired many of the reserved tickets and were selling them at inflated prices, four dollars for two dollar seats and six dollars for three dollar seats.

A crowd of 38,281 packed the Polo Grounds, setting an attendance record for a baseball game. The series pitted Baker against his teacher and former teammate Buck Herzog. Prior to the game, Baker, Herzog and Giants coach Wilbert Robinson, a former member of the Baltimore Orioles, posed for the *Baltimore Sun* photographer. Other photographers saw the opportunity and snapped photos of the trio for four of five minutes. Certainly, it was a thrill for the two of them to meet in the World Series just six years after playing for the Ridgely, Maryland club. The presence of both Baker and Herzog, both native Marylanders, in the World Series captured the attention of baseball fans throughout the state. The *Baltimore Sun* greatly expanded its coverage of the 1911 World Series compared to its coverage of the 1910 World Series. Readers were interested in knowing every detail about Baker and Herzog. While a handful of Eastern Shore fans had taken the train to Shibe Park to witness Baker in the World Series in 1910, many more were considering making the trip this October. Some even talked about traveling to New York.

The opening game featured Bender of the Athletics matched up against Mathewson of the Giants. The game was scoreless in the second inning when Baker walked out of the dugout, toting his heavy black bat to the plate. Fans yelled encouragement to him as he stepped into the batter's box, bent down to rub his hands in the dirt and wiped them on his uniform. His nervousness quickly disappeared as he jumped on Mathewson's first pitch, a fastball, sending a scorcher to right field for a single. Baker advanced to second on an infield out, took third on a passed ball and scored the first run on Harry Davis's single.

With two outs in the third inning, Rube Oldring doubled over third base and Collins walked. Baker strolled to the plate, looking to expand the A's' lead. The Trappe slugger, however, fanned on three bad pitches.

The Giants tied it in the fourth as Fred Snodgrass reached first base after one of Bender's pitches grazed his hand. He advanced to second on an infield out. McGraw put on the hit-and-run and Herzog hit a hard grounder to Collins. The ball hopped out of his glove and caromed out of his reach. Snodgrass raced home and beat Collins's throw to the plate, tying the game 1–1.

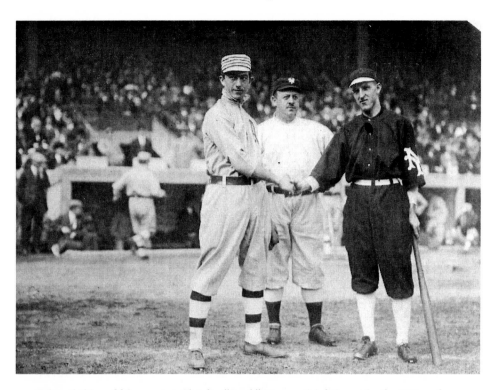

Baker (left) and his mentor Charles "Buck" Herzog (right) met in the 1911 and 1913 World Series as the Philadelphia Athletics battled the New York Giants. Here they shake hands as Giants coach Wilbert Robinson looks on. Baker was 19 when he played for Herzog, who managed the Ridgely, Maryland, team in 1905. Herzog switched Baker to third base and later recommended him to the Reading, Pennsylvania, team in the Tri-State League. Baker credited Herzog for helping him get to the major leagues. BROWN BROTHERS.

Baker figured in another key play in the sixth inning. Snodgrass was hit by the pitch for the second time and Red Murray sacrificed him to second. Fred Merkle fanned and Snodgrass broke for third base. Thomas's throw was in plenty of time as Snodgrass barreled into Baker, spikes first. Baker held his ground and Snodgrass spiked him in the left forearm, knocking him down and causing him to drop the ball. The A's trainer ran onto the field and patched up Baker, whose arm was bleeding. The trainer brought a new pair of pants to replace Baker's which had been ripped from knee to hip. Baker changed on the field behind a blanket and stayed in the game. Snodgrass's spiking of Baker seemed to be part of the Giants' strategy to intimidate the third baseman, who was said to be spike shy. The Giants had spent time during the pregame warm-ups sharpening their spikes with files in full view of the Philadelphia bench — sending a clear message: Stay out of our way. Herzog walked and when the Giants tried a double steal, Thomas threw to Collins at second to nab Herzog, who then rifled the ball back home in time to retire Snodgrass.

With one out in the seventh, Meyers slammed a pitch over Lord's head in left field. It hit the fence about a foot from the top and Meyers ended up on second with a double. Devore followed with a double over Baker's head to score Meyers, making it 2–1. Matty made the score hold up as he finished the game with a six-hitter. Bender had been just as masterful, allowing just five hits while fanning 11.

The turning point of the game, according to Mathewson, was when he fanned Baker with two men on base to end the third inning. The Athletics, who many observers felt stole the Cubs' signs in the 1910 World Series, were apparently onto the Giants' signs early in the game. Matty believed the A's scored in the second inning because Davis knew a curve ball was coming. McGraw countered by switching the Giants' signs.

In the crucial third inning, Matty believed Oldring was tipping the signs to Baker from second base. But they were the signs the Giants had used the previous inning. Baker fanned on three bad pitches, apparently not getting the pitches he was expecting.

"That was the turning point of the game," offered Mathewson. "After that point, they stopped trying to get our signals. After the third inning, I saw Barry, Collins and Baker with their heads together and I knew they were talking about what went wrong."[9]

Mathewson said the Athletics were the best offensive team he had ever faced. He added that they were smarter than any National League club when it came to stealing signs.

Matty's win in the opener was exactly what Mack wanted to avoid. After all, the team which won the first game of the Series had won the last six consecutive World Series. The big right-hander's outstanding performance also fueled the hopes that the Giants could get through the series riding his arm and Marquard's. Matty threw just 93 pitches (only 20 balls) in nine innings compared to Bender's 136 in eight innings.

McGraw was encouraged by Mathewson's strong finish. Baker, Murphy, nor Davis got the ball out of the infield in the last inning. "That is the reason why I think he could beat them twice more," said McGraw. "I think Matty will take three games. I don't care who works against him."[10]

In addition to the record-setting crowd which attended Game 1 at the Polo Grounds, an estimated crowd of 10,000 fans watched the reproduction of every play by the *Evening Telegram* on the Broadway façade of the *New York Herald* building. Thousands of fans were standing in the street an hour before the game started at 2 p.m. The streets from 35th to 36th were so jammed with people that 100 policemen were needed to keep the street open for streetcars and automobiles. The *Evening Telegram*'s Playogram kept fans abreast of the game by flashing a light signaling whether each pitch was a ball or a strike. If the pitch was hit, a ball on the board traveled to the position on the field. If the shortstop threw a batter out, a ball traveled across the field from shortstop to first base. If the batter was out, a light signaled out. If a batter was safe, a cross marked him as a runner. It was the most sophisticated reproduction at the time.

The Athletics returned to Shibe Park for Game two on Monday, October 16, in a matchup of left-handers, Plank versus Marquard. The game attracted 26,286 fans, the largest official attendance for a game in Philadelphia. Many of them had come from the Eastern Shore, Baltimore, and other towns in Maryland to root for Baker and Herzog. There wasn't an inch of room in the park as thousands stood in the outfield and an estimated crowd of 5,000 fans watched from neighboring rooftops, windows, telephone poles and trees.

In the A's' first inning, Bris Lord singled to right and advanced to second as Murray misplayed the ball. Oldring sacrificed him to third and Lord scored on a wild pitch. Marquard didn't surrender another hit until the sixth inning. The Giants tied the game in the second when Herzog doubled over Oldring's head in center, went to third on Fletcher's infield out and scored on Meyers' single to left.

With two outs in the sixth inning and the game tied 1–1, Eddie Collins doubled to left field just inside the foul line. Catcher Chief Meyers walked out to the mound to have a talk with Marquard before Baker came to the plate. The southpaw had struck him out on three pitches in the first inning and gotten him to ground weakly to second in the fourth.

With Collins on second base, the Giants were sure he was trying to steal their signals. Meyers told Marquard to throw two curve balls no matter what he signaled. Meyers was hoping to cross up Collins and Baker. Meyers signaled for two fastballs and Marquard delivered two curves, but Baker failed to swing at either one. Meyers went back to the straight signals on the third pitch. This time Marquard shook off the curve in favor of a fast ball. Despite trying to fool the Athletics, both Meyers and Mathewson believed Collins tipped the fastball to Baker.

Years later, Meyers recalled the 1911 World Series. "They're getting our signals from some place," he told McGraw. "That coach on third base, Harry Davis, is calling our pitches. When he yells, 'It's all right,' it's a fast ball."

"He must be getting them off you," McGraw said.

"But they weren't getting them off of me. I went to Rube and Matty and said, 'Pitch whatever you want to pitch. I'll catch you without signals.' And still the guy was hollering 'It's all right' for the fast ball. He knew something. I never did find out how he did it."[11]

With the count 1–1, Baker crushed a Marquard fastball, sending it over Murray's head in right field; the Giants' outfielder looked up and stopped in despair. The ball cleared the 335-foot wall by 10 feet. The *Philadelphia Public Ledger* described it as "a mighty smash, a terrific drive."[12] Baker started full speed down first base, but slowed to a trot as he noticed the ball clear the fence. He touched each base carefully on his way to home plate. Collins, on second base, raised his hands above his head and broke into a wide smile as soon as he knew the ball had enough distance to clear the field. He danced with excitement from third to home, ahead of Baker.

The crowd erupted into a thunderous ovation. Men screamed themselves hoarse, threw their hats in the air, and danced in the aisles. Horns, cow bells, and noisemakers filled the air with a carnival of sound. The Athletics jumped up off the bench, danced in joy, and ran to greet Baker as he crossed the plate. After countless pats on the back and handshakes, Baker entered the dugout and quietly went over to get a drink of water.

Calm on the outside, Baker was thrilled on the inside. It was his greatest moment. Thirty years later, he recalled the home run, "Thousands of fans on their feet, hands waving, hats in the air, and shouting as you rounded second base is something a man never forgets."[13]

Giants captain Larry Doyle ran from second to Meyers behind the plate and started to berate him for signaling a fast ball. Meyers pointed to Marquard, who was getting lectured on the mound by infielders Fletcher, Herzog, and Merkle. The ovation for Baker didn't stop until Murphy struck out to end the inning.

D.L. Reeves, covering the game for the *Philadelphia Ledger*, correctly predicted the magnitude of the moment. He wrote, "It will live in baseball history as long as the national game survives."[14]

Hal Chase, manager of the New York Highlanders, said, "I never saw Baker wallop a ball any harder than that one ... I don't think a ball could be hit any harder than that was."[15]

World Series home runs like Baker's were still rare enough to merit the description "Over the fence home run" in the headlines of many newspapers. It was only the tenth home run in World Series history.

In his newspaper column, Marquard wrote: "I fully intended to follow instructions and give him curve balls. But after I had one strike on him and he had refused to bite on another curve which was a little too wide, I thought to cross him by sending in a fast high straight ball the kind I knew he liked. Meyers called for a curve, but I could not see it, and signaled a high fast ball. Either he knew the signal from Collins, who was on second, or he outguessed me, for he was waiting for that fast one."[16]

Many sportswriters felt Baker benefited throughout his career with the Athletics from having Collins, a leader in stolen bases and crafty sign stealer, frequently on base in front of him. Collins addressed the issue a number of times, saying, "When it came to hitting, Baker needed help like (Andrew) Carnegie needed money."[17]

Marquard took full responsibility for the loss. He wrote, "Baker deserves credit for the victory, and I will bear the blame, for the fault is mine. I gave him just the kind of pitch he was looking for."[18]

Mathewson, covering the game for the *New York Herald* through a ghostwritten column by sportswriter Jack Wheeler, put the blame for the loss squarely on Marquard's shoulders. He wrote, "One ball pitched to Frank Baker in the sixth inning here today cost the Giants the game. That ball was right on the heart of the plate, came up the 'groove' and Baker hit it over the fence for a home run, scoring Collins ahead of him. If the ball had been pitched on the outside or had been a curve the result probably would have been different.

"The sixth inning was the critical inning of the game — victory hung on that one ball, and Marquard served Baker with the wrong prescription. I don't think for a moment Rube intended to lay the ball over the plate for him, but he did, and this cost us the game."[19]

He wrote that Baker's home run was due to Rube's carelessness. Prior to the game, McGraw had gone over all the Philadelphia hitters in a clubhouse talk, and paid particular attention to Baker. Marquard was told just what not to pitch the A's slugger. The victory took the pressure off the Athletics. With the series tied at 1–1, Mathewson could win two more games and it wouldn't be enough for the Giants to capture the series.

For Game 3 on Tuesday, October 17, at the Polo Grounds, McGraw came back with Mathewson, as expected, and Mack tabbed Coombs, the hero of the 1910 World Series. Many observers felt if Matty lost, the series would virtually be over for the Giants.

With nearly 38,000 fans looking on, the Giants scored their only run in the third inning as Meyers bounced a single over Baker's head at third. Mathewson singled to right, sending Meyers to third. Meyers scored when Devore grounded to shortstop Barry, who momentarily fumbled the ball before forcing Mathewson at second.

Matty worked out of a jam in the eighth as Barry was thrown out at the plate and Lapp was caught in a rundown between third and home.

Fans were already filing to the exits at the start of the ninth inning when Collins grounded out to Herzog at third base. The dangerous Baker calmly stepped to the plate with one out. He was always cool under pressure and enjoyed coming to bat when things looked bad and a big hit was needed. Mathewson gained an early advantage, recording two strikes on curve balls. But, like Marquard, he figured he could cross up the home run king with a fastball. As one account described it, "Baker leaned against the ball with all the gentleness of a battering ram."[20]

He connected for a sizzling line drive that never went higher than 15 feet off the ground over the high concrete right field wall, landing in the next to last tier of the upper grandstand occupied by Philadelphia fans for his second crucial home run in two days. Mathewson had made a mistake of the same magnitude Marquard had made the day before. Baker's blow shook the veteran right-hander's confidence, unsettled the Giants' defense, and changed the entire momentum of the game.

After Baker's homer, Matty angrily kicked the dirt while McGraw couldn't believe Baker had once again trumped his pitchers. The crowd was stunned. Mathewson had surrendered just one run in 44 1/3 innings against the Athletics going back to the 1905 World Series. For him to surrender a run in this situation, much less a homer, was unthinkable.

Fred Lieb, who covered the 1911 World Series, recalled the feeling in the press box and stadium, "Giant fans were aghast; a Baker home run off Marquard could happen, but not off Matty. I can still remember the awesome silence that followed the crash of Baker's bat. It was so quiet that those with especially good hearing could pick up the patter of Baker's feet as he romped joyfully around the bases."[21]

Despite the excitement, Baker, as always controlled his emotions, and he trotted around the bases with his head down, carefully touching each bag. The chills and goose bumps he was experiencing weren't evident to the crowd.

In the 10th inning, Fred Snodgrass attempted to reach first base by sticking his elbow out to get nipped by one of Coombs's pitches. Umpire Brennan recognized Snodgrass's ploy and refused to let him take first. Snodgrass eventually succeeded in drawing a walk from Coombs. On the way to first, he jumped up and down and threw his bat in the air, trying to upset the A's hurler. Murray sacrificed Snodgrass to second. With Merkle at the plate, catcher Jack Lapp dropped a curve from Coombs and Snodgrass dashed for third. Lapp quickly recovered and threw the ball to Baker, who was waiting for the hard-charging Giant.

Baker stood his ground, holding the ball tightly as Snodgrass came in feet first. Snodgrass's spikes ripped his pants and cut his right forearm.

Baker, unnerved, held tightly onto the ball and applied the tag on Snodgrass's stomach. The crowd of mostly Giants fans immediately broke into a storm of hisses and cat calls. Snodgrass's move seemed unsportsmanlike and out of place. Baker wiped the blood from his arm, the trainer came out to bandage the wound, and several of the players gathered around the third baseman with a blanket as his torn pants were pinned. When play was ready to resume, the crowd voiced its disapproval of Snodgrass' actions by cheering Baker. Snodgrass walked toward the dugout amid the uncharacteristic jeers and boos of the hometown crowd. The shouts of disapproval continued for nearly 10 minutes.

The Giants' infield faltered in the 11th inning as darkness approached. With one out, Collins singled to left and Baker sent a hot hopper to third baseman Herzog, who overthrew first base, allowing Collins to go to third and Baker to second. Murphy hit a routine grounder to Fletcher, who fumbled the ball allowing Collins to score. Davis tagged Matty's first pitch for a single to right, sending Baker home to stretch the A's' lead to 3–1.

The Giants managed to score one run in the bottom of the inning as Herzog doubled to left field. Fletcher flew out and Herzog took third as Meyers grounded out. David "Beals" Becker pinch hit for Mathewson. He grounded to Collins, who fumbled the ball, allowing Herzog to score. The game ended as Lapp threw out Beals, trying to steal second base. The A's catcher humiliated the speedy Giants, throwing out all five of their base stealers in Game 3.

The scene on the Athletics bench after the game was one of unrestrained happiness. They tossed their bats, gloves, and sweaters in the air. They hugged each other like long-lost brothers. They had beaten the previously invincible Mathewson, the man who was expected to block their path to World Series victory. They were now convinced they could win it all.

The *Philadelphia Public Ledger wrote*, "In this idol's [Mathewson's] fall, New York has lost its fond hope of a world's championship."[22]

In his ghost-written column after the game, Marquard wrote, "It was the hardest game to lose I ever saw and Matty lost it the same way I lost the game in Philadelphia. When he came back to the bench ... I asked him what it was.

"'The same thing you did, Rube,' said Matty. "I gave Baker a high, fast one. I have been in the business a long time and have no excuse."[23]

Marquard said the home run beat the Giants, instead of merely tying the game. He said the Giants were a beaten team, and they knew it when the score was tied.

"From that moment the luck of the game seemed to change," offered

Mathewson. "We had gotten all the breaks up to that time. After the home run, they got them all."[24] He attributed the Giants' loss to Snodgrass getting thrown out at third base in the 10th inning.

Baker, who considered himself a hitter without a weakness, was offended by both the Marquard and Mathewson columns. After the game, he said sarcastically, "Say, ain't it a wonder I got any kind of average in the American League. I'm a lucky guy to be in the league at all, after reading what they say where I hit 'em and where I miss 'em. I thought I hit for better than .300 this year, but I guess it's all a sad mistake. I've been hitting against some pretty swell pitchers in our league and they've put all kinds of stuff on the ball and for a blind man I guess I've done pretty well."[25]

Snodgrass's spiking of Baker unleashed a barrage of charges and countercharges, practically overshadowing the Philadelphia third baseman's crucial homer.

After the game, a *Philadelphia Evening Bulletin* reporter described the scene in the Athletics' locker room. "Stretched on a board, Baker twitched painfully as the trainer treated his spike cuts. The injuries were no mere scratches. When Snodgrass spiked Baker on Saturday, Baker had wounds on his left arm and left knee, the one on his arm being about four inches long and a half inch deep. The skin on either side was laid back, almost exposing the bone. Tuesday's wounds were just as deep and painful. One of Snodgrass' spikes slipped up Baker's right arm from the wrist to the crotch of the elbow, leaving numerous small cuts, one deep one and a mass of red abrasions. The other cut is on the right leg and is almost as bad."[26]

Hal Chase said, "Snodgrass' spiking stunt is the dirtiest I have ever seen. It was the most cowardly and dirtiest piece of ballplaying I have ever witnessed."[27]

There was no doubt in Baker's mind that Snodgrass's spiking was intentional. "Yes, I believe Snodgrass spiked me intentionally. He jumped across the bag to get me. I was in my right position," Baker told C. Starr Matthews of the *Baltimore Sun*. He said Snodgrass had acted like a "swellheaded busher" and reported that the Giants outfielder said, "If you don't get out of my way, I'll cut you down. I have a new pair of shoes and spikes for you." When asked if he had any idea why Snodgrass would deliberately spike him, Baker replied, "Just to get my goat."[28]

The Giants, who had heard Baker was spike shy, figured he would be unsettled after the incident. Baker traced the problem back to 1909 when Cobb spiked him. Detroit Tigers manager Hughie Jennings reportedly told the Giants that Baker had been nervous ever since.

Mack sided with Baker. "Mathewson and Charles "Red" Dooin [manager of the Philadelphia Phillies] can say what they please, but to my mind it was a deliberate spiking of Baker. They say Frank doesn't know how to tag a man at third. That is not true. Baker knows how to do it as well as any other third baseman in the business. There have been only two men to spike Baker — Cobb and Snodgrass. Snodgrass has done it twice in three days. Yesterday there was absolutely no reason why Baker should have been spiked. Snodgrass went out of his path to sink his spikes in Baker. It was a dirty, contemptible trick."[29]

American League President Ban Johnson didn't have any doubts, either. He said, "It was one of the worst things I have ever seen on the ball field. There's no question in my mind that it was done deliberately and I say that easily because there was no occasion for the act. Baker had the ball long before Snodgrass got to the bag and there was no reason why he should slide with his feet raised, then claw the baseman. Baker's legs are badly cut."[30]

Washington Post reporter Joe S. Jackson disagreed. "There was nothing either deliberate or dirty in the spiking," he wrote. "Snodgrass is somewhat new, and very rough in his work on the paths, but he dove straight at the bag. Baker does not know how to tag a runner and his awkwardness cost him, as it has on several occasions."[31]

The Giants chalked up Baker's spiking to his clumsiness. "There is a right and a wrong way to cover the bag and Baker uses the latter," voiced McGraw. "He doesn't give the runner any leeway to reach the sack, he seems to forget that the runner has the right of way. Baker is going to get badly hurt some of these days in spite of every effort on part of the runner to avoid him."[32]

Mathewson said, "Snodgrass was only doing what he has a right to do. It wasn't dirty ball. Baker had him by 15 feet, but instead of giving him room to slide into the bag in front of him and touching Snodgrass as he came in, Baker sprawled all over the base and blocked the runner completely off the bag. Snodgrass has a right to the base line and he slid in feet first to get a chance at the bag. It was Baker's own fault that he was spiked."[33]

Baker had captured the attention of the nation with his back-to-back homers and his name was on the lips of countless baseball fans. After Game 3, he received hundreds of congratulatory telegrams, letters, and postcards from fans across the country. Of course, Eastern Shore fans from Chestertown to Crisfield delighted in his success. Virtually every one of the 300 residents in Trappe was walking prouder, anxious to tell everyone where they were from. This was the World Series in which Baker put Maryland's Eastern Shore and his hometown of Trappe, described by a New York writer as "a village bypassed by the state highway and it seems to sleep in eternal peace,"[34] on the map. Almost overnight, Trappe became one of the best-known small towns in America. Perhaps only "Gettysburg Eddie" Plank was more closely associated with his hometown than Baker.

The jubilant Athletics returned to Philadelphia following the game. A crowd of several thousand fans greeted them at the North Philadelphia train station. Everyone wanted to see Baker, shake his hand, or talk to him. An American flag and a blue flag with a white elephant (the Athletics' mascot) on it were raised and the players, many accompanied by their wives, walked between them. The crowd grew larger every step of the way. Fans peppered Baker with questions as he traveled to a waiting car. He didn't want to talk, but he briefly responded to a couple questions. "Yes, I was spiked, but not badly," he said. "I am in good shape and will be in the game tomorrow." How about those home runs, he was asked. "What home runs?" he asked innocently. He didn't elaborate.[35]

Chase said, "I never saw in all my life a ballplayer grow so popular over night. But there is a mighty good reason for it. It will be a long time before we see another player hit two home runs in the pinches in such a set of big games as Baker has done."[36]

The *Philadelphia Evening Bulletin* reported that booking agents, safety razor pushers, fountain pen experts, cigar salesmen and motor car experts camped out to ask Baker to endorse their products. Offers for paid public appearances in department stores and other businesses poured in. Baker was offered $600 a week to appear in Vaudeville for 15 weeks at the conclusion of the World Series. The newspaper also reported that 17 babies born in Philadelphia in the week following Baker's homer off Mathewson carried the first name Frank and the middle name Baker.

While Baker was basking in the spotlight, McGraw advised Snodgrass to go home to escape the taunts of the Philadelphia fans. Snodgrass's absence from the Majestic Hotel started rumors that an irate fan had attempted to shoot him. At the same time, a rumor circulated that Baker has suffered blood poisoning from the spiking and had been hospitalized. Neither was true.

Despite the threats, Snodgrass was ready to play and prepared to handle the verbal abuse from Philadelphia fans. "The fans don't bother me," he said. "I have a clear conscience. I won't be worried by a few jeers and cat calls. My goat is not for sale."[37]

Neither McGraw nor Mack planned to announce their starters ahead of time for Game 4, scheduled for Wednesday October 18, at Philadelphia's Shibe Park. McGraw was expected to go with right-hander Leon "Red" Ames, who was 11–10 in the regular season. Although Ames had unusual speed and a deceptive curve, he was unreliable because of his lack of control.

The Giants' manager knew many fans believed that Matty's defeat in Game 3 stacked the odds in favor of the Athletics. Many observers felt Philadelphia's 3–2 win in 11 innings had broken Mathewson's spirit and his confidence.

Rain, however, delayed Game 4 for six days, the longest delay in World Series history. Shibe Park was described as a "virtual quagmire." Although the pitching mound and catcher's box were covered, the Athletics owners had no cover for the field like the one used for the Polo Grounds. The field was thoroughly soaked after two days. Sponges and buckets were used to sop up and carry away the pools of water that had formed along the baselines and elsewhere. Several cartloads of sand were hauled to the diamond to fill up holes in the infield. The outfield grass was trimmed as a measure to help the drying out and 12 men with lawn mowers went to work. Gasoline was burned over the outfield grass to help dry it.

By the time the conditions allowed the A's and Giants to play Game 4 on Tuesday, October 24, in Philadelphia, it was as if it were the start of another World Series. All the Athletics received standing ovations as they returned to Shibe Park, but the ovation for Baker from the crowd of 24,355 "curdled milk in Bustleton, Pa.,"[38] according to the *Philadelphia Evening Bulletin.* For three minutes, the cheers, whistles and foot stomping resonated throughout Shibe Park. The slugger was already being referred to as "Home Run" Baker by the Philadelphia newspapers. Still wearing bandages on his right arm and right leg from the Snodgrass spiking, he responded to the crowd by hitting the second pitch of batting practice over the right field fence. The week in between games had served to magnify Baker's feat of home runs in back-to-back World Series games off two of the National League's best pitchers. Others had hit home runs in the World Series before, but none on a bigger stage or with a greater sense of timing.

The postponements had restored all of McGraw's pitching options. It gave Matty and the rest of the staff time to rest and a chance to rebuild their confidence. Despite the options, observers knew the Giants' fate rode on the arms of Mathewson and Marquard. Game 4 was a rematch of the opener when Bender faced Mathewson.

The Giants staked Matty to a 2–0 lead in the first inning as Devore singled and Doyle followed with a hit to right center that rolled past Oldring on the slippery field for three bases, scoring Devore. Snodgrass flied out to Lord, sending Doyle home.

Matty appeared to be in top form as he struck out Lord and Oldring before Collins singled. Mathewson, Meyers and Doyle conferenced on the mound as Baker came to the plate. They were figuring out whether to pitch to him or not. The boisterous, frenzied fans were hoping for a repeat of Baker's earlier homer off Matty. The Giants decided to pitch to him and Mathewson made sure it was the right decision when he struck out the slugger.

The Athletics got to Mathewson in the fourth inning. Baker started the inning with a lead-off double as left fielder Josh Devore lost his fly ball in the sun. Danny Murphy followed with a double, scoring Baker. Harry Davis joined the hit fest as he doubled, chasing Murphy home to tie the game 2–2. McGraw ordered Marquard, Ames, and Wiltse to warm up in the bullpen. Davis advanced to third on an infield out and scored the go-ahead run on Thomas's sacrifice fly.

In the fifth inning, Collins and Baker continued to torment the Giants' ace. With two outs, Collins singled to center and Baker delivered in the clutch again, slamming a double to score Collins.

After surrendering a pair of hard-hit doubles to Baker, Mathewson walked him in the seventh inning without throwing a ball anywhere near the strike zone. The *Philadelphia Evening Bulletin* wrote, "Mathewson was afraid of Baker. That much was clear."[39]

While Mathewson faltered and was relieved by southpaw George "Hooks" Wiltse in the eighth, Bender got stronger. He shut out the Giants after the first inning and worked out of a jam in the top of the ninth after Merkle doubled with no outs to secure the 4–2 victory.

Philadelphia had beaten the New York ace for the second time in the series and taken a commanding three games to one lead. Afterwards, Mathewson said the Giants had been beaten by "too much Baker and Collins."[40] Once revered and feared, Mathewson was a shadow of himself. In seven innings, he had surrendered 10 hits, including six doubles, and suffered his worst World Series defeat. The *Baltimore Sun* observed that he was no more than an ordinary pitcher against the Athletics and at times during the game he possessed nothing but his ability to think.

The *Philadelphia Evening Bulletin* referred to Mathewson as "the Giants' fallen god." The newspaper added, "Anyone who knows anything about baseball, knows this was the deciding game of the series.... In the final analysis, it will be known as the day of the fall of Christy Mathewson."[41]

The Philadelphia newspapers, however, were premature in writing Matty's pitching obituary. After all, he won 23 or more games in each of the next three years and a total of 84 games before retiring.

After the World Series, catcher Ira Thomas revealed that the Athletics had detected a move Mathewson made that tipped off when he threw his fadeaway (the modern day screwball), an extremely effective pitch against lefthanders. The A's also discovered that he seldom threw the fadeaway for a strike. They decided to lay off that pitch and force Matty to throw more curves and fastballs. Although Mathewson beat the Athletics the first game, Thomas felt as if the club had achieved their goal, forcing the Giants' ace to labor harder. They felt confident he would not beat them again.

Philadelphia's Jack Coombs opposed New York's Rube Marquard in Game 5 on Wednesday October 25, at the Polo Grounds before 33,228 fans. The Athletics scored three unearned runs in the third inning after Jack Lapp singled, Coombs reached on an error and Rube Oldring unloaded a homer. Red Ames relieved Marquard in the fourth inning. The Giants cut the deficit to 3–1 with a run on Meyers's sacrifice fly in the seventh inning.

In the bottom of the ninth, Artie Fletcher doubled with one out. Pitcher Doc Crandall, who had entered the game in the seventh inning as a pinch hitter for Ames, tagged a double between right and center field, high over the heads of Murphy and Oldring to score Fletcher. Devore singled Crandall home to tie the game 3–3. Mack may have paid a price for letting the right-handed Coombs pitch to the Devore, a left-handed hitter. Coombs was laboring in pain, but wanted to finish the game. When Ira Thomas approached the mound, Coombs told him to tell Mack that he could take care of Devore. Southpaw Eddie Plank, who had struck out Devore four times in Game 2, was in the bullpen, but didn't get the call. Coombs had been bothered by intense pain in his groin since the seventh inning, when he twisted his right leg, aggravating an old injury. The pain kept him from throwing a curve ball.

Plank relieved Coombs to start the bottom of the 10th inning. Left-handed hitter Larry Doyle, who had committed a costly error at second base in the third inning, greeted Plank with a double down the left field line on a high pitch nearly at his head. It was his fourth hit of the game. Snodgrass bunted and Plank thought he had a chance to get Doyle at third, but his throw was late. That turned out to be a crucial play. If Plank had gotten Doyle at third, it would have erased a runner in scoring position and given them an out. Red Murray, held hitless in the series, lifted a shallow fly to Danny Murphy in right field, but it wasn't deep enough for Doyle to score. Giant base runners remained at first and third with two outs as Merkle came to bat. He got good wood on the ball and sent a deeper driver to Murphy, who waited until the last possible second to catch it, hoping that it would curve foul. He caught the ball on a hard run very close to the cement wall and was in an awkward position to throw home. His throw was accurate, but too late to get Doyle sliding home with the winning run. Some felt the ball would have landed in foul territory if

Murphy hadn't caught it. Although Murphy was criticized for his decision to catch the ball, the Athletics felt the ball was fair and Murphy made the right decision.

When Doyle slid home with the winning run, hundreds of fans stormed the field in celebration. National League umpire Bill Klem stood at home plate for a few seconds, waiting to see if the Athletics would protest.

While Mack's club was on the train returning to Philadelphia, Klem announced that Doyle slid to the outside of the plate and hadn't come within six inches of touching it. Doyle maintained that he took great pains to touch the plate. The Athletics, however, didn't file a protest. Catcher Lapp was so intent on receiving Murphy's throw, he didn't notice whether Doyle had tagged home plate or not. Official scorekeepers Francis Richter of Philadelphia and J.G. Taylor Spink of *The Sporting News* confirmed that Doyle missed the plate.

Lapp and the Athletics were anxious to get off the field to avoid the mob. Mack and Harry Davis had apparently noticed Doyle hadn't touched the plate, but they made no protest. Mack explained his reasoning to sportswriter Fred Lieb years later. "Jack Lapp and the rest of the players erred by leaving the field so quickly.... Lapp should have noticed that Doyle did not touch the plate, also that Klem made no safe sign. Lapp should have gone after Doyle and tagged him. But he needed to do it immediately." While Mack knew no legal run had scored, he had to consider the moment. He knew that within seconds there would be 20,000 rowdy Giants fans on the field. He believed if he had raised the issue and a ruling was made against the Giants, a riot would have ensued. "I believe they would have torn the place down," said Mack.[42]

Klem said if Philadelphia had filed a protest, he would have ruled the runner out and the game would have continued into the 11th inning. The win gave the Giants renewed hope, but it was short-lived.

Confronted with a must-win situation in Game 6 on Thursday, October 26, in Philadelphia, McGraw didn't have his aces Mathewson and Marquard available. He had counted on the duo all year and they had started all five games, without much success. McGraw decided to go with 29-year-old right-hander Red Ames, who had blanked the A's for four innings in Game 5. It wasn't the card McGraw preferred to play in a crucial game.

Mack was expected to go with Plank, who was well rested. He had won Game 2 10 days earlier and pitched just one inning in Game 5. Both Bender and Plank warmed up for the game. Until the Athletics took the practice field, Plank was expected to start since Bender usually needed more rest between starts. McGraw, in fact, had left-handers Marquard and Wiltse throw batting practice to help his hitters get ready for Plank. Mack surprised everyone, however, by selecting Bender, who had beaten the Giants just two days before. Shortly before practice, Bender approached Mack and told him he felt fine and could work. Mack immediately called Plank and told him the circumstances. The veteran southpaw apparently agreed to step aside and give Bender a shot at closing the World Series.

The Giants took an early lead in the first, as Doyle doubled into the temporary seats in right field, Snodgrass flied out, and Doyle scored as Murphy muffed Murray's fly ball. After that, Bender cruised through the next three innings, throwing just 18 pitches, 17 of them strikes.

The Athletics tied the game 1–1 in the third when Thomas walked, advanced to second on an infield out, and scored on Lord's double. The A's broke the 1–1 game open in the fourth inning with four runs, much to the delight of the 20,485 fans in attendance, the smallest crowd of the World Series. The lack of a capacity crowd reflected the fans' reduced enthusiasm after the week-long rain delay and their certainty that the A's would win.

Baker started the rally with a long single to center and Murphy singled him to third. Davis rapped a grounder to Doyle at second, who tried to tag Murphy en route to second, hoping for a double play. But Murphy stopped in his tracks, foiling the plan. Doyle then decided to try to get Baker at home, but his throw was too late. With runners on first and second, Barry bunted toward first. Ames fielded the bunt and threw to first but hit Barry in the head, sending the ball bouncing into right field. Murray retrieved it and overthrew Fletcher at second in an effort to get Barry. The ball rolled out to left field and Devore chased after it. By the time he picked it up and threw home, all three runners had scored. The Athletics turned the game into a fiasco in the seventh inning, scoring seven runs on seven hits.

Philadelphia was in no danger of squandering a 13–1 lead, but Mack sent Cy Morgan, Plank and Harry Krause out to warm up, rubbing salt in the humiliated Giants' wound. With two outs in the ninth inning, Captain Harry Davis went over to the Athletics' dugout and signaled Stuffy McInnis to take his place at first base. Davis had replaced the injured McInnis as a starter in the series. After McInnis took first base, pinch hitter Art Wilson lined a hard shot to Baker, who threw to McInnis for the final out of the series. The Athletics' 13–2 victory was the most lopsided in World Series history up until that time.

Immediately following the final out, McGraw rushed out of the dugout and shook Mack's hand and said, "You have one of the greatest teams I have ever seen. It must be. I have a great team, too, but you beat us."[43]

Mack grinned and said, "That's squaring ourselves for that trimming in 1905."[44]

After the game, Mathewson wrote, "I freely admit the Athletics were the better ball club ... their pitchers were better than ours and they outhit the Giants."[45] None of the Giants disagreed.

The *Philadelphia Public Ledger* wrote that the Giants were beaten by a team with more stamina, brains, nerve, and pitching. The Giants' biggest weakness was their inability to hit. As a team, the Athletics hit .244. Although not overly impressive, it was nearly 50 points higher than the Giants. Philadelphia's three pitchers surrendered just 33 hits for a combined ERA of 1.29. They held Giants' cleanup hitter Red Murray hitless in 21 at bats.

Baker was one of the major reasons why the Athletics stunned the Giants. Many observers felt his homer in Game 3 against Matty, which had tied the score in the ninth inning, was the turning point of the series. Had Mathewson won that game, the Giants would have been up two games to one and would have held the psychological edge.

Each Athletic received a winning share of $3,654. For Baker, it meant more money he could use to acquire farmland in Trappe.

Baker's clutch-hitting exploits had earned him one of the most revered nicknames in baseball history. He was the hero of the World Series. His two homers were crucial to winning two games and he won another with his bat. For the series, Baker batted .375 with nine hits, including four extra base hits, seven runs, and five RBIs. "Baker is a great hitter and will be the talk of the baseball world for some time," wrote Chase.[46] He would no longer be known simply as Frank Baker. For the next 50-plus years, he would be known as Frank "Home Run" Baker.

FIVE

A Bittersweet Season

After the 1911 World Series, Baker was no longer just a hero to the residents of Trappe, the Eastern Shore and Philadelphia. He was a national hero. Baseball fans from Pennsylvania to California and Maine to Texas had read about his home run hitting exploits in the newspapers. Sportswriters across the country had provided reams of copy about the Maryland farmboy's feat of slugging home runs on consecutive days against the Giants' Rube Marquard and Christy Mathewson in the most reported World Series up until that time. Even though he had destroyed the Giants' hopes of winning the World Series, Baker was surprisingly popular among New York fans. They admired his coolness under fire, his ability to deliver under pressure and his calm and quiet demeanor.

In just three full seasons, the Maryland farmer had established himself as one of the best hitters in the major leagues. Always confident of his ability at the plate, Baker was a natural hitter. His theory of hitting matched Detroit's Sam Crawford, who believed hitting should be done unconsciously. "If you get to studying it too much, the chances are you'll miss the ball altogether," said Crawford.[1]

F.C. Lane, writer for *Baseball* magazine, said he once overheard a conversation between Baker and a scientific friend, who was trying to get to the heart of batting and he mentioned the angle of incidence. Baker shook his head and appeared puzzled. "I don't know anything about the angle of incidence, but I do know that if I swing and meet the ball just right it will sail into the grandstands over there."[2]

A dead pull right field hitter with strong wrists, Baker waited until the last split second before he swung. He was patient, always making the

Baker displays his classic home run swing. The Philadelphia Athletics slugger led the American League in home runs for four consecutive years (1911–1914) with a high of 12 in 1913. From 1911 to 1914, he drove in more runs than any player in the American League. His best season was 1912 when he clouted 10 home runs, drove in 130 runs, scored 116 runs, stole 40 bases and batted .347. NATIONAL BASEBALL HALL OF FAME LIBRARY, COOPERSTOWN, NY.

pitcher throw him the pitch he wanted. He always looked for an inside pitch that he could pull to right field, where most of his home runs landed. He seldom hit outside pitches to the opposite field, unless instructed to by Mack. A low, outside curve ball was his biggest weakness.

The Philadelphia slugger stood with his feet about 18 inches apart with a closed stance. He always placed his back foot on the back line of the batter's box and he never moved around in the box because of who was pitching.

When Baker was asked what it takes to be a good hitter, he replied, "A good eye, nerve and strength. You can't be afraid of the pitcher or of being hit."[3]

Advertisers and commercial businesses were quick to capitalize on Baker's popularity. His image appeared on all sorts of items, ranging from pocket mirrors to magazines. Fans wanted to know more about 25-year-old slugger and sportswriters were quick to oblige. A December 1911 article in *Baseball* magazine described Baker as a "quiet, retiring kind of man, who prefers his country home to city life.... He is a stolid sort of athlete, hates publicity and was rather bashful when he first came up. He does not have much to say on the field, but plays with his heart and soul.... He is devotedly fond of his home and never happier than when playing with his little daughter."[4]

New York writers like Bozeman Bulger of the New York *Evening World* made the arduous train trip from New York to Cambridge, which could take as long as 10 hours, to visit Baker and his wife. They sometimes stayed with her parents in Cambridge during the winter. On one of Bulger's visits, the writer encountered several residents, who all claimed to have given Baker his start in baseball. Baker laughed and told Bulger he could meet a dozen more men who would make similar claims. And they all honestly believed it.

Baker's modesty made him popular with the residents of Trappe. Alfred Kemp, a pharmacist at the Thomas and Thompson's drugstore, spoke proudly of the village's most famous resident. "Frank never talks about what he does or what he can do and Trappe thinks all the more of him for it. He's the most popular guy in Trappe. When he comes home for the winter, he putters around the farm and hunts. He doesn't talk much baseball."[5]

The men of Trappe were delighted every time Baker smashed a home run. It not only meant more recognition for their favorite son and their small town, but another shipment of free smoking tobacco. Every time an Athletic clouted a homer some Philadelphia-area tobacco companies would send him a 10-pound supply of smoking tobacco. Baker, who didn't smoke, requested that all the tobacco be sent to Trappe. The men had an ample supply of smoking tobacco throughout the year.

Like many other baseball players, Baker enjoyed hunting in the winter and spending times outdoors. He often invited teammates down to his farm to go duck hunting. He was as comfortable with a fishing rod and shotgun as with a baseball bat and glove.

Baker savored his time away from the spotlight and the intense scrutiny of reporters. The four months from the conclusion of the World Series and the beginning of spring training seemed to fly by. The Philadelphia Athletics were full of confidence when they headed to San Antonio, Texas, for spring training in March of 1912. Back-to-back world championships against the mighty Chicago Cubs and New York Giants would make any team confident.

The question on most baseball fans' minds was: How great were the Athletics? Were they the greatest team in baseball history? Only the Chicago Cubs in 1907 and 1908 had won back-to-back world championships. Could they do what no other team had been able to accomplish — win three world championships in a row?

The A's hadn't really been pushed. They had won back-to-back American League pennants by 14.5 and 13.5 games. And they had won 8 of 11 World Series games. The future appeared bright. The Athletics were young, talented, confident, and oblivious to pressure. Mack didn't have a starter older than 28 and the only pitchers older than 30 were Eddie Plank and Cy Morgan. Mack's eye for talent and the ability to develop players had produced the top infield and best pitching staff in the majors.

Despite the success, Mack knew he couldn't stand pat. Although he had no major concerns, he wanted to develop another starting pitcher and fortify the catching position where Ira Thomas and Jack Lapp had split duties.

Mack felt that Bender was the best pitcher he ever saw and that Coombs was the equal to Walter Johnson and Ed Walsh. He said, "I think the Athletics have the greatest pitching staff ever pulled together under one management."[6]

Opposite: **Baker, labeled as "clumsy and awkward," was always underrated as a fielder because he lacked the grace of other American League third basemen such as Terry Turner of Cleveland and Larry Gardner of Boston. He quietly improved his fielding through hard work and practice. He led the American League third basemen in fielding percentage in 1911 and 1912. Baker was a fearless and aggressive third baseman. He studied the hitters, knew their tendencies and strategically positioned himself to make hard plays look easy.** TRANSCENDENTAL GRAPHICS.

But Mack wanted to get some younger pitchers into the rotation. He had hopes for lefthander Harry Krause, 24, who had won 18 games as a rookie in 1909. But the little lefty had gained considerable weight and had arm problems since his impressive debut. He had posted a 17–14 record over the past two seasons. Lefty Russell, 21, had loads of potential, but only one major league win since making his debut late in 1910.

Hoping to find a diamond in the rough, Mack invited more than a dozen hurlers to spring training. Among the pitchers were Dave Danforth, Roger Salmon, Carroll "Broadwalk" Brown, Byron Houck, and Bob Shawkey.

The Athletics infield of Baker, Barry, Collins and McInnis was considered the best ever. In early March, Mack said, "There have been some great infields, but we have one that has to bow to no one ... right now, they excel anything on the face of the earth."[7] The Philadelphia foursome became known as the "$100,000 infield." The $100,000 — a princely sum in those days — was what Mack said he would turn down for the infield.

The outfield was set with Danny Murphy, Rube Oldring, and Bris Lord. The *Philadelphia Public Ledger* deemed Murphy the best all-round outfielder in the American League with the exception of Ty Cobb. The newspaper felt Lord, who hit .310 in 1911, had the strongest arm in the league. Amos Strunk was the fourth outfielder. Mack, however, touted Harl Maggert, a speedy left-handed hitter, as a possible future star.

Baker and the other veterans arrived in training camp on March 6. The following day, Baker hit four consecutive balls over the fence off teammate Danny Murphy during batting practice. The last one cleared the right field fence and hit the top of a house outside of the ballpark.

With World Series fame and the newly acquired nickname "Home Run," had come increased pressure and expectations from fans. It would take much of the enjoyment out of the game for Baker, who inevitably would disappoint fans by not walloping a home run.

Mack addressed the issue early in training camp, "All the fans across the country are waiting for Baker to crack a home run every day. Well, they will be disappointed. Frank could duplicate that feat of the World Series with the same conditions in front of him. But he is not going to break any home run records and fans shouldn't ask him to.

"He is the hardest hitter in the American League and I do not except Sam Crawford, Tris Speaker or Nap Lajoie. But Frank, as a rule, hits the ball hard on the line and does not loft it over the fence as much as fans seem to think."[8]

It didn't take long for the pressure to take a toll on the young slugger. During the Athletics-Phillies city series in early April, Baker was admitted to the hospital with severely sprained stomach muscles as a result of trying to hit home runs. The pressure, however, wasn't just on Baker; it was also on the Athletics. Every team was gunning for the World Champions.

The Athletics were clearly the favorites to win the 1912 pennant, but Mack refrained from such a prediction. He figured five teams— Philadelphia, Boston, Detroit, Cleveland and New York — would be in the race. He labeled the Red Sox as the most serious contender. Although Boston had finished fifth at 78–75 in 1911, it had the best ERA in the league and a staff headed by 22-year-old Smoky Joe Wood, winner of 23 games the previous year. The youthful outfield of Harry Hooper, Tris Speaker, and Duffy Lewis averaged .317 and was the best in the majors. From time to time, the Red Sox had shown their potential, but injuries had always sidetracked them. With a new manager, Jake Stahl, and a new ballpark, Fenway Park, the club was more optimistic than ever.

Mack wanted to get off to a quick start to avoid the poor starts of 1910 and 1911. Unfortunately, it never happened. The season opened in fine fashion as Jack Coombs outpitched Walter Johnson of the Senators in Philadelphia. The Colby College hurler held the Senators without a hit for seven innings en route to a 4–2 win. Cy Morgan followed with his own pitching gem as he held the Senators to a scratch single.

The pitching continued to shine as Plank beat Boston 4–1 on a six-hitter. The following day, however, Harry Krause lasted just one inning while Smokey Joe Wood, who was to enjoy one of the greatest pitching seasons in baseball history, struck out 11. The Athletics' inability to beat the Red Sox turned out to be one of the major differences of the 1912 season. The Red Sox were clearly superior, defeating the A's in 15 of the 22 games.

Mack's pitching staff struggled early in the season. Bender didn't start until the ninth game and Coombs was injured in his second start. Coombs crumpled on the mound in the seventh inning against the Senators and had to be carried off the field with what was later diagnosed as a pulled groin muscle. It was the same injury that plagued him in the fifth game of the 1911 World Series. It was feared that he would miss the rest of the season, but he missed just three weeks.

Philadelphia's pitching was unsettled when the club visited Boston in late April. The Red Sox won three of the four games as Eddie Plank was the only Athletics' pitcher to notch a victory. Pitching, however, was one of the Red Sox's strengths. Five hurlers won at least 14 games. Although Joe Wood posted an incredible 34–5 mark, it was far from a one-man show. Twenty-two-year-old teammate Hugh Bedient went 20–9. Tom "Buck"

O'Brien (19–13), Charley Hall (15–8) and Ray Collins (14–8) kept the Red Sox from losing more than three games in a row until late September when they lost five in a row.

Offensively, Boston was led by centerfielder Tris Speaker, who batted .383, third behind Ty Cobb's .410 and Joe Jackson's .395. Speaker rapped 222 hits, including 53 doubles and 10 home runs, second to Baker's 12. He also led both leagues in on-base percentage and was third in the American League in slugging percentage.

The Athletics were involved in the first players' strike on Saturday, May 18, when the Tigers, in support of Ty Cobb, walked off the field before the start of the game. American League President Ban Johnson had indefinitely suspended Cobb for jumping into the stands in New York and pummeling a fan, who allegedly yelled vile epithets at him. His teammates protested what they saw as an injustice.

Jim Delahanty explained, "The assassin who shot President McKinley was given a trial. Cobb was suspended, but he was afforded no opportunity for explaining. And no player is afforded that right. He is chucked from the game, assessed with a heavy fine or subjected to a humiliating rebuke. It is only in keeping with the sportsmanlike principles of the game to give each and every player a square deal."[9]

Detroit manager Hughie Jennings quickly recruited some collegians and semiprofessional players, paying them $50 each. He dressed them in Tigers' uniforms, and sent them out to face Jack Coombs in front of 15,000 fans in Philadelphia. Predictably, the Athletics had a field day, routing the makeshift team, 24–2, as Aloysius Travers, a seminary student at nearby St. Joseph's College, pitched the entire game for Detroit. Upset with the Tigers' actions, Johnson cancelled Monday's game and met with the regular Tiger players. He threatened to ban them from organized baseball unless they played at Washington the next day. The regular Tiger players took the field on May 22 to end the strike. Cobb had encouraged them to play, saying he appreciated their support, but they shouldn't jeopardize their careers over the issue. Cobb's 10-day suspension stuck and the striking players were fined $100 each.

Approaching the end of May, the A's were off to another slow start with a mediocre 15–15 record and in third place. Mack had used eight starters in the first 30 games. Plank, his most dependable hurler, had started seven games, but Bender had started only three times.

Despite the record, Mack was confident his club would eventually win the pennant. He thought they were the class of the league. "Chicago has a great club, but the Athletics have the best team man-for-man," he said.[10]

He was patiently waiting for Bender, Morgan, and Coombs to round into their top forms. Bender started the season out of shape and the cold weather had hindered his progress. Morgan was a mystery and Coombs was battling back from an injury. Despite the slow start, Mack figured his club would be in first place by July 4. He didn't believe the White Sox or Red Sox could maintain their winning pace.

"Repeating is one of the hardest things to do and we are up against that this season," said Mack. "Every club, even Washington and St. Louis, saves its best stock of pitchers for us, for they know that we are the one club they have to whip. I have confidence in the Athletics and I'm convinced that we are a long ways from beaten in the race."[11]

The Athletics proved their mettle on a 23-game road trip that took them away from home from May 24 to June 19. Philadelphia posted a 15–8 record and moved into second place behind Boston. Road trips and home stands were typically long in those days because all travel was by train. Western trips for American League teams usually consisted of traveling to Cleveland, Chicago, Detroit and St. Louis. Traveling conditions were often rugged as players were crammed on trains and jostled for hundreds of miles. Players would frequently wake up covered in cinders from the coal-burning engines. Hotels were not the best and players spent countless hours away from home with an inordinate amount of time to kill. Travel was one aspect of being a major leaguer that Baker disliked.

Traditionally a slow starter, Baker had started to heat up by mid–May. On June 3, he homered against rookie right-hander Oscar "Rube" Peters of Chicago in Comiskey Park. On June 15, he came to bat in the first inning against Detroit right-hander Joe Lake at Tiger Stadium. After fouling over a dozen pitches, he caught one and slammed it to the top tier of the right field bleacher seats. No one had hit a ball further than the lower corner of the stand and only one had gone that far. The ball came close to clearing the wall entirely.

By June 10, Mack's men led the American League in everything but the standings. Their team batting average of .277 was 17 points higher than the Red Sox and 38 points higher than the White Sox. They led in team slugging average. Baker was fourth in extra base hits while McInnis was eighth. Collins led in stolen bases, while he and Baker were among the Top 10 in runs scored. Plank was 8–1 and Coombs, recovered from his groin injury, was 9–2. Baker was hitting .328, Collins .327, McInnis .320 and Murphy .315.

Shortly after the Athletics embarked on their road trip, J. Ed Grillo, a reporter for the *Washington Star*, wrote that according to the Detroit Tigers, the Athletics were feuding internally. "The most serious clash is said to have taken place between Barry and Collins some time ago, and according to reports, McInnis and Baker have taken a hand in the trouble with the result that there are no words exchanged between the two sides of the infield," wrote Grillo.[12]

Grillo reported that Mack had supposedly failed in trying to smooth things over. The feud was cited as one of the reasons why the A's had not been able to take over first place. At the time, the rumors were dismissed as the work of Tigers' manager Hughie Jennings in an effort to stir up the Athletics. The Philadelphia newspapers assured fans that the Athletics were getting along.

By mid–June, Philadelphia was 28–21 and in fourth place, trailing Boston, Washington and Chicago, but Mack was still confident. "I expect to win the AL pennant," he said. "But it is going to be a hard fight and it will be July before we take the lead, unless some of the top teams fall hard in a slump."[13]

Mack knew he needed a couple more dependable pitchers. Plank and Coombs had been carrying the load. Although Bender (4–2) was starting to round into shape, at age 28 he wasn't the dominant hurler of the past. Of all the young prospects Mack had brought into training camp, Carroll Brown and Byron Houck were the only ones remaining. If Mack could get some production out of them, it would be the key to the season. He knew he couldn't keep going with Plank and Coombs throughout the summer and doubleheaders. The toll would be too great. Mack was caught in a tough position. He needed to use Brown and Houck, but it was too risky because every game was critical.

The Athletics returned home to Shibe Park riding a hot streak, having won 9 of 12 during a successful three-week road trip. The Washington Senators, the surprise of the 1912 season, brought a 17-game winning streak to Philadelphia. Under first-year manager Clark Griffith, the youthful Senators were led by Arnold "Chick" Gandil at first base and speedy Clyde Milan in center field. Always dependable Walter Johnson was getting help on the mound from Bob Groom and Tom Hughes.

The clubs were scheduled for back-to-back doubleheaders. The prospect drew more than 20,000 fans both days. The four games served as a high point of the season for the Athletics and Baker, who looked their best and played well under pressure.

The A's snapped the Senators' 17-game winning streak and swept the back-to-back doubleheaders as Baker played a key role in all four games. Mack's club got a break as Walter Johnson was ill and stayed in Washington.

In the opening game on June 19, the Senators' 12-year veteran right-

Frank Baker was a national baseball hero after his home run hitting exploits in the 1911 World Series. This pin is just one of many collectible items that featured his photograph. He was besieged with requests from numerous companies to endorse their products and appear in their advertisements. COURTESY OF HUNT AUCTIONS.

hander Tom Hughes was one strike away from securing a 1–0 win and stretching the club's mark to 18 straight wins. Hughes had out dueled Coombs, limiting the A's to five hits. With two outs in the bottom of the ninth, Baker was the Athletics' last hope. Hughes worked him to a 2–2 count. Then Baker tipped a foul that hit squarely in catcher John Henry's mitt, but rolled out, giving him new life. Baker battled back, fouling off two more pitches.

Then Hughes tried to fool Baker and the slugger made him pay the price, just as he had made Marquard and Mathewson pay. He slammed the ball to right field, clearing the fence by a couple of yards to tie the game 1–1. "It is doubtful if the scene that followed was ever duplicated at Shibe Park," wrote the *Philadelphia Evening Bulletin* reporter. "It was only rivaled by the reaction to Baker's home run against Marquard in the World Series."[14]

The crowd was on its feet, waving whatever they had, cheering Baker as he rounded the bases. The Athletics tossed coats, sweaters, bats and gloves into the air. Shibe Park was a madhouse. The Senators were stunned at the turn of events. Hughes, however, calmed down, regained his composure and struck out Amos Strunk.

Coombs, who had surrendered just five hits, retired the Senators in the top of the 10th. With one out in the bottom of the inning, Barry beat out an infield single. Jack Lapp lashed a double down the right field line; Danny Moeller retrieved it and threw to second baseman Ray Morgan, who relayed the throw home. Barry, who had gotten a big jump toward second on the hit-and-run play, raced home. Henry tried to block him off the plate, but the little shortstop threw himself at Henry and dove between his legs. Henry applied the tag, but not before Barry touched home. Umpire John Egan signaled him safe. This unleashed a flood of protests by the Senators, who surrounded Egan and pleaded their case to no avail. The upset Henry lunged at Egan, but was restrained by his teammates.

In the second game, Bender faced 31-year-old right-hander Barney Pelty, who was making his debut with the Senators after being acquired from St. Louis. With the Senators leading 3–2 in the sixth inning, Baker tied the game with a RBI-single.

Baker doubled down the left field line to start the rally in the bottom of the ninth inning. He advanced to third on Strunk's sacrifice and scored the winning run when McInnis singled to left. He finished the doubleheader with two singles, a double and a home run.

The following day, Mack sent Eddie Plank to the mound and Griffith countered with 19-year-old southpaw Joe Engel. It was no contest as the veteran 36-year-old Plank had plenty of stuff and stamina and blanked the Senators on five hits. Stuffy McInnis's two-run triple in the sixth prove to be the Athletics' big blow. Baker collected two singles and scored a pair of runs in the 5–0 victory.

In the second game, Carroll Brown faced right-hander Carl Cashion. Baker continued his hot clutch-hitting as he put the A's on the scoreboard in the first inning with RBI-triple. In the third inning, Collins snapped the 1–1 tie with a RBI-single. With bases loaded, Baker followed with a deep drive to right, scoring two runs.

Baker bolstered his reputation as one of the game's most dangerous hitters as he collected nine hits in 15 at bats, including six singles, a double, a triple, and a home run, scored six runs, and drove in three.

The Senators rebounded by winning the next two games, knocking Philadelphia back to fourth place. In the last game, Baker continued his torrid hitting, homering off Hughes to tie the game in the fifth inning. The ball landed in almost the same spot where he had deposited his earlier homer.

At the end of June, Baker was hitting .346, sixth best in the league behind Speaker (.391), Jackson (.383), Cobb (.375), Lajoie (.362) and Collins (.357).

The Athletics trailed Boston by six games as they prepared for the biggest series of the season — a six-game series against the Red Sox at Shibe Park over the July 4 holiday. The Red Sox won four of six games, coming from behind in all four. They clearly established their superiority and deflated the hopes of the A's, who had won 21 of 30 games in June, most of them on the road.

On July 9, Mack received the bad news that Captain Danny Murphy would be out for the season. He had injured his knee sliding into home plate in Chicago in early June. Mack said, "It's a great blow to us, we need him."[15]

By July 22, Philadelphia was in third place, 11 games behind the Red Sox. Mack's outfield and pitching staff had been the source of problems. The outfield, which had hit a collective .319 in 1911, had underperformed. The loss of Murphy hurt and Lord and Oldring both were in season-long slumps. Mack had moved Lord to right to replace Murphy, started Harl Maggert in left, and given Strunk more playing time while keeping Oldring on the bench. Pitching was the same problem it had been all year. Mack had been counting too heavily on Plank and Coombs. Bender and Coombs were battling sore arms; Brown had been sick and Morgan had been a major disappointment. Mack had been forced to use his youngsters— Houck, Brown and Pennock — because his veteran starters were over-worked. The youthful trio had gained experience, but they couldn't be counted to carry the club down the stretch.

The Red Sox were playing at an impressive .696 clip, but most of the Athletics expected them to fade, much like the Tigers did in 1911. "It's a long race and we have the power to get better from now to the finish," said Collins.[16]

"If we get within five games of them (Red Sox) in the next three weeks, we will get them for sure," offered Lord.[17]

From July 22 through August 15, the Athletics won 16 of 21 games. The Red Sox, however, won 15 of 22. Philadelphia swept a doubleheader from Cleveland on August 14 to move past the Senators and into second place, eight and a half games behind the Red Sox. Mack's men had their last chance to make a move against the Red Sox with a three-game series at the end of August in Fenway Park.

Prior to the Red Sox series, Mack acquired Eddie Murphy and Jimmy

Walsh from the minor league Baltimore Orioles of the International League, hoping to improve his outfield. Both were hitting .350 or better for Jack Dunn's club. Mack sent disappointing pitcher Cy Morgan, outfielder Bris Lord, and infielder Claude Derrick to Baltimore. The move showed that the veteran manager was determined to catch the Red Sox.

Walsh was considered one of the finest minor league outfielders in the country. He could throw, hit the long ball and run the bases. Murphy was considered a diamond in the rough "with the potential to another Ty Cobb or Joe Jackson."[18]

In anticipation of the crucial series, Mack juggled his pitching rotation for two weeks to assure that Plank, Coombs and Bender would be available. Red Sox manager Jake Stahl had Ray Collins, Hugh Bedient, and Tom "Buck" O'Brien ready.

The Red Sox won the battle of the southpaws in the opener, 8–1, as Collins allowed only six hits and beat Plank. Boston tallied four runs off of Plank in the fourth, bunching a walk and four hits. The Athletics were never in the game after that.

Mack started Coombs in Game 2 against Bedient. The Athletics tagged Bedient for four runs on seven hits, including triples by Walsh and Barry, in the first three innings. The Red Sox scored two runs in the third and tied the game in the fourth on relief pitcher Charlie Hall's RBI single and Harry Hooper's sacrifice fly. Bender relieved Coombs in the fifth and held the Red Sox in check until the seventh when they broke the game open on Jake Stahl's two-run single.

Mack came back with Coombs against O'Brien and the two swapped six-hitters. The Red Sox built a 2–0 lead on O'Brien's RBI-single and a throwing error on Speaker's attempt to steal third. The Red Sox completed a sweep of the series, posting a 2–1 victory.

After the game, Mack conceded the pennant to the Red Sox and predicted they would easily win the World Series. He said he didn't realize how strong Boston was until this series.

The final chapter of the Athletics' dissatisfying season came on September 6 when Mack suspended and fined outfielder Rube Oldring and ace right-hander Chief Bender when they showed up late to the ballpark in New York for a game against the Highlanders after a "joy ride all over town."[19] Mack met them in the dressing room and a heated discussion followed. The veteran manager accused them of breaking the rules of discipline, not only in New York, but in other cities. He declared that their behavior had cost the A's many games. He told Bender and Oldring to take the first train back to Philadelphia. The two players were thought to be on the trading block as the result of their actions.

The Improved Collar Buttonhole

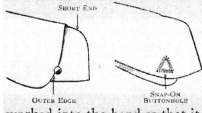

SHORT END

OUTER EDGE

SNAP-ON BUTTONHOLE

It's the newest buttonhole—the strongest and most practicable

THIS latest closed-front shape has the LINOCORD "SNAP-ON" BUTTONHOLE which is worked into the band so that it will neither stretch nor break in the laundering process, and no matter how moist the collar becomes during the hot days it will not spread or pull apart, and when placed on the collar button it cannot slip off. It is simple to adjust to the collar button, as it snaps on and off with ease. It holds the collar together in front and gives it that much sought for straight, closed-front effect every time it is worn. Has Ample Scarf Space.

Ide *Silver* BRAND

Collars 1/4 Sizes — 2 for 25¢

In Canada, 3 for 50c

in hundreds of impartial tests have proved they last longest in the laundry—and we have the proof.

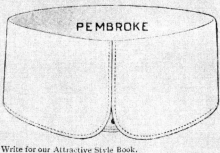

PEMBROKE

Write for our Attractive Style Book.

GEO. P. IDE & CO., 491 River Street, Troy, N. Y.

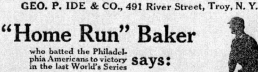

"Home Run" Baker

who batted the Philadelphia Americans to victory in the last World's Series **says:**

Gentlemen: Your Silver Collars have certainly made a big "hit" with me. The buttonholes are the easiest and best ever.

Yours truly,

(Signed) FRANK BAKER.

Ide *Silver* BRAND Collars

Frank Baker advertisement for Ide Silver Brand Collars from the July 6, 1912, *Saturday Evening Post*.

The incident partly explained Philadelphia's failure to win the pennant in 1912. Bender and Oldring had been problems for Mack all year and their poor performances had weakened the club. The *Philadelphia Public Ledger* wrote, "Ever since the season started, Mack has been forced to deal with internal dissension until yesterday when patience ceased to be a virtue."[20]

It was a disappointing year for the Athletics, who finished third at 90–62, 15 games behind the Red Sox and one behind the surprising Senators. Boston finished 105–47 and set a record for the most wins and highest won/lost percentage in American League history. Again, the American League was without a close pennant race.

Finishing third was particularly bitter pill for Mack to swallow. Years later, he called the 1912 Athletics the most talented team he had ever managed.

"The club had speed, hitting power, pitching skill, and more brains than one ordinarily finds on three clubs; but it didn't win. We still had our big pitching three — Bender, Plank and Coombs — and Eddie had one of his greatest seasons for me, winning 26 games and losing only six. [Stuffy] McInnis came along fast that year, as did [Amos] Strunk, and in the latter part of the season we acquired Eddie Murphy and Jimmy Walsh from Baltimore to give us additional outfield strength."[21]

Mack said the team suffered from overconfidence, believing they were unbeatable. The club felt as though it could win whenever it decided to. They laughed off the poor start and Mack said he may have been complacent, too, figuring his team would realize the Red Sox were going to be difficult to beat. The season slipped by without the A's snapping out of their slump. "By August we were playing the Red Sox and they already were chiding up as the ex-champions and there was nothing we could do about it," he said.[22]

Baker recalled Mack's effort to motivate the team in 1912. "He pulled no punches in making it known to us just which guys he felt were living off last year's reputation. He made no bones about the fact they were dogging it. In fact, he put a detective on their trail after telling them they couldn't drink beer and play ball, too. But it didn't work. The game didn't mean as much to them as it did the previous year when we beat the Giants."[23]

Mack's infield, however, couldn't be blamed for the subpar season. McInnis hit .327, Baker .347, and Collins .348. Barry managed a .261 average, but made up for it with his brilliant defense and leadership qualities.

Baker recorded one of the greatest seasons ever for a major league third baseman. He rapped out 200 hits, scored 116 runs, drove in a record

130 runs, clouted 40 doubles, 21 triples, and led the league in home runs with 12. Plus, he stole 40 bases. His slugging percentage of .541 was fourth, behind Cobb (.586); Jackson (.579); and Speaker (.567).

Late in the season, the *Philadelphia Evening Bulletin* observed that Baker had been "consciously working on improving his power by trying to master swinging up on the ball to loft it instead of swinging down on it."[24] It was an indication that the Athletic slugger was well aware of how to take advantage of the livelier baseball.

Despite Baker's impressive offensive numbers, his performance is often overlooked because the A's finished third. Even the Philadelphia newspapers during the 1912 season didn't accurately portray the magnitude of his production.

His 130 RBIs were the major league record at the time. Babe Ruth eclipsed the mark in 1920 with 137 runs batted in. Baker's season-high RBI total wasn't surpassed by a third baseman, however, until future Hall of Famer Eddie Mathews of the Milwaukee Braves drove in 135 runs in 1953. He accomplished that with the benefit of 47 home runs, compared to Baker's 12. Kansas City Royals' Hall of Famer George Brett is the only other third baseman to hit .300, and tally triple figures in runs and RBIs and double figures in home runs, doubles, triples, and stolen bases in a season. Brett accomplished the feat in 1979.

For Baker, 1912 was a bittersweet season. He enjoyed his greatest individual season, but it was one of the most disappointing for the Athletics.

SIX

Redemption

The Philadelphia Athletics had plenty to prove in 1913. Their egos had taken a beating in 1912 as they had been forced to watch the Boston Red Sox beat the New York Giants in seven games in a poorly played World Series, which produced 31 errors.

Mack was convinced he still had the best team. His challenge was to motivate his players and make sure they didn't become lackadaisical and overconfident again. He hoped they had learned a lesson from the previous season.

The Athletics had no pressing needs for 1913, if they could avoid injuries. Mack had improved the team's depth with younger pitchers who had gotten some valuable experience and the acquisition of outfielders Eddie Murphy and Jimmy Walsh.

When the A's departed the North Philadelphia train station on February 24, for another training period in San Antonio, Texas, spirits and expectations were high among the players and the fans. Baker did not make the initial trip south, having received permission from Mack to report to spring training on March 9 in order to take care of some business matters. Baker, like many other players, was not particularly fond of spring training and throughout his career he found some reason to report late. Players did not get paid during spring training. They started to receive their regular paychecks when the season began. There was, however, never any concern about Baker's physical condition because he was one of the best conditioned players in the major leagues from plenty of off-season exercise.

After arriving in spring training, Baker didn't take long to prove he was in midseason form. In his first game, he pounded out five hits—three singles, a double and a triple — as the Athletics thumped the San Antonio Broncos of the Texas League at Block Field, 17–1. The A's completed a six-game sweep the following day.

Baker was the hitting star once again when the Athletics defeated Dallas of the Texas League five days later as he slammed two singles and a double. The club moved on to Texarkana, where more than 1,000 fans turned out to see if he could drive a ball out of Texas into Arkansas against the Texas and Oklahoma League club. The outfield fence at Hilly Ball Park was the dividing line between the two states. Baker failed to clear the fence and wallop a ball into Texas, but collected a single, double and a triple that hit the top of the fence.

Philadelphia ran its winning streak to 12 straight with a victory over Memphis of the Southern League. While the opposition hadn't been of major league caliber, it was clear that Mack's team wasn't taking anyone lightly. A seriousness had replaced overconfidence.

Baker got fans buzzing again when he homered in Nashville, another Southern League team, on March 20. His blast easily cleared the 30-foot high right field fence, which was on a 20-foot embankment. It was the longest home run ever hit at Nashville Park. The Athletics continued their winning streak in Nashville and Louisville, where they played an American Association team. Mack's men had won 18 games in a row by the time they arrived in Philadelphia. They tuned up for the city series against the Phillies by beating the University of Pennsylvania team. The Athletics followed by winning four straight games from the Phillies. The fifth game went 18 innings and ended in a 2–2 tie. The A's won the sixth game to stretch their streak to 23.

On April 9, the day before the regular season started, the A's traveled to Baltimore to play the International League Orioles. Twenty-three-year-old right-hander Bob Shawkey, a former Athletic, started for Baltimore and held his former teammates to three hits as the Orioles dealt Philadelphia its first loss of the spring. Baker went hitless in three trips. Despite the setback, the Athletics had delivered a message for how they were going to approach the season.

If Mack's club was going to regain its status as the top team in the American League, it would have to beat out the Red Sox and Senators, teams that finished in front of them in 1912. Both clubs had dominant pitchers, Smoky Joe Wood and Walter Johnson, who were coming off their best seasons. The Red Sox suffered a major blow to their pennant chances in spring training, however, when Wood slipped fielding a bunt and broke the thumb on his pitching hand. His victory total fell from 34 to 11 and his innings pitched dipped from 344 to 146.

In 1913, the Athletics finally got off to the quick start that had eluded them in previous years. They opened the season with six games against the defending champion Red Sox, two at Fenway Park and four at Shibe Park. The A's won five of six, averaging six and a half runs per game. At the beginning of the season Mack showed a tendency to go to his bullpen often and to rely on his starters to take on plenty of additional responsibility as relievers.

Mack increasingly went to the bullpen, but never more so than in 1913. Jack Coombs started the opener and Bender and Plank relieved. Plank also relieved in the second game. Bender started the third game and relieved in the fourth game. Plank started game five. Mack decided to take advantage of his pitching depth, going with his youngsters as long as he could and then bringing in a veteran from the bullpen. Mack had added 20-year-old "Bullet" Joe Bush and 21-year-old Weldon Wyckoff of Bucknell University to his returning staff which included Herb Pennock, 19, and Duke Houck, 21.

Philadelphia raced out to a 15–3 record, settling in first place on April 24. They didn't relinquish the lead for the rest of the season. Although Coombs started the first two games of the season, he was sidelined with typhoid pneumonia and was expected to miss the rest of the year.

Of the first 18 games, Carroll Brown and Houck started eight games, one more than Plank and Bender combined. The experience they gained from 1912 was paying off and it was giving Mack other dependable starters.

Although the Athletics were dominating the early action, they weren't getting much help from Baker's bat. He was off to his typical slow start, hitting just .217 in early May. By the middle of the month, it was obvious the A's were the class of the league.

On May 16, the *Philadelphia Ledger* reported that hard-luck Jack Coombs was "critically ill and may never pitch another game." Coombs had left the opening game in the fifth inning and according to the newspaper, "he has practically been an invalid ever since."[1] He had nursing care around the clock and his situation was apparently life threatening. After remaining in the hospital for three weeks, he was transferred to his home in Philadelphia.

The A's were 22–10 on May 24, but Mack was concerned about his

Opposite: **Walter Johnson of the Washington Senators called Baker "the most dangerous hitter I ever faced." Baker slugged five career home runs off the dominating right-hander. In 1913, when Johnson won 36 games and compiled a minuscule 1.14 earned run average, Baker batted .318 against him and smashed a pair of home runs. Transcendental Graphics.**

pitching because no one seemed to be able to throw a complete game. Then the Athletics reeled off a 15-game winning streak, taking four games from Washington, New York and Detroit and three from St. Louis. The A's were 37–10 and in first place when their streak ended on June 11.

By now Baker's bat was heating up and he played an instrumental role in the club's winning streak. On May 29, he homered in the seventh inning against the Yankees' right-hander Ray Keating to tie the score. With two outs in the ninth, he doubled down the first baseline and scored the winning run on McInnis's single.

Baker homered and doubled as the Athletics swept a doubleheader from the Yankees on May 30. In the first inning, he touched right-hander Ray Fisher for a two-run blast to left field. Baker continued to feast on Yankee pitching the following day as he unleashed his third round-tripper in as many days, this time against right-hander Ed Klepfer, as the A's romped 12–2.

He continued his power display against the Senators and Walter Johnson as Philadelphia swept a doubleheader on June 2. In the fourth inning of the second game, Baker broke open a 0–0 game as he clouted a solo homer to right field to continue his early career success against the American League ace. He later doubled and scored a run.

The club reeled off seven more wins against Detroit and St. Louis before the Browns halted the streak on June 11. The Athletics didn't have any time to dwell on the loss since they had to prepare for a crucial four-game series with Cleveland. Although the A's had played at an amazing .770 pace, the Naps had played at a .700 clip. They were paced by right-hander Cy Falkenberg, who started 10–0, and lefty Vean Gregg, who was 9–3. Joe Jackson was hitting over .400 and Nap Lajoie was hitting .344. Three other Naps were hitting above .300. Pitching dominated the series as the Athletics won three of the four games, padding their first-place lead to six games over the Naps.

Baker continued his torrid streak with the bat as he rapped out three hits, including a home run against right-hander Jim Scott of the White Sox on June 17. On June 22, he drove in five runs against the Red Sox with what the *Philadelphia Public Ledger* described as "a terrific triple, a slashing double, and a screaming single."[2] Three days later, the Philadelphia slugger roughed up Washington's Walter Johnson again as he clouted a two-run homer in the third inning and finished the day with three hits. The following day the A's swept a doubleheader from the Senators as Baker went 5-for-9, lifting his average to .300.

The Athletics followed with a four-game sweep of the New York Highlanders, virtually locking up the pennant by July 4. They were 51–17 and

10 games ahead of second-place Cleveland. The only time they had lost two games in a row was June 20 and 21 against the Red Sox.

Mack's club was hitting .285, 25 points higher than the second closest team. They led the league in extra-base hits and fielding, had three of the top 10 sluggers, three of the top 10 base stealers, and four of the top 10 run scorers. The only question at this point was who Mack would select to start the World Series— Bender or Plank.

The Athletics were coasting by mid–July, but Senators' manager Clark Griffith tried to stir things up, proclaiming, "Philadelphia will not win the AL pennant; they will crack any day now.... We [Washington] will pass the Naps in 10 days and the rest will be easy," he said. "I expect the A's to win barely half of their remaining games."[3] He predicted that Plank and Bender would cave in soon and Mack's young pitchers would not be able to carry the burden.

Griffith was close on his latter prediction. Philadelphia went 29–28 from August 1 through the end of the season. Neither the Senators nor the Naps, however, could take advantage of their mediocre performance.

Philadelphia won 96 games and could have easily surpassed 100 wins if Mack had not had to juggle their lineup so much in the second half. They still had a chance to reach 100 wins after clinching the pennant, but lost eight of their final nine games as Mack experimented, giving other players time in the lineup. Bender and Plank started only one game after September 13.

Mack had five pitchers earn double-figure wins. Far from being washed up, Bender led the way with 21 wins and 12 saves while Plank added 18 wins and four saves. Houck, Brown, and Bush accounted for 45 wins. During the year, Mack's top six pitchers started 135 games and made 95 relief appearances.

The Athletics scored 794 runs, 163 more than the Cleveland Naps, the second-best run-producing team in the AL. Mack's men became the first team in the 20th century to score more than 100 runs than the next best team. Only 13 teams have accomplished the feat in baseball history. Four players— Collins, Baker, Eddie Murphy, and Rube Oldring crossed the plate 100 or more times. Eddie Collins led the way with a .346 average while McInnis batted .326.

Baker turned in another splendid year. He led the league in home runs with 12 (his career high, no other player had double figures) and RBIs with 117. He scored 116 runs, second behind league-leader Eddie Collins with 125. He collected 190 hits, third behind Joe Jackson (197) and Tris Speaker (193). He slammed 34 doubles, second to Jackson's 40. He batted .337 and stole 34 bases. In a year when Walter Johnson won 36 games and compiled a minuscule 1.14 earned run average, Baker batted .318 against him and slugged a pair of home runs.

Prior to the start of the World Series, noted newspaperman Hugh Fullerton assessed Baker. He wrote, "Baker ranks among the greatest batsman of recent days. As a fielder, he has improved wonderfully during the last two years. He fields and bunts well, gets as many foul flies as any third baseman in the game and can now handle thrown balls splendidly.... He is neither as slow nor as awkward as he appears." [4] Fullerton focused more on his fielding and throwing than hitting, trying to dispel a number of myths about the third baseman. He praised Baker's strong and accurate arm, his ability to knock down hard drives and recover to throw out runners, and his ability to field bunts.

Baker, always labeled as clumsy and awkward, had quietly improved his fielding through hard work and practice. He led American League third basemen in fielding percentage in 1911 and 1912. The Trappe native studied the hitters, knew their tendencies, and strategically positioned himself to make hard plays easily. He was a fearless and aggressive third baseman, running out to shallow left field to make plays, chasing balls in foul territory and charging bunts.

Baker's fielding was always underrated because he lacked the grace of some of the other third basemen in the American League such as Larry Gardner of Boston and Terry Turner of Cleveland. Additionally, his hitting overshadowed his fielding. Baker's fielding statistics belied the perception of his defensive abilities.

Assessing Baker after his career, Mack said, "I've heard many people comment that Baker was an ordinary third baseman. They said he was clumsy and used his body to stop hard-hit balls. That wasn't true. Baker was a great third baseman. Maybe Jimmy Collins was better. But from 1909–1914, he was the best in the American League. To me, he was a third baseman almost without a flaw."[5]

In a 1913 article rating all the major league third basemen, sportswriter F.C. Lane named Baker the greatest. In regards to his fielding, Lane wrote, "He (Baker) is a good if not brilliant fielder.... His deficiencies in the field, which are not great, are far more counterbalanced by his excess of batting power."[6]

In the same article, two of the greatest American League stars selected Baker as the top third baseman. Walter Johnson said, "Anybody who can cover third base and hit as he does is a wonder" and archrival Ty Cobb added, "There may be prettier fielders, but Baker has a long reach and covers a good deal of ground."[7]

Fielding in Baker's era was a much more challenging task than it is today. Gloves were small, lacked padding, had no webbing between the fingers and were flat without a natural pocket. A fielder couldn't just stick his hand out and catch a ball, he had to play it almost perfectly. Additionally, infields were not as well manicured as they are today and bad hops were more common. Many of Baker's errors came on throws to first. Making accurate throws was difficult when the ball was sometimes covered with saliva or tobacco or was lopsided.

From 1901 to 1910, the American League committed 2,277 errors for a .954 fielding percentage. From 1911 to 1920, the league made nearly 300 fewer errors and lifted its fielding percentage to .960. The 1920 season saw the single greatest revolution in glove design with the appearance of the Bill Doak model, which featured a preformed pocket and reinforced webbing. Fielding percentage continued to increase in each succeeding decade.

In the 1955, Cambridge *Daily Banner* sports editor Bobby Layton recalled seeing Baker's glove that he used with the Athletics. "I thought it belonged to his grandchild or some six-year-old. It was in fair shape, but it looked like a kid's glove you buy in a dime store. It had no pocket, but was flat all over and about two-thirds the size of a regular ball player's glove. I had read about how poor the gloves were in Baker's day, but I had no idea of how poor."[8]

In the National League, John McGraw's New York Giants coasted to its third consecutive pennant, beating out the Philadelphia Phillies by 12.5 games. The club won 101 games on the strength of its pitching. Christy Mathewson, Rube Marquard, and Jeff Tesreau all won 20 games and Al Demaree added 11. All three 20-game winners were well rested, healthy, and confident. While McGraw's staff produced the league's lowest earned run average, his club didn't lead the league in any offensive category. Catcher Chief Meyers was the only regular to bat over .300. No Giant drove in more than 73 runs or scored more than 81 runs.

At the end of August, Mack predicted, "This will be the hardest-fought World Series this country has ever seen."[9] For the first time, Mack didn't have a proven, veteran staff. Weak pitching had plagued his club all year. But Mack had masterfully juggled his rotation during the regular season, working in his young pitchers and using Bender and Plank when he needed them. Many observers didn't believe he could do that in the World Series, where every game was critical and there are fewer opportunities. The Giants' main strength was its pitching staff. The big question was 'Could the Athletics' offense offset the Giants' pitching."

Most observers and sportswriters didn't think so. In a survey of 30

Baker was a thorn in the side for New York Giants manager John McGraw, left, and pitcher Christy Mathewson, right, in the 1911 and 1913 World Series. Baker slammed a crucial game-tying home run off Mathewson in the bottom of the ninth inning in Game 3 of the 1911 World Series after blasting a game-winning home run off Rube Marquard the day before. Those two home runs, delivered under intense pressure against two of the game's best pitchers, earned the Trappe, Maryland, native the prestigious nickname "Home Run." The A's defeated the Giants in 1911 and 1913 as Baker collected 18 hits in 44 at bats for a .409 average. NATIONAL BASEBALL HALL OF FAME LIBRARY, COOPERSTOWN, NY.

prominent baseball writers, 18 voted for the Giants, nine for the Athletics and three were undecided.

McGraw, under intense pressure after losing two consecutive World Series, predicted his club would win the 1913 World Series. He believed his staff was the best in the majors. He expected Mathewson to dominate the Athletics as he had in 1905 when he pitched three shutouts. Matty, 33, surrendered just 21 base on balls in 306 innings during the 1913 season. He was never more impressive than when he went 68 consecutive innings without a walk from June 19 to July 18.

Mack's youngsters, however, weren't to be taken lightly. Tris Speaker of the Red Sox predicted that 20-year-old pitcher Bullet Joe Bush would be the surprise of the series. He compared him to Walter Johnson, rating his fastball a close second to the Big Train's. Bob Shawkey had posted a 2.35 ERA in 18 games. Mack was handicapped because 17-game winner Carroll "Broadway" Brown had injured his knee late in the season and 14-game winner Duke Houck was still considered too wild to pitch in a crucial game.

Mack had great faith in his youngsters, despite their lack of experience. That was good because he was going to be forced to use them. And, their performance would likely hold the key to the series. If the A's could match the Giants' pitching, they would gain the advantage because they were superior in every other category.

In the 1911 World Series, it had been Mack who had wanted revenge; this time it was McGraw. The Athletics and Giants rosters were similar to those of the past World Series and they knew each other well. The A's had 13 players who had played in the 1911 World Series and the Giants had 12.

Perhaps smarting from losing the pennant, Cleveland's Joe Jackson said the A's didn't have a chance of winning. He picked the Giants to win in four straight. He said Bender wasn't as effective as he used to be; Plank was washed up; and that the young pitchers couldn't last more than three innings.

His manager, Joe Birmingham, wasn't of the same mind. Although he felt Plank and Bender weren't as good as they were two years ago, he believed Bender could beat any team in the World Series. He was also high on Bush and Shawkey, figuring they would give the Giants trouble. "Mack has a tribe of murderous hitters," he said. "Candidly, I don't think even Mathewson can stop them."[10]

Walter Johnson, who had faced the Athletics seven times in 1913, had high praise for them. He believed the A's would win the Series because they were stronger offensively than the Giants. "I don't believe the Giants will have any more success against Bender and Plank than they did two years ago," he said. "My experience has been that unless I'm right in every sense of the word and pitch shutout ball, they have beaten me."

According to Johnson, Philadelphia didn't have a weakness. Everyone in their lineup, including their pitchers, could hit. He considered Baker and McInnis the two most dangerous hitters on the team. "If either has a weakness, I don't know what it is. Both will go after bad balls and make base hits when a pitcher least expects it. Usually, too, they do it when a hit means a run."[11]

Johnson felt the A's were a better all-round team than they were in 1911. He expected Bender and Plank to handle most of the pitching. If, however, any of the younger pitchers held the Giants to three runs or less, he felt the Athletics would win.

Although the World Series was set to start on Tuesday, October 7, at the Polo Grounds, there was talk that it could be halted. The recently formed Baseball Writers of America was protesting the practice of players writing articles for newspapers. Baker and Collins both wrote articles during the World Series. Actually, the articles were ghostwritten and appeared under the player's byline. August Herrmann, chairman of the National Commission, said the World Series could be called off if players refused to halt the practice. American League President Ban Johnson said players could write their own stories, but that lending their names to the stories without writing them should stop. The issue was quickly resolved in the players' favor.

One new rule, however, was put into effect for the 1913 World Series. No photographers would be allowed on the field except for those employed by the daily newspapers and they must be off the field before the game began. Another new practice was that no spectators would be allowed to watch the game sitting in the outfield. In the past, spectators crowded wherever they could on the field and they were roped off from the playing area. Ground rules were established for balls that bounced or landed into the crowd. Now, however, the players would be the only ones allowed on the field and every hit would be what the player could get.

As always, winning the opening game of the World Series was important. This year, however, it would be a key advantage to Mack more so than McGraw. A victory would give Mack an opportunity to work the pitching to his advantage. It would mean he would less likely have to put one of his young pitchers in a must-win situation.

As expected, the excitement level by the start of the World Series was at a fever pitch. The Athletics and Giants represented the greatest matchup in sports. In New York hotels, bars, and restaurants there was one main topic of conversation: Who would win the World Series? And, just about every fan was willing to place a bet on his favorite team.

A near-record crowd of 36,291 attended the opening game at the Polo Grounds on Tuesday, October 7. Hundreds of fans stood in line all night waiting for the ticket windows to open at 10 a.m., two hours later then anticipated. The crowd stood 10 deep for six blocks. When the ticket windows closed at 1 p.m., one hour before game time, there was still an estimated crowd of 10,000 to 15,000 fans in line. Many of those who weren't fortunate to purchase tickets were among the 15,000 in Times Square who followed the game through information related to the *New York Times* 18-foot by 24-foot electric scoreboard, the top of which was 46 feet above street level.

Once again, Baker and his mentor Buck Herzog, third baseman for the Giants, met in the World Series. Prior to the game they shook hands and posed for photographs. The band played "There's a Girl in the Heart of Maryland." In batting practice, all eyes were on Baker, who had won his third consecutive home run title. The slugger put on an impressive exhibition during batting practice, smashing several balls over the fence.

Mack and McGraw, always trying to gain any edge they could, played their probable starters close to the vest, not wanting to reveal who would start until the last possible minute. For the opening game played under threatening skies, McGraw had both Mathewson and Marquard warming up while Mack had Plank and Bender working on the sidelines. McGraw decided to go with Marquard 15 minutes before the game. He figured the southpaw's fastball would be more difficult for the A's to pick up on a cloudy, overcast day and be tougher on left-handed hitters. Mack countered with Bender.

The Giants tallied the first run in the third inning on Merkle's single, a sacrifice and Larry Doyle's RBI single. The Athletics wiped that lead out in the fourth as Eddie Collins tripled to right center and Baker followed with a smash off of Doyle's glove at second base to drive home Collins. With two outs and a runner on first, Jack Barry doubled to chase Baker home with the second run. Switch-hitting rookie catcher Wally Schang blasted Marquard's offering to right center. Arthur "Tillie" Shafer, normally an infielder, was playing center for the injured Merkle who had been moved to first base. Shafer misjudged the ball, hesitated briefly and then ran for it. He barely got his glove on the ball, managing to knock it down. Schang slid into third base with a two-run triple, giving Philadelphia a 3–1 lead.

Baker stepped into the World Series spotlight again in the fifth inning. With one out, Marquard walked Collins, bringing the feared left-handed slugger to the plate. Baker let Marquard's first pitch pass as Collins stole second. Then the southpaw threw him a high, inside pitch which he hit solidly. From the crack of the bat, players and fans knew it was a home run. "Like a rocket, it shot to right field,"[12] described the *Baltimore Sun*. Red Murray raced back to the concrete grandstands and stood watching the ball sail over his head. Ironically, Baker's blast cleared a big advertising sign, half of which borne the inscription "Champion of the World." Thousands of fans jumped to their feet to cheer him. The Athletics tossed their bats high in the air and danced with joy. Collins waited for him at home plate, grabbed his hand, shook it enthusiastically and patted him on the back. Baker was once again a dramatic Giant killer.

The Athletics' 5–1 lead looked secure, but the Giants rallied. Merkle singled and Harry "Moose" McCormick, pinch hitting for Marquard, singled. They advanced as Collins threw out Shafer. Merkle scored on Collins's throwing error and Artie Fletcher's single scored McCormick. With runners on first and third and one out, Baker made a brilliant defensive play as George Burns smashed a wicked grounder between third and short. Baker seemed to come from nowhere, grabbed the ball with one hand and threw to second for a force out. Collins' relay throw to first barely missed doubling up Burns. A run scored on the play, making it 5–4. Herzog, however, popped up to Collins to end the inning.

Baker and Collins, however, weren't finished with their heroics. In the eighth inning, they teamed to plate an insurance run. Collins bunted for a single off Otis Crandall, who had relieved Marquard in the sixth inning, and Baker followed with a line drive to left center. Stuffy McInnis pushed home a run with a double.

After the 6–4 victory, Baker was modest about the role he played and his home run. In his column, he wrote that Bender, Schang and Collins should get credit for the win. After all, he was only directly responsible for two or three runs. As for his home run, he wrote, "I hit a curve ball that cut the plate in the groove." Even though it was the longest home run in World Series history, he considered it "more like a lucky punch than anything else."[13]

After the game, McGraw cited Baker's defensive play as the key to the game. "I figured we had the score tied when Baker flashed over and grabbed the ball with one hand," he said. "If Burns' hit had gone through, I am confident we would have come through right there, because I would have pushed Tesreau into battle."[14]

Giants' captain Larry Doyle said, "Two men beat us yesterday — Baker and Collins. Somebody told us they couldn't hit lefthanders. I wonder what lefthanders they have been facing."[15] McGraw also was surprised how hard the A's had hit Marquard.

Losing the first game was bad enough, but the Giants had failed to take advantage of the always-hard-to-hit Bender on a day when he lacked his best stuff. The Giants' strategy was to be patient and make Bender throw a lot of pitches. The Giants reached him for 11 hits, which usually would have been enough to win. Lacking his best fastball, the big Indian relied on his experience, change of pace, and control.

Victimized by Baker for a second time, Marquard shouldered the responsibility for the loss. "I alone lost the first game for the Giants," he said. "I make no apologies or alibis. If I had had control, we would have won the game."[16] Marquard blamed his downfall on nervousness and lack of control. The Giants' southpaw also admitted he had crossed up Meyers up in the fourth inning by throwing a fastball instead of a slow ball when Schang tripled.

The series moved to Philadelphia for Game 2 on Wednesday, October 8. Fans packed Shibe Park and boys who didn't have ticket money climbed to the crosstrees of the nearby telephone poles, risking electrocution. In practice, Giants' Chief Meyers was injured when Buck Herzog threw a ball that hit the catcher's right thumb, cutting the flesh down to the bone of the first joint. Meyers was expected to miss the rest of the series. Larry McLean, who had caught just 28 games, replaced the veteran. Fred Snodgrass replaced Merkle, who had sprained his ankle in the first game, at first base.

McGraw and Mack continued their chess game of starting pitchers as McGraw warmed up Mathewson, Tesreau, and Demaree while Mack sent out Plank and Brown. Most observers knew Mathewson and Plank would be logical choices. Although McGraw and Giants fans were supremely confident in Matty, he had lost four consecutive World Series games and was no longer a sure thing.

The Athletics received a rousing, standing ovation from the crowd of 20,563 when they took the field. After Plank retired the Giants in the first, Mathewson faced his first crisis of the afternoon. Eddie Murphy reached on an error by Doyle and Rube Oldring singled. Collins advanced them to second and third with a bunt. That brought Baker to the plate. Fans gave him a thunderous hero's welcome, clapping and stomping their feet. As the commotion died down, Matty delivered his first pitch, a ball, to Baker. The Athletics' slugger proceeded to foul off the next two low pitches. Mathewson fooled him on the third pitch with a slow fadeaway. The crowd groaned as Baker went down swinging.

Hundreds of fans were crammed at Broad Street and Columbia Avenue to watch the *Public Ledger*'s electric scoreboard. When Baker came to the plate in the first inning, John Sherrick yelled, "Give us another home run, Baker." When Baker struck out, avid baseball fan Sherrick collapsed on the sidewalk and died from an apparent heart attack.[17]

In the third, Snodgrass lined sharply past third in what could have been a double, but the injured Giant limped down to first base. Mathewson followed with a single and Snodgrass hobbled around to third. This convinced McGraw to send in pitcher George "Hooks" Wiltse to pinch run for Snodgrass. Wiltse stayed in the game and played first base.

Plank and Mathewson dueled each other through eight scoreless innings. Plank worked out of a jam in the ninth after Fletcher singled and Burns walked with one out. The left-hander responded by retiring Shafer and Murray.

The Athletics missed a golden opportunity to win the game in the bottom of the ninth. Amos Strunk lined a single and Barry bunted to Doyle, who made a wild throw to first base, allowing Strunk and Barry to advance to third and second. After Doyle's bad throw, the Giant infielders flocked around him. Herzog raced over from third, patted Doyle on the back and pushed the others gently away and tried to settle everyone down. Mathewson knew he needed a couple of ground balls to get out of the jam. The confident A's were already packing up their equipment, figuring the winning run was just moments away. Then Matty baffled the Philadelphia batters. Jack Lapp, batting eighth, lined a grounder to Wiltse at first, who fielded it flawlessly. He threw home to McLean to nail the sliding Strunk in a close play. Plank walked to the plate, but Oldring approached him to say that a pinch hitter would take his place. Captain Danny Murphy, however, signaled from the bench for Plank to go ahead and hit. The pitcher rapped a hard grounder to Wiltse, who again threw home to trap Barry between third and home. Barry was tagged out in a rundown as Plank advanced to second and Lapp to third. Murphy grounded back to Mathewson to end the inning.

In the tenth, Plank began weakening. McLean singled to right and McGraw sent Eddie Grant in to pinch-run. Wiltse sacrificed him to second. Matty helped his own cause, delivering his second single of the game to drive in the game's first run. Herzog grounded to Collins, who threw wildly to second, allowing Mathewson to go to third and Herzog to second. Plank hit Doyle to load the bases. Fletcher bounced one over Baker's head at third, scoring two runs. The veteran southpaw recovered by striking out Burns and getting Shafer to fly out, but the damage had been done and Philadelphia trailed 3–0.

Matty refused to wilt in the bottom of the tenth. Oldring grounded out and Collins fanned. Baker, hoping to start a rally, rifled a nasty grounder down the first base line. As it was hopping over Wiltse's head, the six-footer leaped up and managed to knock it down. Second baseman Doyle, who was backing Wiltse up, recovered the ball in time to toss it to him and retire Baker for the final out.

"It was the greatest victory of my life and it will probably remain so,"[18] said Mathewson, who had won more than 335 games at this point in his career.

It was a tough loss for Plank and the Athletics. Plank, 38, the oldest pitcher in the majors, had given it his all. For nine solid innings he had matched Matty and was superb. *Washington Post* reporter Joe S. Jackson described the scene as Plank walked off the mound after the 10th inning. "Dejected, tired, and bitterly disappointed, Plank walked slowly to the bench. They patted him on the back and tried to cheer him up. It was no use. He looked at Mack and Mack looked at him. There was no word of reproach, no reference to the great southpaw's collapse. Plank was sorry he had lost the game, but Mack was sorry for Plank."[19]

"Mathewson is the greatest pitcher who ever lived,"[20] boasted McGraw afterwards. A win over Plank boosted the Giants' confidence as they prepared to return to the Polo Grounds. Not only had the Giants beaten one of Mack's aces, but they had done it with a pitcher playing first base, a second-string catcher and an infielder playing center field.

Mathewson had handled Collins and Baker masterfully. He worked the corners, kept them off balance and fooled them with his curve. The *New York Herald* considered the popular right-hander's victory over the A's as the most remarkable game played since the start of the World Series.

Giants Captain Larry Doyle said, "Matty deserves all the credit for the win. He is the greatest money pitcher in any league in the world."[21]

Marquard assessed Mathewson's performance, saying, "Matty pitched the greatest game of his life, without making a mistake in judgment. He outguessed Collins and Baker throughout the game."[22] Marquard said Mathewson had changed his style of pitching after the A's had said he tipped his pitches in the 1911 Series. He covered up every pitch, making it more difficult for the Athletics to figure out what was coming. He struck out Collins twice and Baker once on curves when they were looking for fastballs.

The unflappable Mack said, "Mathewson pitched a wonderful game against us, but I do not think one pitcher can win the World Series."[23]

Baker also praised Mathewson, crediting him with pitching one of the smartest games he had witnessed. He lamented striking out in the first inning with two men on base. "I feel sorry for Plank because he pitched a good game and deserved to win," he said.[24]

Philadelphia also had squandered opportunities in the fourth and eighth innings when one hit would have meant a run. It was the ninth inning, however, that sealed their fate. Mack was understandably second-guessed and criticized for failing to pinch hit for Lapp and Plank in the ninth with runners on second and third. Marquard said all the Giants thought Mack would send veteran Harry Davis to hit for Lapp and another pinch hitter for Plank, who batted .105 during the regular season and appeared to be out of gas. Mathewson said, "When Mack let Lapp and Plank hit in the ninth, I felt sure we would win. I am inclined to think for once in his life, Mack guessed wrong."[25]

When Mack was asked why he didn't pinch hit for Plank, he said, "I had my reasons of course, but do not care to give them. Let others criticize. That's their privilege. We lost the game and that is all there is to say."[26]

Fifty-seven wires and nine cables had flashed the results of each play around the world. Newspapers from as far away as Kansas City, Toronto and Cuba sent reporters. More than 300 newspapermen covered the series and the number would have been greater if intercity series in Pittsburgh, Chicago, Cleveland and St. Louis weren't being played at the same time. In all, more than 120,000 words were clicked off by operators.

The stage was set for Game 3 at the Polo Grounds on Thursday, October 9. It shaped up as the most crucial and intriguing games of the series because Mack would be forced to start one of his youngsters. If he could steal the win, he would have the series advantage with veterans Bender and Plank ready to go again.

After Joe Bush, Bob Shawkey and Weldon Wyckoff warmed up, Mack called on the right-hander Bush, who was still almost two months shy of his twentieth birthday. Jeff Tesreau and Al Demaree warmed up for the Giants, but six-foot-two right-hander Tesreau got the call. With 36,896 fans in the Polo Grounds and so much on the line, Bush was understandably nervous as he sat in the dugout waiting for the game to start. His teammates, however, tried to put him at ease as they pounced on Tesreau, a veteran spitballer and 22-game winner, for three runs in the first inning.

With one out, Oldring and Collins singled, putting runners at second and third as Baker came to the plate. Philadelphia's best clutch hitter smacked a 0–2 pitch past Fletcher at shortstop to score Oldring. When McInnis came to bat, Mack signaled for the hit-and-run. McInnis swung and missed, but Collins and Baker completed a double steal. Catcher McLean was so surprised, he fumbled the ball and didn't get a throw off. Strunk grounded to Fletcher deep in the hole at shortstop and he threw wildly to first base, allowing both Collins and Baker to score.

Even with a 3–0 lead, Bush was shaky in the first inning. With one out, he surrendered a single and hit a batter before the Athletics' infield bailed him out with a double play. Part of the Giants' strategy was to rattle the inexperienced youngster. The bench and coaches hurled personal remarks at Bush, trying to upset him. At one point, umpire Cy Rigler warned Snodgrass, coaching on the bases, to refrain from his personal remarks or he would be banished to the dugout for the remainder of the game. When Bush came into the Athletics' dugout after the first inning, he wisely sat next to Mack, who had a knack for calming down young players.

The A's boosted Bush's confidence even more in the second inning when they plated a pair of runs on Collins's two-run single to center field.

The Giants snapped Bush's shutout bid in the fifth as Red Murray singled, stole second and scored on McLean's single. Philadelphia put the game out of reach in the seventh as Collins unloaded his third hit of the afternoon, an RBI triple, and scored on Baker's sizzling line drive past Doyle at second base. Catcher Wally Schang added another highlight when he clouted a prodigious home run to the farthest corner of the right field bleachers off of Crandall in the eighth.

"Plain slugging and the ability of Bush to hold us, beat us,"[27] explained the Giants' Doyle after the 8–2 setback. The young right-hander baffled the Giants as he mixed his dazzling fastball and puzzling curve. It was the first time the Giants had faced him and he kept them off stride, limiting them to five hits. The Philadelphia outfield accounted for only three of the 27 outs and the lead New York batter reached base only twice.

Marquard said Bush outguessed virtually every hitter in the Giants' lineup. "When we looked for a curve, he threw a fastball and vice versa. He seemed to have superhuman knowledge of what our batters were expecting and he double crossed them just as Matty did in Philadelphia."[28]

While Bush was outguessing the Giants' hitters, the A's had no trouble figuring out Tesreau. The Athletics had studied Tesreau and detected a peculiar movement he made with his fingers when he was going to throw his spitter. That allowed them to either sit on his fastball or spitter. Armed with the information, Mack's men jumped on Tesreau for five runs in the first two innings.

McGraw felt the first inning was the key to their downfall, citing the A's double steal as the break of the game. It ended up giving Philadelphia three runs instead of one. Without the double steal, McGraw said either Strunk wouldn't have come to bat or Fletcher would have had an easy play at second base.

McGraw also paid homage to Collins, who collected two singles and a triple while handling nine fielding chances flawlessly. "The great playing of Collins was directly responsible for the defeat of the Giants." McGraw said Collins had no weakness and he considered him, "by far the most dangerous man in Mack's lineup. He is the greatest player in a pinch that I ever saw."[29]

The series moved back to Philadelphia for Game 4 on Friday, October 10. The Giants needed to win to keep their hopes alive. Both managers were undecided about who their starters would be. Most observers felt Mack would go with 22-year-old right-hander Shawkey and save Bender for Game 5. McGraw had to decide between going with Marquard again or 13-game winner Al Demaree. McGraw's confidence in Marquard had understandably waned because the southpaw hadn't had any success with the Athletics, despite his persistent contention he could beat them. McGraw went with the right-hander Demaree while Mack pulled a surprise and sent Bender to the mound.

Philadelphia drew first blood in the second inning as McInnis singled to center, just out of reach of Snodgrass and went to second on a sacrifice. Barry popped to Merkle in foul territory, but he muffed the ball, giving the little shortstop a second chance. Barry made the most of it, doubling to the extreme left field corner, chasing home the first run.

Philadelphia padded the lead in the fourth with a three-run outburst. Strunk lined one to third base that was too hot for Herzog to handle. Barry lined solidly to left center, pushing Strunk to third. Schang plated two runs with a stinging drive just out of Doyle's reach. After taking second on the throw-in and third on a passed ball, Schang scored on Bender's slow roller to Merkle that he bobbled.

Down 4–0, the Giants threatened in the top of the fifth. With runners on first and third and one out, Moose McCormick pinch hit for Demaree. He lined hard to left field, but Oldring came in at top speed, reached down and grabbed the sinking liner off of his shoe tops. If Oldring had missed the ball, it would have cost the Athletics two runs. With two outs, pinch runner Claude Cooper was thrown out trying to steal.

The cocky Marquard relieved Demaree in the bottom of the fifth, but he soon found out his luck hadn't changed. With two outs, Strunk walked on four pitches and Barry doubled to left. Schang continued his fine work with the bat as he touched Marquard for a two-RBI single, giving the A's a seemingly insurmountable 6–0 lead.

Bender had surrendered just two hits in the first six innings. But he got into trouble in the seventh. Burns and Murray both singled and scored on Merkle's home run shot into the left field bleachers.

The big Indian was in hot water again in the eighth inning. With a runner on first base, Fletcher hit a hard one-hopper back to Bender, who was able to block it. He picked it up, whirled and rifled the ball to Barry covering second. The throw was wide of second and it caught Barry going the wrong way. But the agile shortstop was able to push off the bag and reach the throw while keeping his toe intact with the bag for the force out. That play looked bigger as Burns doubled along the left field line, scoring Fletcher. Shafer then cracked a triple to make it 6–5. New York had the tying run on third base with two outs. Captain Danny Murphy walked to the mound to confer with Bender and the other infielders while Ira Thomas checked on the status of Brown and Shawkey in the bullpen. Bender apparently convinced Murphy he could get out of the jam. With the Athletics on the ropes, Murray swung at Bender's first offering and grounded out to Collins, ending the threat.

"My team died scrappy, and that's the most encouraging sign of the afternoon,"[30] offered McGraw, who pointed to two defensive plays as the turning points in the game. The first was Oldring's diving catch of McCormick's ball in the fifth inning and the second was Barry's catch of Bender's wide throw in the eighth. "Nineteen out of 20 times a ball like that would have ricocheted off him and gone for a hit," said McGraw. "If Barry had missed the ball, Doyle would have scored and Fletcher would have advanced a base."[31]

Chief Meyers wrote that Oldring's catch was the turning point of the game. "If Oldring missed the ball, it probably would have been a triple. Bender deserved some credit for the catch because a few seconds before he had moved Oldring in about 15 or 20 feet."[32]

McGraw's gamble to go with Demaree hadn't panned out. "We didn't have much trouble with Demaree, who showed us nothing but a little dinky curve," said Baker. "Marquard didn't look much better than he did in the opener."[33]

Baker's confidence was sky high after Game 4. "We all believe we have the series won now and there was a lot of kidding in the clubhouse after the game. Everybody was happy and the boys are planning to start home on Sunday. Most of us feel Plank is going to win, even if the Giants throw Matty. He can't come back as strong since he's only had two days rest," he said.[34]

Although the Giants' pitching was supposed to have been far superior to the Athletics, only Matty had been able to contain the Philadelphia hitters. Once again, the do-or-die pressure was on Mathewson in Game 5 in the Polo Grounds on Saturday, October 11. Mack, however, had the option of going with Shawkey or Plank. If Shawkey failed, the A's would still hold a three games to two advantage, Plank would have one more day's rest, and the Series would return to Shibe Park. Mack boldly went with Plank with the idea of ending the Series in five games.

The Athletics wasted little time getting on the scoreboard. Eddie Murphy opened the game with a single. Oldring attempted a sacrifice bunt but Murphy was forced at second. Collins singled to right, moving Oldring on third. Baker lined to Burns in left field, who tried to throw Oldring out at the plate, but his throw was high.

Murphy started things again in the third with a single through short. Oldring followed with a hard smash to Doyle, who fumbled it. Collins moved the runners up with a sacrifice. Baker swung hard at the pitch, but barely nipped it, dribbling it down the first base line toward Merkle, who picked up the ball, ran a few feet toward the plate and faked a throw home. Murphy slowed up and headed back to third. It was then that Merkle decided to chase Baker, who had just run past him. He turned to either run after him or throw to Doyle, who was covering first, but it was too late. That's when Murphy dashed home. Catcher McLean yelled for the ball and Merkle threw home, but it was high and Murphy slid home safely under the tag and scored. McInnis sent a deep fly to Burns, scoring Oldring on the sacrifice.

Staked to a 3–0 lead, the experienced Plank didn't allow a runner to reach base until the fifth inning when he issued his only walk of the afternoon to Tillie Shafer. On a hit-and-run signal, Shafer lowered his head and darted for second. Murray lifted a 50-foot fly ball above the pitcher's mound. Plank signaled for it, but Baker apparently did not hear him or see him wave everyone off. Baker crossed in front of Plank and as the ball made contact with the pitcher's glove, Baker bumped him. Plank dropped the ball and it rolled toward first base. Shafer had already reached second base and it would have been an easy double play, if Plank had been able to hold on to it. McLean followed with a single, making the score 3–1 and erasing Plank's shutout. The A's hurler surrendered only one more hit— a single to Mathewson in the sixth.

New York couldn't muster a threat against Plank, despite the wishes of the 36,632 screaming fans at Polo Grounds. Disappointed fans started to stream from the stadium late in the game, sensing there was no hope for a comeback against the brilliant southpaw.

After striking out Schang to end the top of the ninth inning, Mathewson started to trot to the clubhouse in far right center. When the fans realized he would not bat in the bottom of the ninth, they rose and gave him a standing ovation that didn't cease until he disappeared from view. The masterful Matty had succeeded many more times than he had failed and he was still one of the greatest major league pitchers of all time.

The *Philadelphia Public Ledger* described the scene from there, "He never looked backward, never stopped running until he reached a small squad of players, A's and Giants, in extreme center field. Then he came to a walk and as he approached pitcher (Art) Fromme, the latter tossed him a Mackinaw coat. With no intent to be rude or churlish, but because his big brave heart had been crushed, he dropped the coat to the ground and passed through the gate without a word. A great, commanding figure, even in defeat."[35]

In the bottom of the ninth, McGraw sent Otis Crandall to pinch hit for Mathewson, who had pitched brilliantly, surrendering just six hits. Crandall grounded out to Collins, Herzog flied to Barry, and Doyle flied to Murphy to end the game. The Philadelphia Athletics were baseball's World Champions again. Thousands of fans poured onto the field and rushed toward the Athletics bench to congratulate Mack and all of his players. The A's congratulated each other and everyone tried to hug Plank. They hoisted him on their shoulders and carried him from the visitors' dugout to the players' gate in the far outfield as thousands of fans surged around him. Plank wore a rare smile as he left the field.

"Gettysburg Eddie" had never pitched a better game. He baffled the Giants all day with his mix of fastballs, curves, and cross-fires. The performance didn't resemble one by a pitcher who had considered retiring in midseason and had retirement on his mind going into the series.

"They told me Plank couldn't come back so quickly, but he pitched every bit as well as on Wednesday," said Chief Meyers. "Throughout this series the A's have shown wonderful consistency, both offensively and defensively. They have hit our pitchers as hard and timely as any team that ever faced them."[36]

After the game, McGraw elbowed his way through the crowd to reach Mack and congratulate him. "The best team won and you deserve all the praise that can be given you,"[37] he said. McGraw said that the A's were as good as any of the great teams he had seen in the past. Mack thanked McGraw for his words and wished him better luck in the future. Then Mack and McGraw went to the field box where Ben Shibe, owner of the A's, was sitting. There, they shook hands again.

McGraw later shook hands with Eddie Collins, telling him he was the greatest player. The Giants' leader praised Collins, labeling him a steady and brilliant fielder, one of the fastest thinkers and the most dangerous hitter on the club. It irked McGraw that he had missed signing Collins, who had attended New York's Columbia University.

"The players in these games for New York deserve credit for being the gamest fighters that have ever taken part in a similar series,"[38] offered McGraw. Injuries to Snodgrass, Merkle and Meyers limited the Giants' moves and cost them on the field and the bases. But, McGraw knew that wasn't the main reason for defeat. "The letdown can not be explained."[39]

"It broke our hearts that Matty lost the way he pitched," offered Marquard. "Mathewson was nearly as brilliant as Plank. Burns' poor throw from the outfield in the first inning, Doyle's bobble and Merkle's misplay in the third, all led to runs."[40]

The A's victory was a crushing blow to the Giants, who had been so highly touted and wanted badly to stop their losing streak in the Series. Mack's club wasn't given much of a chance because of New York's supposed pitching superiority. Yet, Matty was the only Giants hurler who was able to shackle the Athletics hitters. Without Mathewson on the mound, the Giants seemed like a second-division team.

The Athletics outhit the Giants, .264 to .201. Baker collected nine hits in 20 at-bats for a .450 average and he drove in a series-high seven runs. In three World Series, Baker had amassed 27 hits in 66 at bats in pressure situations for a composite batting average of .409, bolstering his reputation as one of the game's greatest clutch hitters. Collins had eight hits in 19 at bats for a .421 average and Schang hit .357. Schang, 23, made an outstanding impression with his hitting, throwing, and defensive work. The Athletics' team ERA was 2.15 compared to the Giants' 3.80. Philadelphia hitters rapped New York pitchers for 46 hits in 45 innings.

With three World Championships in four years, won in convincing fashion, the Philadelphia Athletics were the greatest team baseball had known. They were a dynasty.

SEVEN

Turmoil and an Upset

For Connie Mack, the Philadelphia Athletics and the rest of the major league, 1914 was a year of upheaval. Most of it could be blamed on the upstart Federal League, a third organized league that challenged the American League and the National League.

In March 1913, the Federal League announced it would play in Chicago, Cleveland, Pittsburgh, St. Louis, Covington, KY (across the river from Cincinnati), and Indianapolis. Not much attention was paid to the league because it was not of major league caliber. In August, James Gilmore replaced John Power as league president and obtained the support of other wealthy businessmen, restaurateur Charles Weeghman of Chicago, Robert B. Ward, owner of Tip-Top Bakeries in Brooklyn, and Phil Ball, who built refrigeration plants in St. Louis. The millionaires brought considerable financial strength to the league, giving it credibility and negotiating muscle. Gilmore also convinced the league to expand to Eastern cities and build eight new ballparks.

Initially, the league targeted only those players whose current contracts had expired. In mid–November, however, Gilmore announced the Federal League would not honor the major league's reserve clause, which made a player property of the club that held his contract. Players in the major leagues were accustomed to not having any negotiating power to compare offers from two or more clubs: They either accepted the salary their current club offered or retired. And, even if they retired, they were still property of the club, even if their contracts had expired.

George Stovall, player/manager with the St. Louis Browns, was the first major leaguer to sign with the Federal League. His case illustrates the restraints ballplayers faced. The 10-year veteran of the major leagues wanted his unconditional release from the Browns in order to sign with the Federal League, but team owner Robert Hedges refused to grant it. Instead, he said Stovall could purchase his unconditional release for $3,500. Stovall took his case to American League President Ban Johnson, who predictably sided with Hedges. He told Stovall that he was Hedges's property and the owner was entitled to benefit from any trade. Stovall made up his mind that he would never consent to be sold. "No man should submit to be bartered for like a broken down plough horse,"[1] he said.

As part of its strategy to lure major league players, the Federal League offered higher salaries and no reserve clause. This understandably appealed to players, particularly the superstars, most of whom were underpaid. Detroit Tigers' Ty Cobb was one of the first players to test the reserve clause when he held out after the 1912 season. He had hit .383, .420 and .409, while collecting the same $9,000 salary each year. He had won six consecutive batting titles and he knew he was worth more than owner Frank Navin was willing to pay. Although Cobb wanted $15,000 a year, he signed a one-year contract for $12,000 after missing the first couple weeks of the 1913 season.

In January 1914, the National Commission, the three-man governing body of Organized Baseball, recognized the Fraternity of Professional Baseball Players of America. It agreed to 11 conditions, including that teams would pay for uniforms. David Fultz, an attorney and former American League player, organized the Fraternity with the idea of getting owners to grant a series of concessions and give players a voice in their own careers. The reserve clause, however, wasn't among the concessions.

In mid–January, a legal battle ensued between the Federal League and Organized Baseball. The Chicago Whales of the Federal League signed catcher Bill Killifer, a five-year veteran whose contract with the Philadelphia Phillies had expired. A week later, however, Killifer changed his mind and signed a contract with the Phillies. That created a legal battle since both teams claimed his services.

The scope of the battle between the Federal League and Organized Baseball became clearer on January 18 when the *New York Times* reported the Federal League had offered Cobb, the game's highest paid player, $15,000 a year for five years. Cobb, however, assured the Tigers he would sign with them for 1915.

The ambitious Federal League owners gave Mack one more thing to worry about. Spring training was slightly more than two months away and he wasn't sure if two of his biggest stars— Baker and Eddie Plank — would return for the 1914 season. An article in the *Cambridge Daily*

Frank Baker was one of the game's most dangerous sluggers and clutch hitters. The powerful third baseman is shown here with his 52-ounce black bat which wreaked havoc on opposing pitchers. The bat was nearly 20 ounces heavier than those used by today's hitters. Jack McGrath of the Louisville Slugger Company said Baker's bat was antiquated even for its time. It was short with a thick handle, almost as round as the barrel. There was no flex and it was almost like a piece of lead. NATIONAL BASEBALL HALL OF FAME LIBRARY, COOPERSTOWN, NY.

Banner (Maryland) on October 23, 1913, carried the headline, "'Home Run' Baker May Quit Base Ball — Athletics' Third Baseman May Leave the Diamond." A report from Philadelphia indicated that in a telephone interview, Baker was debating the possibility of quitting baseball to tend to his farms full-time.

Although Baker was only 27 and at the peak of his career, he had talked about retiring from baseball as early as the fall of 1911. Shortly after the World Series ended, Alfred Kemp, a Trappe resident who had played on the town team with Baker, told reporters, "Frank has a $100 bet with teammates (Eddie) Collins and (Harry) Davis that he will not spend more than one more year in baseball. I believe he intends on quitting."[2]

Baker didn't like traveling and being away from his family. Road trips frequently meant traveling on a train for three or four weeks. He preferred spending time on his farm and in the small-town atmosphere of Trappe. He considered quitting baseball on a number of occasions over the next 10 years.

In mid–January, Mack made a rare trip to Trappe and accompanied Baker duck hunting. Although they bagged a couple blackhead ducks, Mack's main purpose was to sign his star third baseman to a new contract. When the Athletics' manager left Trappe he had Baker's signature on a new three-year contract.

"I have decided to play baseball another year," Baker told the *Easton Star-Democrat*. "This is probably the last year that I shall play. I do not expect to continue playing longer than this season."[3]

In mid–February, Plank acknowledged he had returned his contract unsigned to Mack and said money wasn't an issue. He had wanted to quit at the beginning of the 1913 season, but Mack said he needed him because of the injury to Coombs. Plank, 38, had more and more trouble each season getting into pitching shape and he wanted to retire before people considered him washed up. Despite what Plank said, Mack was optimistic his ace left-hander would report to Jacksonville, Florida for spring training. On February 24, Plank announced he would throw his hat in the ring for another season with Mack's club.

By early March, American League President Ban Johnson said, "The Federal League must be exterminated.... Personally, I think the Federal movement is a joke. We are determined to put the Federals out of business."[4] He declared war on the upstart league and said there would be no consideration of a truce or peace.

Prior to the start of spring training, however, it was obvious the Federal League was of consequence, even though some owners like William Baker of the Phillies didn't initially take the league seriously. Baker's attitude changed, however, after he lost six players to the Federal League, including Tom Seaton, a 27-game winner with the 1913 Philadelphia Phillies. The right-hander signed with the Brooklyn Federals for a reported $7,000 a year for three years and one year's salary in advance. The Phillies president vowed to fight to prevent Seaton from joining the Federal League.

Other Phillies who jumped ship included second baseman Otto Knabe, pitchers Adie Brennan and Howie Camnitz, outfielder Vincent Duncan, and shortstop Mickey Doolan. The loss of these players had a crippling effect on the Phillies, who the Feds targeted because it was well known that many of the players were upset with management.

Shortstop Doolan had accompanied Charles Comiskey, White Sox owner, and Giants manager John McGraw and a group of players, featuring White Sox and Giants, on a world tour after the 1913 World Series. The tour ended in mid–March and the Federal League had representatives there to meet them. Tris Speaker, Sam Crawford, Ivy Wingo, Steve Evans, Lee Magee and Doolan were offered contracts. Doolan, Magee and Evans jumped to the new league.

McGraw returned home from the world tour to a guaranteed $100,000 offer from the Federal League. Given the outrageous sum, McGraw had to consider it. In the end, he turned it down, believing the Federal League would fail. The Federal League was desperate to sign a big name that would give the league credibility and drawing power. The Brooklyn Federals were willing to pay Mathewson, who was earning around $12,000 a year, any amount of money to manage their club. Although tempted, Matty remained loyal to the Giants, refusing to use the Federal League's offer to negotiate a better contract.

To ensure that none of his players jumped to the rival league, McGraw ordered raises for them. Few of the Giants were interested in jumping because McGraw saw to it that they were among the best paid players in the game. They also had benefited from three consecutive World Series checks. Although the A's had won three world championships in four years and were considered the best team ever, they were not as well paid as the Giants. Mack had earned a well-deserved reputation as being tight with his money. His approach was to try to sign as many players as possible to multiple-year contracts with little or no raise. At the time, most players signed year-to-year contracts with little security from one year to the next. A multiyear contract offered security, an unusual commodity for a major league ballplayer.

The Federal League signed 42 big leaguers for the start of the 1914 season, including Joe Tinker, who went from a $5,500 offer from the Cincinnati Reds to a $12,000 offer plus stock with the Chicago Whales; the Yankees' Hal Chase, who moved from $6,000 to $9,000 with Buffalo; the Yankees' Russ Ford, who signed for $10,000 with Buffalo; and the Cubs' "Three Finger" Brown, who signed for $10,000 with Brooklyn.[5] Major leaguers who signed with the Federal League, however, risked being blackballed by Organized Baseball. They were told they would never play again in the American or National League. If the Federal League folded, some players faced the possibility of being left without a livelihood. The money was good, but it was not without risk.

Shortly after the Athletics arrived in Jacksonville for spring training, Mack named catcher Ira Thomas captain and released 14-year veteran Danny Murphy, who had held the title, to Baltimore of the International

League. Murphy had fallen out of favor with Mack because of his decision to have Carroll Brown pitch all 18 innings of an exhibition game on a cold, windy day against the Phillies prior to the start of the 1913 season. The outing was detrimental to Brown, who never regained his form. Murphy also was criticized for letting Plank pitch the 10th inning in the second game of the 1913 World Series. In the past, Mack had used Murphy, Thomas and Harry Davis as his assistants, which were nonexempt roster positions. They were occasionally used to pinch hit or start if injuries took their toll on the regulars. Mack decided, however, he couldn't afford to have three assistants.

Naming Thomas captain may have been a source of friction on the team because some observers thought Mack would bestow that title on Eddie Collins, who was the team leader and sparkplug. Mack went with the more experienced Thomas. Within a week of being released to Baltimore, however, Murphy signed a three-year contract with the Brooklyn Federals to be their bench manager.

"The Feds offered me more money in advance than I ever received for a year's play with the Athletics," said Murphy, explaining his decision. "I figured I was almost through as a player and there was no sentiment about the affair. I didn't believe the Feds would make good on their offer, but when they began to count out the money in ten and twenty dollar bills and I saw the pile it made, I grabbed it and signed the contract."[6] Murphy had neatly summed up the appeal of the Federal League. The same week Murphy signed with the Brooklyn club, six members of the Chicago Cubs were reportedly wavering on offers from the Federal League.

By mid–March, the Federal League filed a petition with the United States District Court for the Western District of Michigan asking for an injunction to restrain Bill Killifer Jr., former Phillies catcher, from playing for any other team than the Chicago Federals. Joe Tinker, manager of the Federal club, felt the league couldn't lose, regardless of the judge's ruling. If the contract was declared valid, then Killifer would be theirs. If not, then it meant that baseball contracts would have no validity, opening the door for the league to offer inducements to players already under contract.

The Federal League and its attempt to sign players from Organized Baseball was the major story of 1914 baseball season. It was a hotly contested issue that daily stirred players, managers, reporters, and owners. Its presence was overwhelming; it was a front page story every week in the baseball tabloid *Sporting Life* from spring training up to the World Series. It was an emotional issue that divided players into separate camps. Some saw the baseball war as an opportunity to get what was due them and others saw league jumpers as traitors.

Baker followed the Federal League news and its ramifications closely from his farm in Trappe. The slugger did not report to spring training until mid–March due to his wife being ill. Shortly after reporting, he accompanied the Athletics to Savannah for an exhibition game, where he assumed a new role — that of actor. As part of the feature film *The Short Stop's Double,* he made a daring rescue of a woman in the city, pulling her out of the path of an oncoming automobile. The camera crew also filmed him at the ballpark. Filming continued the next day as the A's traveled to Charleston, South Carolina. Baker became the first famous athlete to perform in a feature with a plot.[7]

The A's arrived in Wilmington, North Carolina, on March 25 to play a game against Jack Dunn's International League Baltimore Orioles. Dunn was showcasing his club in an effort to prove they were as good as a major league team. He also was proudly showing off his 19-year-old southpaw, George "Babe" Ruth, who started against the Athletics' Carroll Brown. Although the A's collected 12 hits off of Ruth, they could only manage two runs as they stranded fourteen in a 6–2 loss, their first of the spring. Baker was the batting star against Ruth, rapping three singles and a double in five trips. Ruth silenced him in a pinch, however, forcing him to line out to center field with runners on second and third and two outs. Earlier he had gotten Wally Schang to tap back to the mound with the score tied, bases loaded and two out. He also struck out Eddie Collins with two men on and two outs.

Three days later, the two teams matched up in Baltimore with Ruth on the mound against Weldon Wyckoff for Mack's club. This time, Dunn's phenom was less impressive. The Athletics tallied seven hits and four runs off of him in four innings. Ruth surrendered three consecutive doubles in the first inning as the A's went on to win 12–5. Baker had four hits, including a double off of Ruth. In two games against the highly touted southpaw, the left-handed swinging Baker had five hits in seven at bats.

With Opening Day two weeks away, Ira Thomas announced Philadelphia would win the American League pennant and the World Series. The prediction shocked no one. The Athletics were a veteran team, set at every position. The biggest question mark was how much Mack could count on two of his former workhorses— 38-year-old Eddie Plank, 30-year-old Chief Bender, who was entering his twelfth season, and Jack Coombs, who had been sidelined practically all of 1913.

Most observers felt the 1914 A's were stronger than the 1913 team, which had to overcome a slow start. Mack had masterfully handled his pitching staff and developed Bush, 21, and Shawkey, 23, who were expected to give him more stability in the rotation. Other young pitchers included

Weldon Wyckoff, 22, Duke Houck, 22, Herb Pennock, 20, and Rube Bressler, 19. Two of the Athletics' toughest contenders in the American League in 1913 suffered losses to the Federal League. Cleveland lost Cy Falkenberg (23–10) to Indianapolis and Washington lost Bob Groom (16–16) to St. Louis.

On April 1, the Federal League published the rosters for its eight clubs, revealing that 59 players had jumped. Thirty-nine were from the National League and 20 were from the American League. The Feds had wanted at least five major leaguers on each team and they exceeded their goal, averaging seven major leaguers on each team. The Phillies lost nine players, the most in the National League, and the New York Yankees lost four, the most in the American League. The Athletics lost only Murphy. As the season progressed, more players signed with the Federal League.

Judge Clarence Sessions ruled on the Killifer case on April 10. He denied the Federal League petition on moral rather than legal grounds. He ruled both contracts were valid and chided Killifer for not being a man of his word. Both sides considered the decision a victory. Organized Baseball was pleased the Federal League petition had been denied. The Federal League believed the judge's ruling, based on "moral rather than legal" considerations invalidated the reserve clause. This increased the possibilities of players jumping from one league to another. After the ruling, Gilmore informed all Federal League clubs to pursue any player whether they were under contract or not. It was akin to the South firing on Fort Sumter to start the Civil War.

The Federal League planned to stagger its league opening games to generate more publicity. Baltimore attracted the largest opening day crowd as nearly 30,000 fans jammed Terrapin Park to watch the Terrapins beat Buffalo 3–2 on April 13. Across the street, the International League Orioles were playing an exhibition game against the New York Giants. Despite the presence of Baltimore native Babe Ruth on the mound and manager John McGraw, a former Baltimore Oriole, the game drew only 1,500 fans, many of whom hadn't been able to purchase seats for the Federal League game. Pressed for money because of declining attendance, Dunn later sold Ruth to the Boston Red Sox in July along with pitcher Ernie Shore and catcher Ben Egan for a reported sum between $25,000 and $30,000.

The Athletics opened the season against the New York Yankees on April 14 in the Polo Grounds before 15,000 fans as Joe Bush was saddled with an 8–2 setback. The season was underway, but the Federal League rumors didn't stop. Four members of the New York Giants had reportedly informed Federal League President James Gilmore they would jump if the terms were right. The likely candidates included Rube Marquard, Jeff

Tesreau, Larry Doyle, Fred Merkle, Larry McLean, Red Murray, and Harry Stock.

Philadelphia dropped the next two games, a 4–0 loss to the Yankees and a 1–0 loss to the Red Sox in a lifeless manner. Once again, it looked as if the A's might be their own worst enemy. Mack didn't take long to deliver a fatherly heart-to-heart talk to his club. He told them to stop thinking they couldn't be beaten and that they could wait to come from behind and win the pennant. They had to protect themselves from overconfidence. Mack hoped the early-season talk would prevent a repeat of the disappointing 1912 season. The Athletics responded by winning seven of the next nine games.

In Philadelphia's first 14 games, only two starters were over age 23. Brown was 29 and Bender was 30. Bender didn't start until the 10th game of the season and Plank didn't get his first call until the 14th game. In the first month, Mack used seven different starters and his club went 5–5. The inability of Bender and Plank to take their regular turns forced Mack to depend on his youngsters and their work hadn't been good enough to win the majority of the games. The *Philadelphia Public Ledger* observed that Bender and Plank were the Athletics' biggest handicap early in the season.

On May 8, the Athletics and Senators played to a 9–9 tie, which was called after 10 innings because of darkness. While the game didn't mean anything in the standings, it had a tremendous impact on Baker and his future performances against Walter Johnson. Baker always feasted on Washington pitching and hit Johnson better than anyone else in the league. He was a tough out, no matter which Senator pitcher was on the mound. Washington hurlers tried to stymie Baker's production by brushing him off the plate, either with inside pitches or pitches around his head.

Johnson came on in relief, but the A's battered him for six runs in three innings. The big right-hander was amidst the worst relief performance of his career when Baker, whom he called "The most dangerous batter I have ever faced,"[8] stepped to the plate. Encouraged by catcher Eddie Ainsmith, Johnson "let fly a high fast one which almost put the home run king into a state of dreamless slumber."[9] Baker hit the ground with a thump as Johnson's 90-plus per hour fastball whistled by his head, less than an inch away. "It was duck or no dinner,"[10] Baker later recalled. According to the normally mild-mannered Johnson, it was the only time he threw at a batter in his 20-plus year career and he always regretted it.

The single, frightening pitch had a lasting result. In his first five seasons, the Trappe slugger had batted .385 against Johnson with four home runs, three triples and six doubles. In his seven remaining seasons starting in 1914, Baker averaged just .207 facing Johnson, with a home run and double as the only extra-base hits in 111 at bats.

A couple weeks after the incident, the *Washington Post* reported that "Frank Baker's head is the target for every pitcher used by the Nationals with the exception of Walter Johnson, who never throws at anyone's head."[11]

Washington southpaw hurler Joe Boehling reportedly remarked, "All you have to do to get Baker is to send a beaner at his head and then give him three strikes."[12]

Mack started to see some encouraging performances in mid–May as Eddie Collins was hitting .353, Barry .323, and McInnis, .305. Baker was riding a hitting streak that started on April 23 and lasted until May 18. During the 17-game span, he rapped 23 hits in 58 at bats for a .382 average.

On May 14, Ban Johnson reported, "The Federal League has forced us to increase salaries beyond all just proportions. [Red Sox star center fielder Tris Speaker had renegotiated his contract and doubled his salary from $9,000 a year to $18,000 a year, for two years]. But I maintain the Federal League has done all the damage it possibly can."[13] Johnson said the American League had signed every star player on its rolls to ironclad contracts (most for multiple years) without the 10-day option release clause. The clause was controversial because it allowed a club to release a player any time with 10 days' notice and not be obligated to pay the player beyond that time.

That didn't stop the rumors. A week later, Walter Johnson, Eddie Ainsmith and Clyde Milan of the Senators flatly denied they had agreed to sign with the Pittsburgh Federal League club at the end of the season. While manager Clark Griffith didn't believe the reports, he and every other manager in the league were concerned about Federal League activity. On the same day, Mack released 22-year-old Byron Houck to Baltimore of the International League. Ten days earlier, Houck had been shelled for 16 hits and 13 runs in an exhibition game against the Brooklyn Dodgers. That convinced Mack that Houck's future wasn't with the Athletics. Houck said he would likely jump to the Federal League rather than report to Baltimore. He accepted a three-year contract from Brooklyn, reportedly for twice as much money as he made with Philadelphia.

Within a week of the dismissed signings of three Senators, Walter Johnson added to the frustration and panic of American League officials when he revealed he had talked to three Federal League teams, including the Chicago Whales. The ace declared the Senators would have to beat the Federal League's offer for 1915 and he expected the Feds to offer him a substantial increase over current salary.

"I am in the game for coin," Johnson told *Washington Post* reporter Stanley Milliken. "If the Federal League and Washington offer the same, I'll stay here, otherwise I intend to jump. I will pitch for the one that gives me the most money."[14] The soft-spoken Johnson, winner of 36 games in 1913 and arguably the game's best pitcher, was no radical or rabble-rouser. He was looking at the game from a businessman's perspective.

By this point in the season, signs already existed that 1914 was going to be a dismal one for Organized Baseball. Adverse weather conditions, players jumping to the Federal League, nearly daily rumors of Federal League threats, and unsettled conditions in Europe related to war-time activity kept fans away from the ballparks. The Athletics' attendance was poorer than the previous year and on par with second-division teams instead of pennant contenders. Boston Braves manager George Stallings said the New York Giants were one of the few teams making money, the rest of the teams were losing an average of $1,000 per week.[15]

Despite impressive Opening Day crowds, the Federal League attendance was poor. Pittsburgh and Brooklyn cut their general admission prices from 50 cents to 25 cents. The Federal League needed more stars— a Cobb, Mathewson, or Johnson — to attract crowds. And, when it came to stars, the Athletics had more than their share. With three World Championships in four years, Plank, Bender, Collins and Baker were high-profile players and heroes to many fans nationwide. As the season continued, the pressure on the Federal League to sign star players increased.

The Athletics started to round into shape when they won two out of three games from first-place Detroit, May 21–23, at Shibe Park. Baker missed the series with a bruised thumb and Cobb was sidelined with fractured ribs. Philadelphia moved within two games of first place and one-half game behind second-place Washington, but Tigers' manager Hughie Jennings wasn't overly impressed. "Mack has a good team, but he has to depend too much on Plank and Bender. His young pitchers are not as classy as most people believe."[16] Jennings felt if the Tigers held the lead through mid–June, the A's wouldn't catch them.

The Athletics moved into first place for the first time on May 29 when they swept a doubleheader from the Yankees to start a 29-game road trip that lasted until June 24. It was the first of five consecutive doubleheaders necessitated by numerous rainouts. The first spell of decent weather was the week of May 25 when no games were postponed. On June 8, Baker's two-run homer off of lefty Tiller "Pug" Cavet in the fourth inning gave the A's a 5–4 win in Detroit's Tiger Stadium. Baker slugged his second homer in as many days as he touched right-hander Jean Dubuc for a solo shot in a 7–3 win. On June 14, Baker was hitting .353, the second highest regular in the league, trailing only Clarence "Tilly" Walker of St. Louis. His thumb was still bothering him, but he didn't want to rest. Mack's reluctance to use Bender and Plank was evident on the road trip as both combined for only four starts. Mack's club went 17–12 and returned to Philadelphia in first place, one and a half games ahead of Detroit.

The Athletics hosted the Senators in a doubleheader after nearly a month on the road. Philadelphia won the first game by forfeit after Washington manager Clark Griffith pulled his team off the field in the fourth inning in a dispute with home plate Ollie Chill. The Athletics won the second game 6–5 in 10 innings as Baker took offensive honors with a pair of two-run homers off rookie right-hander Yancy "Doc" Ayers and a sacrifice fly that scored a run. It marked the second time he had homered twice in a game and the first time he had hit two homers off the same pitcher in a game.

By mid–June the Federal League had gained momentum as Eddie Collins, Walter Johnson, and Ty Cobb were believed to be seriously considering offers. Brooklyn reportedly had offered three-year contracts to Collins and Johnson, for $25,000 and $13,000 a year, respectively. Chicago had supposedly offered Cobb a three-year contract for $25,000 a year. Federal League president Gilmore predicted 40 players would jump to the Federal League at the end of the season. He said the Federal League had been assured by lawyers that players who still had the 10-day clauses in their contracts, could easily abrogate their contracts by giving owners 10 days' notice.

A's second baseman Eddie Collins admitted he had dinner with Robert Ward, president, of the Brooklyn Federal League club, to discuss what terms would be acceptable. Collins said the rumored amount of $25,000 a year for three years was way too high. He ruled out switching leagues in mid–season and said he would not jump without giving the Athletics a chance to bid for his services. "I think a player is foolish who will not listen to a reasonable offer, providing he is playing fair all-round," he said.[17] Although optimistic about the league's future, the astute Collins said he would insist on much of the money when he signed and the remainder guaranteed by a bonding company and placed in the bank subject to the fulfillment of his contract.

Former Athletic Danny Murphy, one of the top recruiters for the Federal League, predicted Collins would jump. He had been talking to Collins and four or five other Athletics, trying to induce them into joining the Brooklyn club next year. He intimated that Baker, McInnis, and perhaps a veteran pitcher would follow Collins. Brooklyn owner Ward said his club would not sign a player who was already under contract.

Mack read the newspapers and heard the daily rumors. Federal League scouts milled around hotel lobbies and at the ballparks, feeling out the players. The games seemed like interruptions and players were understandably distracted. According to some sportswriters, talk of high salaries and the elimination of the 10-day clause caused players to become indifferent and that led to sloppy play. Some observers felt the poor attendance was linked to the poor quality of baseball.

As if the Federal League didn't present enough headaches for managers and owners and distractions to players, the Clarence Kraft case stirred things up even more in July. David Fultz, president of the Players' Fraternity, ordered a strike of all players under contract to the American and National Leagues on July 19 in protest at the National Commission's ruling on the Kraft case. It was the first time there was the threat of a possible strike involving the majority of the players since the National and American Leagues were formed. Teams were split about the strike. The *Philadelphia Evening Bulletin* reported that the Athletics and New York Giants were expected to oppose it while the Phillies, Tigers, Braves and Pirates favored it. The Cubs, Cardinals, Reds and Indians appeared evenly divided, according to the newspaper. It didn't say how the other six teams felt.

Fultz had asked for the Athletics' support and Ira Thomas, captain and director of the Players Fraternity, said he regarded the situation as a joke and he thought few players would listen to Fultz. The frustrated president of the association then wrote Eddie Collins a letter asking for support. The Athletics were one of only two teams (the other being Cleveland) that would have played, if a strike had been called. This offended many of the others teams, who recognized the need for solidarity in order to beat the owners on issues. Bitter feelings toward the Athletics resulted.

The case of Clarence Kraft centered around the Cincinnati agreement, which provided a major league player must be offered to all Class AA teams when being demoted from a major league club before he could be sent to a Class A team.

Brooklyn had drafted Kraft from the Nashville Southern Association Class A club in 1913. In the spring, Brooklyn released him to the Boston Braves, but later recalled him. Brooklyn president Charles Ebbets agreed to release Kraft to Nashville under an optional agreement. Nashville accepted the proposition, but later withdrew its acceptance when the Brooklyn club delayed the transaction. Brooklyn then released Kraft to Class AA Newark of the International League, causing Nashville to file a protest. The National Commission ruled Kraft should go to Class A Nashville, which meant his monthly salary would be cut by $150. Kraft refused to report to Nashville and was suspended without pay.

Ban Johnson appeared to be eager to confront the players. He declared that if American League players went on strike, every stadium would be closed, all salaries would be stopped, and the striking players would be heavily fined. He vowed that the strike would be the last one conducted by Fultz and the Players Fraternity since the owners were prepared to keep the stadiums closed the rest of the season, no matter how much money it cost them.

"It's about time that this fraternity nonsense should end," he said.[18] Ban considered the Kraft case a "trivial matter" and felt it wasn't worth the players risking their careers. The strike was avoided when Ebbets, representing the Newark club, agreed to purchase Nashville's interest in Kraft for $2,500. Ebbets had not conferred with Fultz or the National Commission before making the decision to avoid trouble between the owners and players. He admitted the settlement would be seen as a victory for the fraternity.

While the Kraft case was dominating the off-field activities, Mack sensed his pitching rotation was starting to settle down and he expected the club to play better. On July 15, the Athletics raised the 1913 pennant flag at Shibe Park after a doubleheader with the Browns was rained out. The hoisting of the flag seemed to signal a new day as the A's won 38 of 44 games over the next six weeks, winning at an incredible .863 pace. They increased their lead over the Tigers from two and a half games to 12.5 games.

Mack surprised nearly everyone on July 21 when he announced second baseman Eddie Collins, a prime target for the Federal League, had signed a multiyear contract. Neither Mack nor Collins disclosed the amount or the length of the contract. Collins's signing came the same day Federal League President Gilmore told club owners to sign all the players they wanted. He said the league had 15 American and National League players under contract ready to jump for the 1915 season.

During this six-week stretch the club looked unbeatable as Mack got strong performances from all of his starters and Philadelphia plated twice as many runs as its opponents. Baker helped spark the team during the streak, going 23-for-50, hitting at a .460 clip. By mid–August, it appeared as if the A's had the pennant clinched, but the club didn't let up on its unbelievable pace until the beginning of September.

Even though the Athletics were dominating the league and Baker was playing a key role, he was not playing at 100 percent. The third baseman was suffering from pleurisy, inflammation of the membrane that covers the lungs and lines the inside of the chest cavity. Pleurisy causes sharp, knifelike chest pain that worsens with breathing or coughing. Baker was running high temperatures at night and subnormal temperatures during the day. He also suffered from headaches, dry coughing and loss of appetite. His weak hitting from mid–July to the end of August had some observers believing his career was on the downslide. Few people knew that there were some days when he could hardly walk, but he refused to come out of the lineup. Baker was treated by a physician, who most likely used mustard plasters, cupping, flaxseed poultices and other old remedies to treat the painful condition. On road trips, he visited physicians to continue his treatments. "It was a miserable season for me," recalled Baker, years later. "Frankly, it was the hardest I had experienced."[19] His illness dramatically affected his home run production. He smashed nine through the end of July, but none the remaining two months of the season.

While the Athletics were demolishing the American League competition, the Boston Braves were making their miracle drive in the National League. The Braves, under manager George Stallings, were 31–41 and trailed the New York Giants by 11.5 games on July 11. They won 39 of 52 games over the next six weeks and passed New York in the standings on September 3 as they swept a doubleheader from the Phillies and the Giants lost to Brooklyn. Although the Braves played at a .750 clip, the Athletics were even hotter. For the same period, Mack's club won 41 of 50 games for a .820 winning percentage. Stallings predicted that if the Braves won the pennant they would give the Athletics "the hardest fight of their lives in the World Series."[20]

The two teams played differently down the stretch, reflecting the managers' different philosophies. Mack believed in resting his regulars once the pennant was secured while Stallings pushed his players to the end to prevent them from becoming lackadaisical. The A's closed out the season with a 17–15 mark in September and October. The Braves finished much stronger, posting a 31–8 mark.

Unreliable early in the season and only 2–2 at the end of June, Bender was the ace of Mack's staff in July, August and the first half of September, reeling off 15 consecutive wins. His streak ended on September 12 at the Polo Grounds when he lost to the Yankees 2–1, as catcher Ed Sweeney clubbed a game-winning homer in the bottom of the ninth.

When Philadelphia struggled down the stretch, the race tightened as the Red Sox pulled within five and a half games. The Detroit Tigers were charged with laying down to help Boston during a five-game series, September 20–23. The Tigers, who had won 10 of 11, dropped four games and tied one. Even the weakest Red Sox hitters pounded Detroit pitchers, long drives invariably got past the outfielders for extra bases while the Red Sox ran wild on the Tiger catchers. Why would the Tigers want to help the Red

Sox beat the Athletics? The Red Sox were members of the Baseball Players Fraternity while the A's had steadfastly refused to join. Philadelphia
snapped out of its slump, reeling off a five-game winning streak to widen
their first-place lead.

In late September, Mack sent Bender to scout the Braves playing a
series against the Giants in New York. Encountering Bender near Shibe
Park when he was supposed to be at the Polo Grounds, the surprised manager said, "I thought you were supposed to be in New York."

"Oh, I didn't see any need for scouting that bush league outfit," replied
Bender.[21]

While much is made of this story, Bender wasn't the only one that
Mack entrusted to scout the Braves. Baker and Collins traveled to Boston
to watch the Braves play the White Sox on September 28. Jack Barry and
Harry Davis scouted the Braves in a doubleheader against the Giants on
September 30.

The Braves completed their unbelievable drive on September 29 as
they defeated the Chicago Cubs 3–2, while the Giants dropped a game, 5–2,
to Pittsburgh at the Polo Grounds. There was nearly a hysterical celebration in Boston, but fans in Philadelphia were subdued when the A's
clinched their fourth pennant in five years. They had come to expect it.

Whatever slim chances the Braves appeared to have to win the World
Series seemed to evaporate on October 7 when third baseman James "Red"
Smith, one of only two Braves to hit over .300, broke his leg sliding into
second base in a meaningless game against Brooklyn. Stallings's philoso-
phy of not resting his regulars had proven costly. Charlie Deal, 22, a strong
defensive player who hit .210 for the season, was tabbed to replace Smith.
The Braves responded to the serious blow by saying they would win the
World Series anyway.

To make matters worse, the Braves would not have a true home field
advantage in the World Series because they would play their games in Fenway Park. Red Sox owner Joseph Lannin had offered his park to the Braves
in September to accommodate the larger crowds. South End Grounds, a
bandbox ballpark, had a seating capacity for only 11,000 and left and right
field fences were much shorter than other ballparks. Additionally, the first
two games of the World Series would be played in Shibe Park, giving
Philadelphia a chance to build an early advantage.

The Braves also lacked World Series experience. Only second baseman Johnny Evers and outfielder Josh Devore, who had played with the
Cubs and Giants, respectively, had seen postseason action. Devore had been
limited to 52 games with the Braves.

Mack's club finished 99–53 and won the pennant by eight and a half games over the Red Sox. Despite his health problems, Baker led the league in home runs for the fourth consecutive year with nine and drove in 89 runs, his lowest total since 1910. He batted .319, second highest on the team to Collins' .344. He had enough speed to hit 10 triples and steal 19 bases. Stuffy McInnis led the team in runs batted in with 95 and batted .314. Collins scored a league-high 122 runs. The Athletics scored 749 runs and batted .272, both league highs. Their batting average was 14 points higher than Detroit's and they scored 134 more runs than Detroit, their closest offensive challenger. It marked the second consecutive year that they had scored 100 more runs than the second closest team. The 1930 to 1931 Yankees are the only other team to accomplish the feat.

For the first time since 1909, the A's didn't produce a 20-game winner. Seven pitchers, however, won double figures. Bender (17–3) and Bush (17–12) earned the most victories while Shawkey (16–8) and Plank (15–7) were close behind. Pennock and Wyckoff each won 11 and Bressler won 10. Although the staff led the American League in shutouts with 24, its earned run average of 2.78 was higher than three other teams. Mack had gotten 65 wins from five starters who were 23 or younger.

Even though the Braves didn't take over first place until September, they won the pennant by 10.5 games over the Giants, posting a 95–59 mark. Outfielder Joe Connolly (.306) and third baseman Red Smith (.319) were the only Braves who batted over .300. No player scored or drove in 100 runs. The 32-year-old Evers led the team with 81 runs and light-hitting five-foot-five shortstop Walter "Rabbit" Maranville (.246) drove in a team-high 78 runs.

The Braves pitching centered around the impressive trio of right-handers Dick Rudolph and Bill James and southpaw George "Lefty" Tyler. James, 22, posted a 26-7 record with a 1.90 ERA. Rudolph, 27, went 26–10 with a 2.35 ERA while Tyler, 24, chalked up a 16–13 record with a 2.69 ERA.

The 1914 World Series shaped up to be a lopsided affair. If McGraw's Giants and Chance's Cubs hadn't been able to beat Mack's Athletics, how could Stallings' band of miracle men do it? Many observers felt the Braves winning the pennant only showed the weakness of the National League, which was smarting from four consecutive losses in the World Series. The Braves were getting no more respect than the Athletics did in 1910 before facing the Cubs. The question wasn't, "Who would win the World Series?" but "Would the Braves win a game?"

To Stallings and his players, it mattered little what the experts thought. They were supremely confident. "What the A's did in other years means nothing to us," proclaimed Stallings. "I refuse to admit that the A's are superior to Boston in any branch of the game."[22] He was willing to bet that Joe Connolly would outhit any player in the series. He believed Evers and Maranville were equal to Collins and Barry, Hank Gowdy was as good a catcher as Schang and his outfield was equal to Mack's.

No matter how good Stallings thought his team was, they didn't stack up to the Athletics in the opinion of most sportswriters and fans. *Washington Post* reporter Stanley Milliken, however, cautioned American League fans not to take the Braves too lightly. "The Braves are a stronger team than the average fan would suppose," he wrote. "They are not a flashy team, but they are hustling all the time. They have a better chance against the A's than the Giants did last year."[23]

The Braves were a hungry team, driven by the scrappy, high-strung veteran Evers and by Stallings, who had taken over the managerial reins in 1913. He was Boston's eighth manager in seven years. He inherited a team that had finished last for four consecutive seasons. The 47-year-old Stallings, a Georgia native, graduated from the Virginia Military Institute and studied medicine for two years at Baltimore's College of Physicians and Surgeons. He gave up a career in medicine for baseball. His major league career consisted of seven games in the 1890s. He was described as superstitious, temperamental, brilliant, abusive, and profane. He was known for his tongue-lashings and his constant movement on the bench. Stallings had gotten rid of any players who weren't willing to hustle, play together as a team or listen to him. He ruled with an iron hand and his players were as afraid of him as of a rattlesnake.

Stallings had managed the Yankees from 1909 to 1910 and was familiar with most of the Athletics. Having played them more than 40 times, he knew Mack's tendencies and those of his players. This gave him a great advantage in preparing to meet them. Stallings admitted that beating Mack's club was his greatest ambition.

"The Braves have gone over the A's with a microscope and Stallings has mapped out our plan to battle against each Philadelphia pitcher because he knows them well and he thinks he knows how to beat them," said Evers.[24]

Stallings planned to use his knowledge to thwart Bender and Plank, two pitchers the Braves had to beat if they were to win the World Series. Winning one of the first two games was key. "The baseball world is going to be surprised by how we handle Bender and Plank," offered Evers.[25] The fiery second baseman said the Braves planned to make both pitchers work hard so that it would be more difficult for them to come back on short rest. He promised that neither one would have an easy game.

Stallings said no one believed the Braves had a ghost of a chance to win the pennant on July 4, so he wasn't bothered that few believed they had a chance in the World Series. He felt if the team kept playing the same way as it did down the stretch of the pennant race, it had a good chance of winning the Series. His team didn't fear any pitcher. The Braves figured they would defeat Bender and Plank the same way the Athletics had beaten Mathewson and Marquard of the Giants. They were anxious to prove their season wasn't a fluke.

When asked if it would be a difficult World Series, Stallings shot back, "Yes, for the A's."[26] Asked about the Series on the eve of its start, Stallings boasted, "We will win for sure. My team is as good as Mack's any way you look at it and we are going to hand a lot of people a big surprise."[27]

The Braves' hopes of winning rested solely on their pitching staff, which meant the big three of Rudolph, James and Tyler. They had carried Boston in the second half of the season and Stallings didn't expect that to change. He expected to beat the A's at their own game — pitching. He had unlimited confidence in his pitchers and expected they would offset the explosive Philadelphia offense. He figured three runs a game was all the Braves needed to win. The question was, would the Braves' trio have enough left for the Series after the grueling pace of the second half of the season?

Evers said, "We will keep on winning games when we meet the A's. We are going to surprise the Mackmen in several ways. The A's have hit the ball harder and more frequently, than we have, but that won't make a difference in a seven-game series. The A's will find that our pitchers are better than many of those they faced this year."[28]

The Braves looked to gain an advantage over the Athletics in two ways. They wanted to prevent them from stealing their signs, something other teams hadn't been able to do. And, they wanted to upset their opponent with relentless verbal harassment.

Evers said neither the Giants nor the Cubs went after the A's. The Braves rode every team during the season, hoping to rattle their players. Stallings' club could be crude, cruel and cutting with their remarks. Led by Evers, they had perfected their unnerving banter during the season. No player was safe from their barbs. And, the bigger the star, the more they rode him.

"We want to get the opposing players up in the air and we will mention anything about their baseball careers of which they may not be very proud to try to get them to answer back. We know a lot of things about the A's that we are ready to pull. I understand that Mack's team is not fond of being 'ridden' either,"[29] said Evers.

To prevent the Athletics from stealing their signs, Stallings discarded the team's already complicated set of signs and devised a new one, just as complicated. His pitchers and catchers practiced them constantly, on and off the field.

In assessing the 1914 World Series, Ty Cobb wrote that it was a matchup between a machine (Athletics) and lucky hope (Braves). "The Boston club is at best a makeshift team," he wrote. "It is just a lot of ballplayers and no tried stars except Evers."[30]

Cobb credited Stallings's shrewd handling of the club and platooning as keys to winning the pennant. Without Stallings, Cobb doubted if the Braves would have finished in the first division. Cobb also expected the Athletics to have trouble with the Braves' trio of starters. Mack's men were great fastball hitters, but were the weakest against a spitter or slow ball. James was the only starter to count on speed but he also had an effective spitter. Rudolph and Tyler were both smart slow ball pitchers. Cobb labeled Rudolph as the smartest pitcher in the National League, next to Christy Mathewson.

Every National Leaguer seemed to be willing to help the Braves in their effort to beat the Athletics. Phillies manager Pat Moran scouted Mack's team the final 10 days of the season and filed a report with the Braves. Giants star Christy Mathewson offered his advice, telling the Braves they needed to stop Collins and Baker. "This pair more than the whole team put together will give you fellows the most trouble." Matty considered Collins harder to pitch to than Baker because he had no weakness. Baker's weakness was a low curve ball on the outside. "But, he is most dangerous at all stages,"[31] he warned.

The Giants star agreed with Cobb that spitballers James and Rudolph would trouble the Athletics and that left-handers would pose more of a problem than right-handers for Boston. The Braves, however, had lost only one time to a left-hander since July 4, according to Stallings.

Walter Johnson of the Senators was rumored to be conferring with the Braves, sharing his information on the A's. Why would Johnson be aiding the National League? He was reportedly upset with Philadelphia's failure to support the Players Fraternity. Ever since the Braves had been in contention for the National League pennant, Stallings reminded his team the A's had refused to sanction a strike of all major leaguers when Fultz asked for a strike vote. The Athletics hadn't won any friends with their position and the Braves saw the series as a chance to extract a measure of revenge against what they considered a scab team. The club had sent a telegram to the A's in the summer calling them quitters for not supporting the Players Fraternity.

The miracle Braves didn't seem to be as much of a threat to the powerful Athletics as overconfidence. When asked about it, Eddie Collins responded, "We had had it fired in our faces enough times that overconfidence and indifference beat us out of a pennant in 1912, when we should have won in a walk. If we lose, it won't be because of overconfidence. If we were playing the Giants, who we have beaten twice, I could understand the talk of overconfidence. But, not with the Braves."[32] Despite Collins's statement, most of the A's had little regard for the National League. They didn't believe there was one National League club they couldn't beat.

When tickets for the World Series went on sale at 9 a.m. at Gimbel's department store at Ninth and Market Streets in Philadelphia on Tuesday, October 6, there was a line six blocks long. Many of the fans had gotten in line the night before. Despite the presence of more than 100 policemen, the crowd was unruly and a number of fights broke out as people pushed toward the Gimbel's entrance and others tried to jump in line. Some ambitious youths got in line early and sold their places to businessmen for $1. When ticket sales stopped at 2 p.m., more than 6,000 unhappy fans were turned away. Speculators were willing to sell tickets to those denied or businessmen for $5 for the $2 seats and $8 for $3 seats. Although interest in baseball had waned during the regular season, it returned in full force for the World Series, creating the greatest demand for tickets ever in Philadelphia.

Stallings, a master psychologist and motivator, picked a fight with the revered Mack on the eve of the opening game. He requested Mack's permission for his team to practice at Shibe Park in the afternoon so his players could get accustomed to grounds and the angle of the sun at that time. Mack had already arranged for the A's to practice in the afternoon and the field wouldn't be available. He did, however, offer to have the Braves practice at Shibe Park in the morning. Stallings refused and practiced at the Phillies ballpark instead. He went away, apparently satisfied, according to Mack. The following day, however, the Braves' manager called Mack and berated him for what he termed "unsportsmanlike conduct." Mack offended Stallings by telling him he had been satisfied with the arrangements the day before. Stallings responded by calling Mack "a liar" and threatened to punch him, if he said the same thing to his face. The incident was one more incentive for the Braves to win and it increased interest.

On the day of the opening game, Friday, October 9, some 8,000 disappointed fans hoping to purchase $1 bleacher seats were turned away from the ticket windows. Hundreds of them headed to the homes outside Shibe Park, stretching along 20th Street to Somerset and west on Somerset to 21st Street, to purchase seats in the temporary "grandstands" erected on rooftops by home owners. Forty houses held grandstands which could seat more than 100 people. The crowd overflowed the rooftops. They hung onto to spouting, peered out of second-floor windows and watched from porch roofs, trying to gain a viewing advantage. Conservative estimates place 5,000 people on the housetops. More than 20,500 fans jammed Shibe Park.

Both managers went with their best pitchers in the opener. Mack tabbed the always dependable Bender while Stallings called on Rudolph, an unimpressive looking five-foot-ten, 27-year-old nicknamed "Baldy." Rudolph had pitched briefly for McGraw's Giants in 1910 and 1911 before being released. After posting a 14–13 record for the Braves in 1913, Rudolph surprised everyone by winning 26 games in 1914. Bender had started and won the opening games of the 1910, 1911 and 1913 World Series. Mack let Plank take batting practice, hoping to dupe the Braves into thinking he would start. Bender didn't appear on the field until 15 minutes prior to the start of the game and then took the time to pose for several photographs.

The Braves started their psychological battle when they walked onto the field. Stallings had told them to ignore the A's, unless they were hurling an insult. The Braves refused to acknowledge the Athletics or shake their hands, upsetting Mack's men.

The Braves had voiced no fear of the Athletics before the start of play and they proved it with their bats. After Bender retired the side in order in the first inning, the Braves plated two runs in the second and never trailed. George "Possum" Whitted walked and scored when Hank Gowdy laced a fastball over Jack Barry's head, sending it all the way to the left field bleacher wall for a double. Rabbit Maranville followed with a single through the box, scoring the second run.

Philadelphia got one run back in the bottom of the inning when Stuffy McInnis walked and Amos Strunk singled to right and the ball went through Herbie Moran's legs in right field, allowing McInnis to score. They wasted an opportunity to tie the game, however, as they failed to score with a man on third and no outs.

The Braves added a run in the fifth after Gowdy opened with a triple to deep right center and Maranville chased him home with a single. Stallings's crew broke the game open with three runs in the sixth. With one out, Evers singled to center and Joe Connolly drew a walk. Whitted lined a triple to deep right center, scoring two runs. Charles "Butch" Schmidt singled through short, scoring Whitted to make it 6–1. That was all for Bender as Mack signaled for Weldon Wyckoff, who was warming up. As the Chippewa Indian walked off the mound and into the dugout a hush fell over the stunned and astonished crowd. "Not a sound was heard except the hornet-like buzz of the hundreds of telegraph instruments which were ticking the tidings of the Indian's downfall,"[33] reported the *New York Times*. His exit marked the first time he had failed to complete a World Series game and the first time an A's pitcher had been knocked out of a Series game. As Bender walked into the dugout with his head bowed, Mack muttered, "Pretty good hitting for a bush league outfit."[34]

Wyckoff pitched carefully to Gowdy and walked him. Maranville grounded to Wyckoff, who threw to third too late to get Schmidt, loading the bases. Charlie Deal grounded into a double play as Baker stepped on third and threw to McInnis. The Braves added a run in eighth to breeze to a 7–1 win.

Rudolph's deceptive delivery had kept the Athletics off balance with a slow ball, lazy curves and an occasional fastball. Cool and collected on the mound, he turned in a brilliant effort. He struck out eight batters, surrendered five hits and allowed only three balls to the outfield. The A's looked like they were fooled the entire game. No other pitcher had made the three-time World Champions look so bad. Rudolph had "tied the A's hitters into knots," just as Stallings had predicted.

John Taylor, former president of the Boston Americans, wrote, "Rudolph had the A's swinging at everything except wild pitches."[35]

While the Athletics were too aggressive, swinging frequently at the first pitch, they may have been trying to cross up Rudolph, who was expecting them to be patient. They thought they would see more fastballs on the first pitch.

Rudolph held Baker in check until the ninth inning. The Trappe slugger popped out in foul territory with a runner on first base in the first inning, struck out in the fourth, reached on an error in the seventh and doubled off the wall in right-center in the ninth.

Cobb attributed some of the Athletics' offensive ineptness to their inability to steal the Braves' signs. Boston, according to Cobb, thwarted Philadelphia's efforts by having Gowdy refuse to give signals when a batter was out of the box. A great trick of the Athletics was to have the batter step out of the box when the catcher was giving his signals, allowing the first and third base coaches to get a better view of the signals. When they tried it against the Braves, Evers yelled to Rudolph, "Take your time. Wait until he gets back into the box." Gowdy surprised the A's by stopping to give his signals.

"We were beaten by superior pitching, but we're still confident," said Jack Barry afterwards. "Rudolph is a different type and style pitcher than we're accustomed to hitting against. I must admit, he had something on us."[36]

Collins added, "We have no excuses to offer. Rudolph pitched a masterful game, but I think we did more to beat ourselves. We were too anxious to hit the ball. Every batter who struck out swung at a bad pitch. There was not a single exception. We could not seem to wait for the ball. Every batter, with the exception of Eddie Murphy, either struck out on bad pitches or hit bad balls that nine times out of ten we would never offer at again."[37]

While Baker and Collins were accustomed to being batting stars, that honor when to the Braves' Hank Gowdy, a .243 hitter during the regular season who singled, doubled and tripled.

Rudolph proved to be a modest hero. He attributed some of his success to an exhibition game he pitched against Mack's club five years earlier and watching them play in New York at the end of the regular season.

"I was just lucky, you know," he said. "I don't know why they didn't hit yesterday. I tried to pitch them where they weren't expecting it, but it is some job to outguess any of that team. I found out what makes the A's such a hitting team. They are all free swingers. The whole batting list is dangerous to any pitcher. To look down that batting list is like looking down murderer's row."[38]

Stallings refrained from saying, "I told you so" to reporters, but he felt vindicated by the impressive opening win. Now, fans would take the Braves seriously. "People have been waiting for us to crack since the end of July, but I guess we can stand the strain of winning for a few days more at least,"[39] he said. He had prepared his team to beat the defending World Champs and his strategy was paying off.

Game 2 on Saturday, October 10, at Shibe Park, featured southpaw Eddie Plank against six-foot-three, 22-year-old right-hander Bill James, who had gone 19–1 since July. His only loss in the final three months of the season was an 11-inning setback against the Pirates on August 22. James was another success story nurtured by Stallings. As a rookie in 1913, "Seattle Bill" compiled a 6–10 record. Who would have thought he would go 26–7 in 1914, posting the National League's best winning percentage? Just as surprisingly, he won only five more games in his career.

The game turned into a classic pitching duel. Plank and James battled each other evenly for eight innings, each refusing to surrender a run. Entering the ninth inning, Plank had given up five hits and James two. Plank, however, was in constant trouble as the Braves had runners every inning, but the seventh.

The Athletics had missed their scoring chance in the sixth inning with

Dick Rudolph, a right-hander who won 26 games for the Boston Braves in 1914, defeated the Philadelphia Athletics twice in the World Series as the "Miracle Braves" swept the highly favored A's in four straight. NATIONAL BASEBALL HALL OF FAME LIBRARY, COOPERSTOWN, NY.

the score tied 0–0. Schang doubled down the third base line with one out for the team's first hit. He tried to advance on a short passed ball, but Gowdy threw him out at third. As Schang stood up to leave the field, the Braves bench loudly jeered him. The young catcher was one of the Braves' favorite targets for verbal harassment during the Series and it seemed to bother him and affect his play.

With one out in the crucial ninth inning, Deal drove a long double over Strunk's head in center. Strunk started in on the ball and then ran back, apparently losing it in the sun. Deal ended up on second with a double. He stretched his lead off of second base, drawing a low throw from Schang to Barry, covering the bag. Deal broke for third on the throw, but Barry couldn't get the ball out of his glove and the Braves' third baseman slid into third safely. After James fanned, Collins and McInnis approached Plank on the mound as Les Mann, a right-hander who was playing right field in place of Moran because a left-hander was pitching, stepped to the plate. Collins made a move with his head, no doubt a signal to other players. Plank was laboring, having thrown more than 130 pitches. Mann worked him to a 2–2 count before lining a Texas Leaguer over Collins's head. The Philadelphia second baseman raced back on the outfield grass and dove for it, barely getting the tip of his glove on the ball. He lay sprawled on the grass as the game's first run scored. Whatever the A's had discussed on the mound hadn't worked. Mann went to second on a passed ball and Evers walked. Plank got out of the jam as Ted Cather bounced into a force play.

Trailing 1–0 in the bottom of the ninth, the crowd was expecting an Athletics comeback, one like they had witnessed many times before. Barry raised the crowd's optimism as he reached first on a walk, James's second of the game. Schang struck out and Barry went to second as Gowdy dropped the ball. With a runner in scoring position and one out, Eddie Walsh was sent to pinch hit for Plank. Walsh coaxed James for a walk, putting the winning run aboard. Philadelphia's hopes, however, were crushed as Eddie Murphy grounded sharply to Maranville, who stepped on second and doubled up Murphy for the final out in spectacular fashion. Evers had directed the little shortstop to play almost directly over the bag moments earlier. The Braves hugged one another and threw their hats in the air. They had incredibly defeated the Athletics twice in Shibe Park.

As soon as the game ended, the 200 members of the Royal Rooters of Boston marched onto the field, carrying banners and celebrating as the Athletic fans sat stunned. A brass band, headed by Boston's ex-mayor Honey Boy Fitzgerald and Braves president James Gaffney appeared on the field. The Royal Rooters grabbed Evers and forced him to lead the parade. They marched twice around the field, singing "Tessie."

While Plank had thrown 148 pitches, James had gotten by with just 92. He faced only 28 batters, one more than the minimum, and allowed only three balls to be hit to the outfield. Of the five runners who reached base, two were picked off of first base, one was thrown out at second on a passed ball, and one was erased on a double play.

James turned in one of the most brilliant pitching performances in World Series history. He did it with a mix of curves, slow balls, change of paces and spitters. He threw only a half dozen fastballs, according to *Washington Post* reporter Stanley Milliken. Most of James's seven strikeouts came on spitters. Before nearly every pitch, James passed his right hand across his mouth, which he covered with his glove. Sometimes he dampened his fingers and other times he didn't. He kept the A's guessing and most of the time they guessed wrong.

James was able to neutralize Baker, who came to bat once with a runner on base. Like the rest of his teammates, the A's cleanup hitter failed to be patient, swinging at the first pitch twice. He fouled out to first, flied to center, and bounced to second in three appearances. In the seventh inning, he came to the plate after Collins had beat out a bouncer to second with two outs. The Braves were expecting Collins to try to steal second to get into scoring position, where he would be in a better position to steal signs. Most opponents felt once Collins got on second, he was a big help to Baker, flashing him signs. James threw over to first twice to keep Collins close to the bag. Baker patiently took a couple pitches, waiting for Collins to make his move. James was well aware of the strategy and kept a close watch on Collins. He caught Collins leaning the wrong way with a quick pickoff throw, nailed him for the third out. That was a crushing blow to the Athletics.

Stallings said, "This was unquestionably the greatest World Series game ever played. Plank gave us more trouble than any left-hander we have faced since the Fourth of July."[40] After months of instilling his players with confidence and convincing his pitchers not to fear the Philadelphia hitters, the astute manager was seeing the payoff.

After collecting just seven hits and one run in two games, the Athletics were doubting themselves. They had overestimated the Braves' weaknesses and had been surprised by their hitting and pitching. Cobb was struck by the A's lack of confidence. He suggested Mack's men were playing as if they were afraid of losing their title. They were being too careful and they didn't appear to be relaxed. He said unless they changed their tactics and mental attitude, they were a beaten club.

Evers figured the Athletics were already a beaten team. He pointed to their decision to have Schang attempt to advance Barry to second with a sacrifice bunt with one out in the ninth inning. That signaled that Mack was playing for a tie at home instead of trying to win the game in the ninth.

The A's voiced confidence they would snap out of their hitting slump. At the same time, the Braves said it didn't matter who pitched for Philadelphia, they could beat them. The tide had definitely turned as the stunned

Athletics, now the underdogs, prepared to go to Boston. Fans had earlier questioned whether the Braves would even win one game in the Series, now there was talk of a possible four-game sweep.

A tumultuous crowd met Stallings's crew at the Boston train station. After catching some sleep, most of the players went out on the town to visit friends and relatives and soak up the adoration. The Athletics, however, stayed secluded in their hotel, thinking about what they needed to do to regain their championship form.

A record crowd was expected at Fenway Park on Monday, October 12. Since it was Columbus Day, a holiday for many residents, and the entire town was in a baseball frenzy. The big question was "Who would start Game 3?" The Braves had already treated Bender rudely and it made little sense for Mack to go back to him with two days rest. Rube Bressler, a young southpaw, was a possibility, especially since Plank had made a strong showing. Shawkey had a good curve ball and the Braves had less success against curves than fast balls. Bush had pitched in the 1913 World Series and made a good showing. Stallings was faced with sending Rudolph back on the mound or going with Lefty Tyler. Rudolph, James and Tyler had pitched regularly during the season and Stallings had to consider if he wanted to disrupt that rotation. Certainly, the pressure was on Mack, who could ill afford to lose the third game.

A record crowd of 35,520 packed every available space in Fenway Park and thousands more stood outside the park. From the top row of the bleachers youngsters yelled the outcome of each play to the crowd below. Two youngsters climbed the flag pole in center field and kept the crowd informed. Bender warmed up for Mack, but Bush started. Stallings went with Tyler, a 25-year-old who had recorded his first winning season in 1914 since debuting with the Braves in 1910.

Mack's men were focused and determined. They made an impression on the crowd by throwing their caps on the ground and practicing bareheaded while the band played "The Star Spangled Banner." The game turned out to be one of the tensest, most nerve-wracking and most dramatic games in World Series history.

The Athletics broke their 15-inning scoring drought in the top of the first as Murphy opened the game with a double, was sacrificed to third, and scored on an error. The Braves tied it in the second as Maranville walked, stole second and tallied on Gowdy's double.

Both teams scored a run in the fourth inning. The two clubs carried a 2–2 tie into the tenth inning. Schang opened with a single and Bush struck out trying to sacrifice him to second. Murphy hit back to Tyler, who whirled and threw to second, too late to get Schang. Collins walked to load the bases. The Braves seemingly preferred to pitch to the left-handed hitting Baker, who had struck out twice and bounced into a double play. Baker crossed up the strategy as he slammed one hard off of Evers' shin, scoring a run. Murphy reached third, but Evers had forgotten that bases were loaded. He picked up the ball, tucked it under his arm and began rubbing his hands. He held the ball so long that Murphy finally darted for home without Evers noticing. After the game, Evers said, "I just pulled a bone. I was caught flat-footed and I didn't even see Murphy running until he reached the plate."[41] The turn of events had given the Athletics a 4–2 lead.

Philadelphia was three outs away from its first 1914 Series victory. Gowdy was the first batter to face Bush. A light hitter during the regular season, the slim six-foot-two catcher had proven dangerous in the World Series. Bush got careless and threw him a fastball on the first pitch, which he promptly deposited over the center field fence. The blow gave the Braves new life. Maranville rushed to the first base coach's box and began to run up and down the line, yelling and celebrating in unbridled fashion. The crowd erupted with applause and thunderous approval. The Boston Royal Rooters band in the center field bleachers began to play "Tessie." The noise in Fenway Park was deafening.

Barry, Baker and Collins made a beeline for the mound to calm the 21-year-old Bush. They reminded him that he still had a one-run lead and needed just three more outs for the win. Don't let them rattle you, they said amidst the noise.

Bush seemed to respond as he struck out Josh Devore, who was batting for Tyler. Bush was starting to tire and Evers yelled from the on-deck circle to Moran to be patient and wait him out. Moran followed instructions and worked Bush for a walk. The veteran Evers was now in a position to atone for his earlier mental error. He took advantage of the opportunity thanks to catcher Wally Schang, who muffed a foul tip that prevented Evers from striking out. With the count 1–2, Evers tipped a pitch foul. Schang had it in his mitt momentarily, but it popped out. On the next pitch, Evers slammed a single to right center to push Moran to third. Connolly flied to center field, deep enough to score Moran with the tying run. Maranville turned flip flops on the sidelines and the players excitedly congratulated each other with back slaps and ran out of the dugout to greet Moran at home. The band continued to play and the crowd went wild. The inning ended as Whitted popped to third.

With the score tied 4–4, James relieved Tyler in the top of the 11th. He retired Walsh and Barry on grounders before walking Schang to get to Bush, who struck out to end the inning. Bush retired the Braves in order in the bottom of the inning.

With darkness coming, the Braves asked home plate umpire Bill Klem to halt the game. He refused, but announced that the 12th inning would be the final one. Approaching five o'clock, it was perhaps already too dark to play.

Murphy opened the 12th with a walk and advanced to second on Oldring's bouncer back to the mound. The Athletics had a man in scoring position with one out and their two best hitters due up. Collins, however, popped to third, Baker was intentionally walked and McInnis forced Baker at second.

As Gowdy strolled to the plate wielding his black bat to start the bottom of the inning, the crowd gave him a standing ovation. He had already earned a place in their hearts, but he had another opportunity for fame. As the game pushed the three-hour mark, Bush was tired from the titanic struggle. Mack had Shawkey warming up on the sidelines for the past couple of innings but hadn't signaled for him

Gowdy ignited the Braves by lining a ball into the left-field temporary seats, which according to ground rules was a double. Mann came in to run for him. Larry Gilbert, batting for James, was intentionally walked to set up the force out at third. The Athletics were expecting Moran to bunt Mann over to third. Bush failed to hold Mann close to second and he got a quick jump before Moran placed a nearly perfect bunt down the third base line. Bush fielded it and knew he had little time to force Mann at third base. Some observers felt he didn't have any chance, even if his throw had been perfect. Rushing, Bush threw wildly to Baker at third. Mann dove head first into third and once he realized there had been an overthrow, he got up and easily scored the winning run.

After Bush's wild throw, the hysterical crowd poured onto the field and embraced as many Braves at they could find. Heartbroken and dejected, Bush made his way under the stands with tears in his eyes and a lump in his throat. Gowdy, with two doubles, a home run and a walk, was once again the offensive star.

"I don't consider the A's have a chance now and I look to see them beaten tomorrow," said Evers afterward. "This club is in a mood where it can't be stopped."[42] Stallings said, "We showed the A's something besides pitching today. Our confidence has soared extremely high and if the Braves do not win four straight games, I'll be disappointed. After exposing every weakness of the A's, I'm prepared for four straight."[43]

The *Philadelphia Public Ledger* was impressed with the Braves' play. "Never has a ball club fought harder, displayed more gameness and fighting ability than the Braves. They came from behind four times to win the game. There was no fluke in their victory."[44]

Cobb added, "I have never seen a team show so much backbone and nerve as the Braves did today. Considered a joke club going into the series, the Braves have earned the respect of the baseball world. I look for the A's to lose four straight."[45]

Despite the disappointment, Baker managed to remain optimistic, "I still think our club will win. If the Braves can beat us three straight, we can beat them four straight. I think they will go with Rudolph and I think we will beat them. It looked like we were starting to break out of our slump today."[46]

Stallings gave the Braves another psychological boost on the morning of Game 4. If the Braves lost, they would have to travel to Philadelphia by train immediately after the game since Game 5 was scheduled the following day. Team secretary Herman Nickerson had made arrangements for the team to take the train in case of a loss. When he told Stallings of the arrangement, the confident manager told him to cancel them. "Why," he asked. "Because we won't be needing them," replied Stallings. Four or five players overhead the conversation in the clubhouse. Stallings refused to pack a travel bag before the game and he made sure his players knew it. "If we had lost, we would have been in a bad fix," he said. "The players got the idea they could win game four and they did."[47]

The Athletics and Braves were at polar opposites on the confidence scale at they prepared for Game 4 on Tuesday, October 13. The previous day's loss was demoralizing. The Athletics were mired in a terrible batting slump, the breaks hadn't gone their way, they had dropped two games at Shibe Park and the Braves had defeated their two best pitchers. Twenty-three-year old Bob Shawkey shouldered the pressure for the Athletics. He was more experienced than Rube Bressler or Herb Pennock, Mack's other possible choices. The previous possibility of a four-game sweep rode with Rudolph, who had baffled the Athletics in Game 1. Could he continue to fool them? Were the A's due to break out of their hitting slump? Would Rudolph become the first pitcher ever to beat Mack's men twice in a World Series?

The capacity crowd of 34,365 seemed subdued, as if they knew there was no way the Braves could lose. Stallings's club got on the scoreboard first with a run in the fourth inning and the A's tied the game in the top of the fifth. In the bottom of the fifth inning, Rudolph singled with one out. Moran laced the first pitch to center for a double, sending Rudolph to third. Evers, the symbol of the Braves' spirit and spunk, was determined to get his pitch from Shawkey. He worked him to a full count and then poked a two-run single over second base. The Braves jumped around in the dugout, hugging each other and cheering their captain. Pennock relieved Bush to start the sixth inning.

Trailing 3–1, the Athletics threatened in the seventh as Jimmy Walsh led off the inning with a walk and went to second on a wild pitch. Rudolph pitched Barry carefully and fanned him. Immediately after the third strike, Gowdy rifled the ball to Evers at second base and caught Walsh off the bag. The play crushed the Athletics. In the morning session, Evers had instructed Gowdy to throw him the ball anytime a batter struck out and there was a runner on second.

As the top of the ninth inning started, hundreds of fans moved toward the exits so they could make their way onto the field after the final out. The Athletics trailed by two runs, but it must have seemed like 20. Philadelphia had Collins, Baker and McInnis due up. Rudolph had scattered seven hits and was in complete command.

Many of the A's could be seen slipping on their blue mackinaws in the dugout, gathering their gloves and bats. They formed a line to watch Collins start the inning, feeling destined to accept their fate and ready to make a quick exit from the field.

Collins, anxious to start a rally, fanned on a low outside pitch that one reporter described as unhittable with the proverbial 10-foot pole. Baker grounded to Evers. When McInnis grounded to third for the final out, the Royal Rooters in the temporary left field stand and fans in the bleachers poured onto the field. The Boston outfielders started for the dugout, hoping to outrun the crowd. The infielders quickly made a beeline for the dugout and the bench players grabbed up the bats and equipment and ducked into the clubhouse. An estimated crowd of 5,000 fans swarmed around the dugout and filled every inch of the field. Evers and Maranville, dressed in street clothes, were the first Braves to appear on top of the dugout to address the crowd. One by one the other Braves appeared.

Captain Ira Thomas led the Athletics over to the Braves' dugout to congratulate Stallings and his team. Collins ran after Evers to make sure he shook his hand and congratulated them. "They proved to be great losers," said Evers. "It was a bitter pill that they had to swallow."[48] Mack chose to stay near the A's dugout, talking to friends.

The Braves had pulled the biggest upset in World Series history, becoming the first team to win in four straight games. The Chicago White Sox "Hitless Wonders" team had upended the more powerful Chicago Cubs in 1906, but they had required six games.

A dejected Mack said, "The Braves are the best team that ever played baseball. We lost fair and square."[49] The upset loss concluded a troubled and unpleasant season for the A's manager.

In his newspaper column, Baker wrote, "The Braves won and they were the better club. They outplayed us from the start. Every one of the four games found us going after bad balls. During the season we made everyone pitch to us. On the bases, we looked terrible. Their catchers were outguessing us and we seemed to fall asleep."[50]

The *Philadelphia Evening Bulletin* wrote, "The A's have no alibis. They will not admit that they were beaten by a better team. The A's were outpitched, outhit, outgamed, outclassed and outlucked."[51]

The *New York Times* sensed the startling loss signaled the end of the Athletics' dynasty. It wrote, "A great change has come over baseball. There is no longer a $100,000 infield in Philadelphia, the far-famed 'Home Run' Baker is no more. Today, he is plain Frank Baker. Collins, 'the greatest player in the world,' is now a private in the ranks. The masterful Bender and the marvel of all southpaws, Plank, are through with World Series. They have had their day: all the gifts baseball can give were once theirs, but a new generation of ball players has grown up. The mighty have fallen."[52]

The Braves had beaten the Athletics on the playing field, but it was perhaps the psychological edge that paved the way. Boston players yelled insults and derogatory remarks constantly at the A's. Evers revealed the Braves rode Baker hard whenever he came to the plate. "Who is that at the bat now?" was the chorus from the bench. "He swings like a busher." That was probably the kindest thing the Braves yelled. Nothing was out of bounds for them —family problems, debts, past shortcomings or character assassination. They were uncouth and unrelenting. Young catcher Wally Schang was a prime target of verbal abuse. The Braves rode him hard and ridiculed him endlessly. Boston stole a record nine bases in four games against the flustered catcher.

Who could have predicted that one of the mightiest offensive clubs would be held to a .172 team batting average in four games? Baker led the regulars with four hits in 16 at bats for a .250 average. Collins hit a puny .214 with three hits in 14 at bats. No other regular batted higher than .200. Murphy (.188), Schang (.167), McInnis (.143), Barry (.071), and Oldring (.067), all failed miserably. The Athletics had averaged five runs a game during the regular season. Against the Braves, they scored six runs in four games.

Gowdy, Evers and Maranville led the Braves. Gowdy collected six hits, including five for extra bases, as he batted .545. Evers rapped seven hits as he batted .438 and Maranville batted .308.

It was a long, silent train ride from Boston to Philadelphia for the humiliated Athletics. When the train pulled into the North Philadelphia station at 10 a.m., four hours late, they found a half a dozen loyal fans waiting to greet them. Two of them were Eugene Davis, son of Harry Davis, and Rev. R.S. Snyder, Davis's brother-in-law.

Of course, there was much speculation as to not only why the Athletics lost, but why they lost in four straight. The three-time World Champions never seemed to recover from their opening game loss with Bender on the mound. Their confidence was inexplicitly crushed. Their determination and will to win seemed to have vanished. Questions arose as to why Mack didn't use Bender and Plank after the first two games. Some observers felt the Athletics were hurt because they didn't face high quality pitching down the stretch after the pennant race had been decided. Others believed they should have tuned up against an all-star team as they had prior to the 1910 World Series. Others believed they overthought the Series.

Had the Athletics had been distracted by Federal League activities? According to the *Philadelphia Evening Bulletin*, Danny Murphy, a Federal League recruiter, spent the greater part of the series with the Athletics and traveled with them on the special train. There was much talk about the Federal League and agents were talking to players throughout the Series.

Cobb probably summed it up best, "The A's defeat can be attributed directly to lack of preparation and overconfidence. Before the series, the A's were rated the greatest team in baseball, while Boston was regarded as not much more than a bush league outfit who had gotten lucky."[53]

It promised to be a long winter for Connie Mack and the Philadelphia Athletics.

EIGHT

Retirement,
a Bitter Feud and Rumors

Mack had been disappointed by the Athletics failure to win the pennant in 1912, but nothing rivaled his bitter disappointment at being swept in the 1914 World Series. To make matters worse, the A's had reportedly lost nearly $50,000 during the season as American League attendance dropped 21 percent from 1913; Philadelphia fans had grown apathetic to the Athletics' winning ways as the sixth-place Phillies outdrew them by nearly 80,000 fans; the Players' Fraternity issue and the Federal League had created internal dissension; several players had leveraged Federal League activity to get Mack to tear up their old contracts and give them new ones with substantial raises. Unfortunately, the outlook for 1915 wasn't much better.

The Athletics had been distracted, divided and overconfident during the 1914 World Series and there were rumors that there would be changes in the off-season. It didn't take long for Mack, who said he knew some of his players had signed with the Federal League or agreed to their terms during the 1914 World Series, to make a move. On October 31, he asked waivers on his three veteran pitchers—Coombs, Plank and Bender. The trio represented 35 years of service to the Athletics and 592 victories. While the three had illustrious pasts, their futures were not as bright. Coombs, sidelined with typhoid pneumonia, hadn't won a game in two seasons. Bender's lackluster performance in the World Series led many observers to believe he was washed up. And Plank, at 39, would have been retired in 1914 if Mack hadn't persuaded him to return for one more year.

Mack had no intention of retaining the three for the 1915 season and asked waivers on them because he suspected he would not be able to meet the Federal League offers. Plank admitted to Mack that he had received a strong offer from the Federal League. He was, however, surprised to be put on waivers, particularly without any notice. He found out about the transaction from a friend, who called him from Philadelphia. By putting the three on waivers, Mack said he was giving the other teams an opportunity to perhaps meet the Federal League offers.

Philadelphia wasn't the only team affected by Federal League activity in 1914. Pittsburgh Pirates owner Barney Dreyfuss blamed the Pirates poor seventh-place finish on the distractions. "Our players talked, played and ate Feds,"[1] he said. During 1914 spring training, Dreyfuss obtained an injunction to keep former Pirate Howie Camnitz, who had recently jumped to the Federal League, from actively recruiting players in the lobby of the hotel and outside the ballpark.

Mack refused to try and outbid the Federal League for players, insisting he couldn't afford to meet the higher offers. Other owners such as Charles Ebbets of the Brooklyn Dodgers took a more aggressive approach to trying to retain their stars.

"After giving the crisis much careful thought, I decided that the war had gone too far to stop it by trying to outbid the Federal moneybags," said Mack, years later. "Nothing could be more disastrous at this time than a salary war.

"There was but one thing to do: refuse to be drawn into this bitter conflict, and to let those who wanted to risk their fate with the Federals go with the Federals."[2]

After not getting any money for Bender and Plank, Mack decided to sell out and start over again. "If the players were going to 'cash in' and leave me to hold the bag, there was nothing for me to do but to cash in too."[3]

Early in December, Plank jumped to the Federal League. Mack told reporters he wasn't sorry to see him go because "he was after the money."[4] Plank received a substantial increase over the $5,000 a year salary he reportedly received from the Athletics.

On December 4, the Federal League announced the signing of Washington Senators ace Walter Johnson, its biggest coup yet. Johnson accepted an offer of $17,500 annually for three years plus a $6,000 signing bonus from the Chicago Whales. Senators' owner and manager Clark Griffith decided to fight to retain Johnson. Within a month, he had convinced Johnson that he was obligated to the Senators. The hurler announced at a press conference that he would return to Washington and fulfill his agreement. He received $12,500 for the 1915 season and was allowed to keep the signing bonus from the Whales.

Johnson's signing with the Feds triggered a monumental move by Mack. American League President Ban Johnson convinced Mack to sell second baseman Eddie Collins to the Chicago White Sox for $50,000, the highest amount ever paid for a player, to offset the Johnson's potential gate appeal with the Chicago Whales. The startling announcement was made on December 8. The famed $100,000 infield was no more and the baseball world was abuzz. Collins signed a contract for five years at $12,000 per year.

Why would Mack sell his most valuable player, who was considered by many as one of the best players in the game? The $50,000 helped Mack recoup much of his loss due to poor attendance and increased salaries and it enabled him to rid the A's of Collins's influence. Collins was the team leader, even though Ira Thomas was the captain. When Mack named Thomas captain it drove a wedge between players on the team. Collins reportedly refused to speak to Thomas on the field. "Thomas is a storm center among ballplayers,"[5] wrote the *Sporting Life*.

The two also feuded after the World Series when Thomas criticized Collins for revealing team secrets through his syndicated newspaper column. Thomas felt it was wrong for Collins to tell how the A's stole the signs of other clubs and picked up on the habits and weaknesses of opposing players. As the result of Collins's columns, other teams changed their signals and were more alert to the A's' tactics. Thomas claimed Collins's information had caused irreparable damage. Christy Mathewson, who also wrote a syndicated column, defended Collins, labeling Thomas's assertions ridiculous. He said Collins didn't write anything the rest of the league didn't already know.

Mack denied the sale had any thing to do with the feud between Collins and Thomas. "As for the reasons for selling Collins, they are my own, and I wouldn't have sold him if I did not think I was doing the right thing."[6]

The *New York Times* quoted an anonymous prominent Athletic as saying that the naming of Thomas as team captain wrecked the club. The player said the A's hadn't been the same since he assumed the role. Many of the veterans felt he was responsible for forcing the popular Danny Murphy out. The players resented Thomas, who barked orders, criticized them, and had a great influence on Mack.

Thomas's stance against the Players' Fraternity also made him unpopular. Ironically, he was named as the Athletics' representative for the Players Fraternity even though he, not the players, was aligned with management and Organized Baseball. He blocked the A's from cooperating with the Fraternity and worked to form another organization in opposition to the Players Fraternity. The club was divided over Thomas and the Players Fraternity, just as they were over the Federal League. It created additional dissension on the club.

Sporting Life's Chandler Richter observed that Mack wouldn't have sold Collins even for the astronomical figure of $50,000, if there hadn't been other reasons. "Friction on the club is evident, despite Mack's comments to the contrary,"[7] he wrote. Mack realized he had to clean house or risk having his entire team wrecked. The team couldn't exist and thrive if it was divided. Mack had great confidence in Thomas, who handled the pitching and other important duties. Getting rid of Collins and his supporters was his preferred option. Richter predicted several other players would follow.

Philadelphia fans were understandably upset about the departure of Collins, Plank, Bender and Coombs, even though Mack contended the team didn't have a chance to win the 1915 pennant with them. Despite the moves, Mack maintained he did not think he was breaking up his club because he had a number of young, promising pitchers in Bush, Shawkey, Pennock, Bressler and Wyckoff. Because of his past success, many fans and sportswriters were hesitant to criticize him. After all, he had built the team from scratch and said he could do it again.

Shortly after the sale of Collins, Phil Ball, owner of the St. Louis Federal League team, announced Baker would jump to his club in the next two weeks. Ball claimed Baker and Mack were at odds because Baker told Mack he wanted a new contract and more money as he had offers from the Federal League. Ball was confident he could obtain Baker without a lawsuit.

"I haven't thought about the Federals and I don't intend to," declared Baker from his home in Trappe in December 1914. "There has been no disagreement between Mack and myself. I am signed with the A's for next year. I have not boned Mack for an increase in salary."[8]

On January 7, a pair of millionaires, Colonel Jacob Ruppert of Ruppert Breweries and Colonel Tillinghast L'Hommedieu Huston, a former Army engineer, purchased the New York Yankees for $460,000 and made a commitment to turn the lackluster team into a winner. The Yankees had not finished higher than sixth in the previous four seasons. Within a month, the New York club was pursuing Joe Jackson of Cleveland, one of the game's top players. Huston and Ruppert vowed nearly unlimited financial support to newly named manager Wild Bill Donovan with the expectation the Yankees would be pennant contenders in two years.

Mack dropped a bombshell at the 11th annual Philadelphia Sporting Writers' Banquet at the Majestic Hotel on Saturday, February 16. When he

Philadelphia Athletics manager Connie Mack and Baker engaged in a bitter feud in 1915. Mack had signed Baker to a three-year contract prior to 1914. Baker announced his retirement from baseball in February of 1915, but later decided to play for Upland, Pennsylvania, in the Delaware County League after saying he wanted more money to return to the Athletics. This infuriated the normally mild-mannered Mack, who said he would not allow Baker to become the property of any other American League team. "I would not sell him for $1 million in cash," he declared. "I'm through with Frank Baker as a player. I hope I never see him again." NATIONAL BASEBALL HALL OF FAME LIBRARY, COOPERSTOWN, NY.

was called upon to respond to a toast, he announced to the crowd of 400 that Frank Baker had quit baseball. Although Mack had received Baker's letter informing him of the decision just prior to sitting down at the banquet table, he had been anticipating the decision for the past two seasons. To protect himself and the A's, Mack convinced Baker to sign a three-year contract prior to the 1914 season. Before Baker signed, however, he insisted upon a clause that read, "If at any time I desire to quit the game, I can do so and not be blacklisted."[9]

In response to the announcement, Baker said, "I have decided to quit the A's for the sole reason that I'm sick and tired of traveling around the country. I want it understood by my Philadelphia friends that I have absolutely no other reason and Mack has treated me fairly. The Federals have nothing to do with my decision and I have not the slightest intention of going with them."[10] Baker, who owned several farms and was financially secure, said if he got the urge to play baseball again, Mack would be the first one he would contact.

Mack had asked Baker about signing another contract, which was much more binding, halfway through the 1914 season.

"There had been some talk of various players negotiating with Federals and again others were getting much more money than they were entitled to. So I figured it would be an excellent opportunity for Baker to make his kick if he felt he was not getting enough money or was not being treated fairly," said Mack. "He came into my office, went over the contract, and without the slightest hesitation, he signed the new contract. Knowing all this, I am sure his decision is exactly what he says it is and there is no ulterior motive."[11] Baker's new contract called for the same amount of money he was receiving and was binding for the 1914, 1915 and 1916 seasons.

Several Athletics refused to sign the new contracts without the 10-day clause, which would theoretically allow them to break their contracts, until they were given raises to prevent them from jumping to the Federal League. Mack considered this a "hold-up" and resented that he had to give them more money. The contract squabbles were believed to be a major reason behind Mack's actions with Plank, Bender, Coombs and Collins.

Mack said any manager seeking Baker's services would have to ask his permission and he would not give it. If Baker changed his mind, he said there was a place for him with the Athletics. A day after Baker's announcement, Mack considered the case closed and said he would not ask the star third baseman to return.

Within a week of announcing his retirement, however, Baker said he would play, if offered a salary increase. "You mean you want more salary?" he was asked.

"That's it," he replied.

"Will a $2,000 increase do?"

"I want much more than that," he said.[12]

"If Baker retired from the game because he wanted more money, I know nothing about it," responded a bewildered Mack. He added that Baker had the same chance as the other players to hold out during last season, if he was unsatisfied. "If Baker wants to play ball and wants more money, it's up to him to come to me and say so, but until I hear from him, I will not believe the rumors."[13]

What changed Baker's salary position? Perhaps it was the realization that Eddie Collins signed a contract for $12,000 a year with the White Sox or that Walter Johnson would receive the same amount from the Senators. Cobb was getting $15,000 a year from the Tigers. Baker was certainly in their class, but his salary was somewhere between $4,500 and $6,500 a year. He had driven in 525 runs from 1910 to 1914, second to Detroit's Sam Crawford's 531. He had led the league in home runs for four years and runs batted in twice. At almost 29, he was one of the biggest stars in the game and a drawing card. One story had Baker being assured his salary was as high as Collins's when he signed prior to the 1914 season only to find out later that it wasn't.

With a three-year contract, the only way the third baseman could get a raise was to ask Mack point-blank (which he would almost certainly refuse) or demand to be traded or sold. Mack had already parted with Collins and he wanted the powerful third baseman to be the anchor for the 1915 club. He wasn't willing, however, to increase his salary.

The *Philadelphia Ledger*'s position was that if Baker was holding out and using his retirement to force his terms, it would be poor policy for Mack, or any other owner, to give him what he asked. It would be an admission by the owners that they were at the mercy of the players and it would add to dissension and dissatisfaction among other players. The newspaper suggested Mack follow the approach of Braves' owner William Gaffney, who allowed three of his players to jump to the Federal League rather than increase their salaries.

Within a week, three teams—the Yankees, Senators and Browns— expressed an interest in Baker. Mack, who hadn't talked to Baker since receiving his letter, quickly made his position clear. "We positively will not trade him to any other club and as far as selling him is concerned that is out of the question. No club has money enough to buy him. There is not enough money in the United States to buy him."[14]

Mack was firm that Baker would play for the Athletics the next two years or not at all. His contract was ironclad and Mack planned to prevent him from signing with an outlaw league.

At the end of February, Mack prepared to take his club to spring training. He was optimistic about the 1915 season, having signed the 41-year-old Nap Lajoie to replace Collins at second base. Twenty-four-year old Billy Kopf, who had played 37 games in 1914, was the most likely candidate to replace Baker.

By March 1, the Yankees had offered Mack $25,000 for Baker and agreed to pay him $10,000 a year. The Yankees, perennially overshadowed by the much more successful Giants, knew Baker would be an ideal clean-up hitter to build an offense around and a drawing card in the Polo Grounds. Mack turned the offer down, saying his selling price was $50,000. Huston and Ruppert declined to meet his asking price, but told fans they were still determined to acquire the players needed to build a winner.

The thought of Baker in the Yankees' lineup appealed to the New York owners enough for Huston to travel to Jacksonville, Florida to meet with Mack. Yankees manager Bill Donovan advised Huston to meet any reasonable terms to acquire Baker. Huston reportedly was prepared to offer $25,000 and Fritz Maisel, considered to be the league's second best third baseman.

While the A's were training in Jacksonville, Baker was in Trappe, practicing with the local high school team and meeting the mail train every day to catch up on the latest sports news. He was working on his farm killing hogs and performing other chores. Friends said he was wavering on his decision and many of them thought he would return to the Athletics. Trappe phone operators and messengers were kept busy taking messages and relaying them to Baker, who had refrained from installing a phone.

As the season opener approached, Baker reinforced his "more pay or I stay on the farm" position. He attended the season opener at Shibe Park against the Red Sox on April 14 and sat in the grandstands along third base with Ira Thomas. After the game, he visited Mack in his office and the two talked for a few minutes. Baker said he would think about returning and let Mack know his decision in a day or two. Mack made it clear that if he returned, it would be under the original terms of the contract. Baker asked Mack if he had any objections to him playing local baseball and the manager said no as long as it wasn't in Philadelphia. A reporter asked him if he was willing to play with the Athletics again. "I'm willing to play, if I'm asked,"[15] he said. Mack replied that he would be glad to have his star player return.

Baker was the captain and the main attraction of the 1915 Upland, Pennsylvania, team in the Delaware County League. The star third baseman, center, front row, batted .377 for Upland with nine home runs. He was enticed to play for the team by millionaire owner John Crozer and manager Frank Miller. As expected Baker was the top player in the league and dramatically boosted attendance. Baker's lifelong friend Tom Kibler, left, front row, is shown wearing an Easton, Maryland, team uniform. DELAWARE COUNTY HISTORICAL SOCIETY, PA.

A week later, however, Baker stunned Mack with the announcement he had agreed to play on Saturdays and holidays with the Upland, Pennsylvania team in the Delaware County League just 10 miles south of Philadelphia. He planned to play with Upland until he returned to the Athletics. Millionaire manufacturer John P. Crozer and manager Frank Miller had convinced the A's home run king to play for them.

The announcement didn't set well with the normally calm and mild-mannered Mack. "Baker can't make a fool out of me," he said. "And if he thinks he can have a little jaunt in the Delaware County League and then report at his pleasure to me and expect to find a place on my team, he has made the mistake of his life,"[16]

Mack hadn't inquired where Baker would play local ball when asked on Opening Day, but he said he wouldn't have agreed if he had known the slugger was going to play in the Delaware County League. His star status would undoubtedly siphon off some of Mack's attendance.

Mack wondered why Baker would travel nearly 100 miles from Trappe to Upland once a week if he didn't like to travel. He swore he wasn't going to give in to Baker nor lose any sleep over him. He was more than willingly to develop another youngster to take his place at third base.

Baker played in an exhibition game with Upland on April 24. He smacked three hits and made two errors in a 13–2 win over Rockdale before a crowd of more than 3,000 fans.

Shortly after he played his first game with Upland, reporters were on Mack's trail again looking for his reaction. "I'm through with Frank Baker as a ball player," he declared from Boston. "It is my intention at the present time not to allow him to become the property of any other team in the American League. I would not sell him for $1 million in cash."[17]

Mack said he would never blacklist Baker, whom he termed a contract jumper, for his actions, but added, "I hope I never see him again. He has treated the club unfairly and I have no time for a man who is not fair in his dealings."[18]

Mack bolstered his position by telling reporters Baker had written him in the summer of 1914 saying he would not play in the 1915 season. Mack, sensing the terms of the contract were unsatisfactory, sent him a letter in early February 1915 asking for his salary demands and what teams he preferred to play with in the American League. Baker replied that he did not want to be traded. He would play for the Athletics, if he played at all, but that his decision to retire was final.

Mack said he could not prevent Baker from returning to the A's since the contract was mutual. "Our sincere hope is that he sticks to his word and remains away," he said. "Still, a man who breaks his word once is likely to do it again. Once for all, I don't want Baker on my club. We miss him terribly and need his services, but I prefer a losing club to having men whose words are unreliable."[19]

At the same time Mack was blasting Baker, E.J. Hackney, president of the Philadelphia Suburban Baseball League, vowed to keep Baker from playing with Upland. Hackney filed a formal protest with Assistant District Attorney Joseph P. Rogers, president of the Interstate Association of Baseball Leagues.

"Baker, if not formally released by Mack, is a contract jumper, pure and simple,"[20] said Hackney. He said one of the purposes of the Interstate Association of Baseball Leagues was to prevent contract jumpers from playing. He felt Baker playing for Upland violated the league by-laws which stated no manager of any club in any league in the association could sign a player of another league until he had been released by that club.

Hackney maintained the association would immediately gain outlaw status if Baker was allowed to play.

Hackney considered Baker playing with Upland unfair to the rest of the leagues in the association, who might play the Delaware County League champions in a semiprofessional championship of the East. Baker could easily be transferred to the league's winning team, creating a disadvantage to the opposing league champions. Hackney was prepared to take the issue to court, if necessary.

Ira Thomas visited Baker for two days at his home in Trappe at the end of April. Although Thomas said he was not representing Mack on the visit, there could have been only one reason why he made the trip. When a reporter asked him about the visit at the train station, Thomas invoked the old adage, you can lead a horse to water, but you can't make him drink. "I don't think Baker wants to play," he said. "Whenever I talk baseball, he talks farming."[21]

Thomas's visit coincided with a rumor that Baker would jump to the Federal League if the National Commission upheld the New York Giants signing of Brooklyn Federal League outfielder Benny Kauff, who hit .370 and won the new league's 1914 batting title. Baker admitted the Federal League hadn't made him a recent offer, but he was willing to listen to any proposition that sounded like real money.

Baker's much-anticipated regular season debut with Upland was delayed when he tripped down a flight of stairs in his home and fractured a rib at the end of April. He sent a long telegram to Upland manager Frank Miller saying he would be unable to play in the home opener, but he would be glad to make the trip and sit on the bench. Miller said that wasn't necessary.

Baker's Upland salary was reported to be $100 per week, but others felt it was considerably more. The home run king admitted his Upland pay was almost as much as he made playing for Philadelphia, the difference being a few hundred dollars.

Baker made his regular season debut with Upland on Saturday, May 8, before the largest crowd ever to attend a game there. He received an enthusiastic reception each time he came to bat. In his first plate appearance, he smashed a hard liner over second for a single for his only hit of the afternoon as Upland defeated Clifton Heights 5–1. Not everyone, however, was thrilled with his performance. The *Chester Times* wrote, Baker's play "was nothing more than mediocre."[22]

Despite playing for Upland, Baker was ready to rejoin the A's, who were 7–12 and in seventh place. Many fans shifted the blame for the club's poor start to Baker, whose bat they felt would make a big difference in the lineup. He and Delaware County League President J. Borton Weeks traveled to Philadelphia on May 8 and met Mack at the train station before the team departed for a western road trip.

Baker offered to join the team on one condition: Mack had to tear up his three-year contract and give him a one-year contract at the same amount of money per year. Baker was willing to play for one year to set things right with Mack. The A's manager, however, was unenthused about the proposal. Baker said he only signed the three-year contract to assure Mack that he would not play for the Federal League.

At a special meeting of the Interstate Association of Baseball Leagues in mid–May, Upland's signing of Baker was upheld. Hackney proposed Baker be barred, but association representatives defeated the proposal 9–7. Immediately following the vote, association president Rogers resigned, saying he refused to be associated with an organization which harbored contract jumpers.

At the end of May, Washington Senators manager Clark Griffith stirred up the Baker case, calling the star slugger "the biggest ingrate in baseball." He added, "Baker's a money-mad baseball player. I hope Mack keeps him on the bench till he has been taught a lesson he'll never forget."[23] Griffith's view was shared by a number of other baseball officials and fans.

Griffith told his version of the Baker-Mack contract negotiations. According to Griffith, Baker signed a one-year contract for 1914 for $4,500 a year. In the summer, he approached Mack about more money for the remainder of the season. Mack countered by suggesting if Baker signed for three years he would increase his salary to $7,000 and the rate would apply for the remainder of the season. When the Feds renewed negotiations with Baker in the fall of 1914, they offered him $10,000 for 1915. Baker approached Mack, requesting to renegotiate his contract. When Mack refused, Baker asked him to tear up the three-year contract and give him a new one for $10,000 a year.

Griffith's attack on Baker drew an immediate response from J. Borton Weeks, president of the Delaware County League, who declared almost every statement was absolutely unfounded. Weeks pointed out that Mack and Baker both had agreed he would not be required to play after 1914, if he didn't want to. Weeks felt Mack was wrong for calling Baker a contract jumper, considering their morally binding agreement. He pointed out that Baker's contract with Upland allowed him to return to the Athletics at any time.

At the end of June, Baker agreed to play with Easton in the Peninsula League, which included Cambridge, St. Michaels, and Salisbury. Opposing towns protested the presence of Baker and several other prominent players on the Easton team. Salisbury proposed Baker play in the games on Easton's home grounds and on the home team of the other clubs once each week.

Baker thrilled Upland fans on June 27 when he blasted home runs in the sixth and eighth innings in a 4–3, 11-inning win over Media, which featured former New York Giants catcher Larry McLean. It was the type of performance Upland fans expected from Baker every game.

Mack continued to dismantle the Athletics as he sold pitcher Bob Shawkey to the Yankees on June 30 for $18,000, shortstop Jack Barry to the Red Sox for an estimated $8,000 on July 1, and outfielder Eddie Murphy to the White Sox on July 17.

In the July 3 issue of the *Philadelphia Ledger* Mack explained he hadn't planned to break up the team but a combination of factors forced him to do it. "The Federal League wrecked my club by completely changing the spirit of the players,"[24] he wrote.

Instead of thinking of victories, Mack claimed the Federal League's offer of astronomical salaries caused his players to think only about money. Although Mack felt his team could keep winning for another five years, he believed he had to break it up sooner than later, particularly since he didn't feel he could retain the players. He said whenever a team dominates for five years or so, players get a feeling of greater importance, and jealousy and dissension occur. He used Ned Hanlon's Baltimore Orioles of the 1890s and Frank Chance's Chicago Cubs in the first decade of the twentieth century as prime examples. He said it was impossible for him to have gone farther with the A's with the conditions that existed. Mack was confident he could build a team greater than the one he broke up. He figured the A's could be competitive again in two years.

Unfortunately, Mack wouldn't field another team with better than a .500 record until 1925. The A's went on to finish in last place every season from 1915 through 1921. Mack had to wait until 1929 before he produced his next pennant winner.

Mack was often asked why he didn't hang on to half of his team that was loyal and start to build up again. He answered, "When a team starts to disintegrate it is like trying to plug up the hole in the dam to stop the flood. The boys who are left have lost their high spirits, and they want to go where they think the future looks brighter. It is only human for everyone to try to improve their opportunities."[25]

On July 21, Mack announced he would sell Baker, but not to any of the top three clubs—Detroit, Boston or Chicago. He did not want to tilt the balance of power to any one team.

Meanwhile in Upland, team officials were making plans for Frank "Home Run" Baker Day, scheduled for Saturday, July 24. New bleachers had been erected, another ticket office had been added to handle the expected record crowd, and the field was in its best shape. The 25-piece Swarthmore Military Band was secured to play before the game and between innings. Fans contributed $1,000 toward the purchase of a Guernsey calf after learning of Baker's desire to add to the herd of cows on his farm. Upland owner John Crozer planned to present it to Baker at home plate in between innings. More than 4,000 fans attended Baker Day as Upland defeated Clifton 5–4 in the highlight of the season. Baker collected two hits, scored a run, but was also picked off of first base.

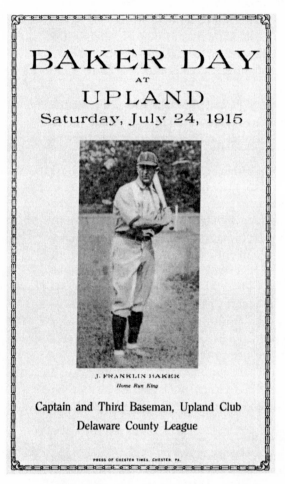

BAKER DAY
AT
UPLAND
Saturday, July 24, 1915

J. FRANKLIN BAKER
Home Run King

Captain and Third Baseman, Upland Club
Delaware County League

PRESS OF CHESTER TIMES, CHESTER, PA.

In early August, Federal League President James Gilmore announced his league was planning another raid on organized baseball and negotiations were underway with 15 stars. He said no amount of money within reason would stand in the way of the league trying to convince players such as Grover Alexander, Baker, Collins, and McInnis to sign contracts.

Baker visited Shibe Park and the A's clubhouse around the same time. It is unknown whether he talked to Mack or not. Baker said three teams were seriously bidding for his services, but Mack had refused to accept

Cover of the Frank "Home Run" Baker Day program. More than 4,000 fans turned out to honor the home run king as Upland defeated Clifton, 5–4, in the highlight of the season. Baker collected two hits, scored a run, but was also picked off first base. DELAWARE COUNTY HISTORICAL SOCIETY, PA.

the $25,000 the White Sox and Yankees were offering. He said he no longer wanted to play for the Athletics and Mack knew it. Was Mack just being stubborn and punishing Baker for holding out?

Upland traveled to Philadelphia to play J.G. Brill on August 8, but Baker did not play because he had promised Mack he wouldn't play in Philadelphia. Prior to the game, Brill manager Frank Clark and Delaware County League President Borton Weeks tried to obtain Mack's permission to let Baker play, but to no avail. Upland defeated Brill 5–3 before its largest crowd of the year.

By late August, Baker was growing increasingly

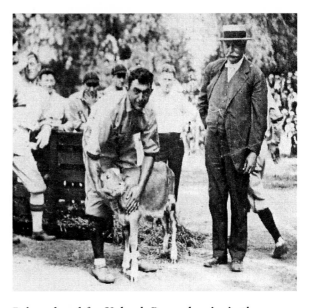

Baker played for Upland, Pennsylvania, in the Delaware County League in 1915 while engaged in a contract dispute with A's manager Connie Mack. The club held a "Home Run" Baker Day on July 24, 1915. Club owner John Crozer, right, presented Baker with a Guernsey calf for his farm. Fans raised more than $1,000 toward the purchase of the prized calf. COURTESY OF KYLE BARRETT.

frustrated, knowing other teams were making offers for him, but Mack kept refusing to accept them. Mack denied he had received any offers for the third baseman. Baker vowed Mack wouldn't keep him out of baseball. "I'm going to play somewhere. The Federal League looks good to me and I am ready to talk business. I will join any league or any club if they meet my figures."[26] Baker reportedly preferred to play for the Federal League Chicago Whales, managed by Joe Tinker. If need be, he said he would sit out the 1916 season in order to be clear to play for 1917.

Baker was keeping all of his options open. He made three trips to Baltimore in August to meet with officials of the Federal League Baltimore Terrapins, fueling speculation he would sign with them.

The American League didn't want to lose Baker, particularly to the Federal League. American League President Ban Johnson was worried the Federal League would put a team in New York City, where the Giants had fallen in popularity and the Yankees had never been a contender. Baker would reportedly join that New York Federal League team. Other rumors had him being sold to the St. Louis Browns. Johnson planned to use Baker to build the Yankees into a marquee team. On September 1, Johnson, Joseph Lannin, president of the Red Sox, Colonel Huston of the Yankees, and Ben Shibe, owner of the Athletics, conferred in New York to discuss the matter. Huston was willing to pay a handsome price for Baker, the Yankees having coveted him since his announced retirement. The group worked out a plan where the Yankees would acquire Baker for $15,000 cash and two or three players to be named later. The sale of Baker was expected to be announced the following day, provided Mack accepted the deal. Mack turned thumbs down, saying Baker wasn't for sale this year. Was he still punishing Baker?

On the field, Baker helped Upland clinch the Delaware County League pennant with a homer in a 9–5 win over Media. On September 4, he unloaded his ninth home run, the longest ever hit at Upland, in a 9–2 win over Media. Ira Thomas was among the 3,000 fans who attended Upland's September 18 game against Columbia.

In addition to playing for Upland, Baker played nine games at third base for Easton in the Peninsula League and compiled 12 hits in 33 at bats for a .364 average. Of course, fans were disappointed if he didn't slug one or two home runs a game.

Baker finished the season batting .377 for Upland with nine home runs. As expected, he was the top player in the league and boosted attendance throughout the league. He had put Upland on the baseball map and was probably worth every dollar Crozer paid him.

The Athletics finished with a dismal 43–109 record, 58.5 games behind the pennant-winning Boston, who went on to defeat the Philadelphia Phillies four games to one in the World Series. After the conclusion of the World Series, the rumors heated up again with speculation that a triangular deal would send third baseman Larry Gardner of the Red Sox to the Athletics; Baker would go to the Yankees, and New York third baseman Fritz Maisel would be traded to the Red Sox. The three-way deal never occurred.

In late October, Detroit Tigers president Frank Navin learned that Chicago White Sox owner Charles Comiskey was willing to outbid any team for Baker. Comiskey had just purchased Joe Jackson from Cleveland for $51,000 and Navin said Comiskey was willing to pay as much for Baker. The thought of Collins, Jackson and Baker in the lineup was an exciting one. Navin, like the other American League owners, was concerned that the acquisition of Baker would give the White Sox a great advantage. Navin joined others in advocating Baker go to a second division club, like the Yankees.

The sports editor of a New York paper wrote, "With a small fortune in prospect for the title to Baker, it is believed that Mack will vent his spleen no further."[27]

By the end of the month, Mack and Baker had agreed he would return to the Athletics. It did not mean, however, he would play for them. The possibility of a sale or trade still existed. The agreement removed Baker's name from the holdout list and ended the impasse. Ira Thomas was responsible for reconciling the two at a meeting in Salisbury, Maryland. The quarrel had been too bitter for Baker ever again to wear an Athletics uniform. By keeping Baker out of the game for a year and turning down offers for him, Mack had made a stand for principle. He showed Baker that he wasn't bigger than the game. The Trappe slugger had made his stand, but had probably miscalculated Mack's response. Despite what Baker originally said about his reason for retiring, it did seem that money was the real issue. He had stayed out of the game for one year in his prime and even though he had played once a week for Upland, it was a far cry from batting against Walter Johnson, Babe Ruth, and the likes.

The saga wasn't over yet. In mid–November, Baker declared he would not play for the Yankees. He told Upland manager Frank Miller that he would play for only one team in Organized Baseball, but declined to name it. There was a possibility he would return to Upland for the 1916 season, according to Miller. Baker may have been using a more than generous offer by John Crozer to cause the Yankees to sweeten their offer. Crozer, who had developed a closer personal relationship with Baker, was willing to pay whatever it took to keep him in Upland. No one knew for sure what Crozer paid Baker in 1915, but a reporter observed that the Maryland farmer purchased another farm in Trappe and a seven-passenger automobile following his season in Upland.[28]

In December, the Yankees, Browns and White Sox were rumored to be pursuing Baker. On December 15, Mack announced he would sell the third baseman to the highest bidder. "There has been so much talk about Baker that I am tired of it,"[29] he said. Baker, however, was demanding a big increase in salary and a slice of the purchase price. According to reports, he agreed to go with the Yankees if he received a three-year contract for $12,000 a year and $10,000 of the money Mack received from the Yankees' owners. But owners were growing cautious about offering too much for any player as the future of the Federal League became more and more clouded. If Organized Baseball and the Federal League reached agreement or the Federal League folded, Baker's value would be much less. On December 18, Mack announced he had received only one offer for Baker and that wasn't enough to buy a decent Christmas present for a nine-year-old boy.

Philadelphia *Evening Bulletin* cartoon of Mack and Baker.

Attendance for 1915 was poor for both Organized Baseball and the Federal League. Combined attendance was at its lowest in a decade. Fans were turned off by the business of baseball and the inferior quality of play. All the leagues tried promotions to boost attendance, but with little impact. The Federal League spent lavishly, but did not acquire enough stars. It had, however, succeeded in pushing baseball salaries to their highest level ever. Before the baseball war, the average salary was $2,500. It rose to $4,000 during the Federal League era. If the Federal League folded, players' salaries were expected to be cut and the average salary would likely return closer to the pre-Federal League level.

As financial losses for all three leagues continued to mount, Federal League owners and members of the National Commission met in Philadelphia during the World Series to consider a possible peace treaty. Robert Ward, owner of the Brooklyn Feds, had been one of the driving forces in keeping the new league going. His death caused the Federal League owners to take a harder look at a possible treaty. In mid–November, the Federal League announced it intended to place a team in Manhattan. That was a major concern to the National Commission and talks were renewed. Another meeting was scheduled for New York in December. At that meeting, a final peace treaty was agreed upon on December 22.

As part of the settlement, Organized Baseball paid compensation to the backers of the Federal League teams. Charles Weeghman, owner of the Chicago Feds, obtained a controlling interest in the Cubs and Phil Ball, owner of the St. Louis Feds, was allowed to purchase the Browns. The Federal League withdrew its antitrust suit and terminated operations. It was permitted to sell its players, who would not be blacklisted or penalized in any way for their actions.

The *Baltimore Sun* reported the Feds had offered Baker a three-year, $40,000 contract. The contract was supposedly modeled after the one L.F. Loree received when he left the Baltimore and Ohio Railroad to become president of the Rock Island system. Loree's contract was for five years and even though he left after only a couple years, he received the full amount of the contract. A man who saw the Federal League contract offer to Baker said he couldn't have lost one cent unless he died before it expired. The Feds agreed to protect Baker in every way. In the event of the death of Harry F. Sinclair, owner of the New York Federal League team along with Pat Powers, Sinclair's estate would have had to pay the money. If the court had decided Baker belonged to Mack, he would have received $10,000 a year anyway.

James Gilmore, president of the Federal League, and Baker met in Philadelphia after several meetings in Baltimore. Gilmore handed him a certified check for $10,000, his bonus for signing with the Feds. He looked at the check carefully for a couple minutes, but said nothing.

"You can buy another farm down in Maryland for that," said Gilmore.

"Yes, I know a piece of property I could buy with it," responded Baker. He couldn't convince himself to jump to the Federal League and handed it back to Gilmore like a hot potato. Gilmore responded, "Frank, you're a sucker if you don't take this check."[30] Had Baker missed his golden opportunity?

Years later, Baker recalled the incident, "It didn't seem right for me to accept that money to jump the A's.... If I was a sucker for not accepting easy money, that's the way it would have to be. I never did things that I didn't believe in. That was a pretty check, but I honestly doubt if I would have signed had the check been for two or three times that amount."[31]

Regardless of the fate of the Federal League, Baker felt he was in a strong position to demand a hefty salary hike from his Philadelphia contract. He was still one of the best players in the league. And, he didn't have to play baseball. He owned three farms in Talbot County and other property, according to the *Baltimore Sun*. He preferred to play in Chicago and join a contender. But, if the American League wouldn't abide by his wishes, then he would be handsomely compensated for going to a team that wasn't his number one choice. Without the threat of a Federal League in Chicago, White Sox President Charles Comiskey consented to give the Yankees a free hand in acquiring the slugger.

The calendar flipped to 1916 without a resolution. Baker's frustration grew greater and he accused Mack of blocking a deal with the Yankees. Mack denied that was the case. Baker said Mack was refusing to give him any of the purchase price he was to receive from the Yankees. "Unless I receive a share, I won't sign with either New York or Chicago," he said. "I will play with Upland again this year, where I have been treated better than Mack ever treated me."[32]

His comments unleashed another barrage of charges between the two. "I'm done with Baker so far as I'm personally concerned," fired back Mack. "He may be sold some day, but the club that gets him will have to pay me my price for him and Baker will get no part of it. I can't see where he has any claim to it."[33] Mack didn't want Baker on the terms of his new contract, saying he couldn't afford him. He told Baker he could quit at the end of the 1914 season, but he didn't tell him he could be a free agent, able to deal with other clubs.

Baker shot back that Mack would either agree to share the purchase money or he would end up with nothing. If he sat out 1916, he would be free of his contract with Mack. Baker said he would return to the Athletics on one condition: Mack had to take back calling him a contract jumper. Mack's response was: Why should I? "Baker said he was not interested in playing baseball, yet he signed with another team and played."[34]

The situation remained unchanged as spring training was less than a month away. The Yankees had spent a record $125,000 for players in their quest to build a pennant contender and they still pursued Baker. Among the players they acquired from the Federal League were outfielder Lee Magee for $25,000, left-handed pitcher Nick Cullop for $12,500, second baseman Joe Gedeon, outfielder Frank Gilhooley, and southpaw pitcher George Mogridge.

"The purse strings are still open," declared Huston. "If we can get more real players, we will pay the price. We want a winner and we will get one if money can buy one."[35]

The Yankees got their man on February 15, paying $37,500 for Baker, who signed a three-year contract for $12,000 a year. It was almost one year to the day since he announced his retirement from baseball. It had been a long year.

After his retirement, Baker said he never regretted declining the Federal League offers. In the end, he believed his earnings totaled much more during his career with the New York Yankees than they could ever have been in the Federal League, even with the $10,000 bonus check.

After sending Baker to the Yankees, Mack announced he had sold his last player. He said he had no other intentions of selling any players after Collins, but once Baker quit he decided to clean house and start all over again. He said if the time came again when he disagreed with his star players, he would give up the game.

Baker credited Vernon S. Bradley, a Cambridge, Maryland, attorney, for convincing him to sign. Bradley told Baker he owed it to himself, Mack and baseball to return to the game. Baker traveled to Philadelphia to sign the contract with the Yankees. The deal was reported to have been consummated during a four-hour conference at Ruppert's brewery between Ruppert, Huston, and Mack.

"I am sure I can play as good ball as I ever did and I am going to give my best," he said. "I have only the kindest feelings for Mr. Mack and Philadelphia and I leave the city with sincere regret."[36]

A week later, Ruppert brought Baker to his private office to hold a session with reporters. When asked why he decided to come back, the Yankees' newest star hesitated. "The dough, of course," blurted out one reporter, helpfully. "Yes, that was it," he replied.[37]

With his salary demands met, it was now up to Baker to help turn the New York Yankees into a pennant contender.

NINE

New York's Hope

After a year-long saga, Baker was still a major topic of baseball conversations heading into spring training. There were numerous questions: "How much had the year away from the major leagues affected him?" "How much would he help the Yankees?" "How many home runs would he hit in the Polo Grounds with its short right field fence?"

Despite the bitterness of their feud, Mack and Baker had supposedly buried the hatchet. Mack predicted Baker would play as well for the Yankees as he did for the Athletics, hit well over .300, be one of the league's best clean-up hitters and the home run champion. Additionally, he would be a drawing card in New York as well as for the rest of the league. After finishing in fifth place and drawing only 265,000 fans in 1915, the Yankees desperately needed an infusion of talent and a boost in attendance. Baker was expected to be the biggest drawing card since Hal Chase.

Boston manager Bill Carrigan talked at great length about Baker and his impact on the Yankees in an interview with the *Boston Traveler*. "The Yankees getting Baker is the biggest and best thing to happen to them in a long time," he said. "Baker going to the Yankees is bigger than Eddie Collins going to the White Sox."[1]

Carrigan believed New York would score a lot of runs with Lee Magee and Fritz Maisel batting ahead of Baker. He thought Maisel would play the same role that Collins had played batting in front of Baker, attracting considerable attention when on first and causing pitchers to lose their focus and get behind in the count. With a left-handed hitter behind him, Maisel, who led the league with 74 stolen bases in 1914, was expected to steal more bases.

"I believe Baker is one of the greatest hitters I ever saw. If he was faster, he would hang up some great batting averages. The Yankees shape up better than the Red Sox every time I start thinking about Baker,"[2] added Carrigan, who may have been trying to put pressure on the Yankees and Baker with his praise.

Not everyone, however, was praising Baker. In his preseason assessment, nationally known newspaper reporter Hugh Fullerton wrote, "Baker is not, never was, and never will be a great ballplayer. He hit some home runs in a World Series and became a hero. He is not a smart man, not a good man for a ball club, and the only thing you can say for him is that he can hit. As a third baseman, he is rather a joke. He is flat-footed, anchored to the base, and only fair in coming in for bunts."[3]

Interestingly, two years earlier Fullerton had praised Baker as one of the game's greatest hitters and a much improved fielder. His revised opinion was seemingly colored by his negative attitude toward Baker for his holdout in 1915. He considered the slugger a money hungry player who put his personal interests ahead of the game. Fullerton's opinion was shared by a number of other writers and baseball fans.

Fullerton, however, conceded the addition of Baker strengthened the Yankees because it would allow them to use Maisel, whom he regarded as being far superior to Baker, at another position, possibly shortstop. Given his harsh criticism of Baker, who did Fullerton consider the best third baseman in the American League? Frank Baker.

Baker was everything the Yankees were looking for — an established star and top run producer who could electrify crowds. He possessed a strong work ethic, knew what it took to win and was a good influence on younger players. The expectations for the Yankees were high, but the expectations for Baker were higher. After all, some of his greatest moments as a batter occurred in New York's Polo Grounds, so those fans were quite familiar with "Home Run" Baker.

How a year away from the game would affect Baker's hitting ability was a major question. Playing for Upland wasn't the same thing as playing in the major leagues, but it helped to keep him sharp. Many people felt he would easily return to his productive ways because he was a natural hitter and always stayed in good shape. James "Nixey" Callahan and Mike Donlin were examples of players who had left the game and returned successfully. After playing 10 years in the majors, Callahan left the White Sox in 1905 at age 31 and was out of the game for five years. He returned in 1911, batted .281 and played another full season before retiring. Donlin, a nine-year veteran, left the New York Giants in 1908 after hitting .334 at age 30. He returned in 1911 and hit .316, splitting his time between the Giants and the Braves.

The New York Yankees purchased Baker for $37,500 from Connie Mack in 1916. His arrival in New York was supposed to turn the Yankees into contenders. Unfortunately, injuries limited his production with the club. In 1916, he fractured three ribs while chasing a foul ball and missed nearly one-third of the season as a result. He never had the same power or swing after the injury.

His best season with the Yankees was in 1919 when he slugged 10 home runs, drove in 83 runs and batted .293. BROWN BROTHERS.

The week before Baker was scheduled to leave for spring training, he seriously injured his right hand while sawing wood on his Trappe farm. A falling log severely smashed the second and third fingers of his right hand. It was originally thought the end of his third finger had been severed. Doctors told him it would be three weeks before he could use his right hand.

Despite the injury, Baker departed for spring training camp in Macon, Georgia, on March 4. Unlike past years, he was anxious to report to spring training because he had a lot to prove. He took batting practice on March 8 with his fingers heavily wrapped. He popped the first ball straight up in the air. He sent the next one to center field and drove the third over the right field fence.

After watching the hitting demonstration, *New York Tribune* writer Grantland Rice wrote, "Baker is a natural hitter. One of the best of all times."[4]

Rice wrote that Baker was a deceptive slugger. Around the hotel in plain clothes there was nothing striking about him. He looked to be an average-size man who might weigh 160 pounds. You wondered how he ever hit a ball over the fence. On the field, in a uniform with a bat, he looked like a big, powerful athlete, at least 180 pounds. He looked taller, broader and more like the home run hero he was.

Whether or not Baker could return to form was one of the biggest questions during spring training. New York reporters kept their readers abreast of almost every swing he took. Fans in New York and on the Eastern Shore were hopeful the former home run king still had long-distance power in his bat. American League players were also curious about how he would fare. Former Washington Senators second baseman Germany Schaefer, a 13-year-veteran, recalled the always dangerous slugger during spring training. "I used to shiver every time Baker came to bat. I took to playing so deep that the temptation to bunt was more than Baker could resist. He'd get some base hits that way, but ... I stopped him from getting a home run."[5]

On March 21, Baker put his hand to the test during a 20-minute field drill where he handled a series of hard grounders. The following day he played his first intrasquad game as a Yankee. With his right index finger bandaged, he doubled off the fence, stole a base, scored two runs and fielded flawlessly. His performance impressed Grantland Rice, who wrote: "If you desire one truth that is self-evident and beyond all rebuttal you can stand by this: John Franklin Baker can hit."[6] Rice informed readers that Baker's love for the game and desire was back. He was enthusiastic about everything he did on the field.

The 1915 New York Yankees had finished in fifth place with a 69–83 record and 32.5 games behind the Boston Red Sox. They were the weakest hitting club in the American League with a .233 average and no player thumped more than five home runs or drove in more than 60 runs. Twenty-five-year old third baseman Fritz Maisel and starters Ray Caldwell and Ray Fisher, who had won 19 and 18 games respectively with ERAs under 3.00, were among the few bright spots on the team. Many observers believed Maisel, a five-foot-seven speedster, was one of the most promising players in the game. In 1915, he batted .281, stole 51 bases and led the Yankees in runs scored and hits. White Sox owner Charles Comiskey offered to trade superstar Joe Jackson, whom he had acquired just months earlier, for Maisel prior to the start of the 1916 season. Jackson had struggled in 45 games with the White Sox, hitting just .272. In April the Red Sox would offer to trade Tris Speaker, whom they were having trouble signing, for Maisel.

The Yankees had taken advantage of the availability of players from the Federal League to strengthen their team. They hoped Nick Cullop, Joe Gedeon and Lee Magee would make valuable contributions. Cullop, 27, was considered the best left-hander in the Federal League, posting a 22–11 record with a 2.30 ERA for Kansas City. Gedeon, a 22-year-old infielder, signed with the Federal League at the end of the season, but never played for them. He batted .317 and hit 19 home runs for Salt Lake in the Pacific Coast League. Magee, a 26-year-old outfielder, hit .323 and stole 34 bases for the Brooklyn Feds after playing four years with the Cardinals.

Other prospects included George Mogridge, who won 24 games for Des Moines; Edward "Slim" Love, a six-foot-seven pitcher who won 23 games for Los Angeles in the Pacific Coast League; and Urban Shocker of Ottawa, who won 19.

The Yankees' outlook for the 1916 season was the best in a decade. They were projected to be a first-division club. Their infield of Wally Pipp at first, Gedeon at second, Roger Peckinpaugh at shortstop and Baker at third rated as one of the best in the league. The outfield of Frank Gilhooley, who hit .322 and stole 53 bases for Buffalo of the International League, Magee and Maisel was considered among the fastest in the majors. The trio combined to steal 141 bases in three leagues in 1915. The starting rotation was expected to feature Caldwell, Fisher, Cullop and Shawkey. The Boston Red Sox were favored to repeat as American League champions while Detroit and Chicago were considered stronger than the Yankees.

The new-look Yankees opened the season on April 13, before 20,000 enthusiastic fans at the Polo Grounds against Walter Johnson and the Washington Senators. Scores of photographers milled around the field prior to the game capturing the players on camera, especially Baker, and managers Griffith and Donovan. Baker rapped out a pair of singles, drove in a run, and started a double play in his debut with the Yankees, which ended in a 3–2, 11-inning loss.

New York hosted Mack's Athletics, described as "a ghost of the old wrecking crew"[7] on April 18. The only recognizable players were second baseman Nap Lajoie, who starred for Cleveland most of his Hall of Fame career; first baseman Stuffy McInnis, outfielders Amos Strunk, and Rube Oldring. The Athletics' infield consisted of McInnis at first base, Lajoie at second, Lawton "Whitey" Witt at shortstop and Charlie Pick at third base. It was an awkward occasion for Mack and Baker. But Baker did no damage to the A's, as he went hitless in four at bats as the Yankees won 4–2.

The Yankees were embarrassed in the Senators' home opener April 20, as they lost 12–4 to Walter Johnson after President Woodrow Wilson threw out the first ball. The Yankees won the next two games against the Senators, but Johnson beat them again in the fourth game of the series. He had beaten them three times in the first two weeks of the season. New York was 5–3, all of its losses coming against Johnson. Baker's bat was cold in a rare, poor four-game series against the Senators, going 1-for-17.

The Yankees visited Shibe Park on April 29 and one of Philadelphia's largest crowds of the year turned out to see their hero in a Yankee uniform for the first time. Baker disappointed the crowd, going hitless in four trips. The A's also held him hitless in four trips the following day. He started to regain his batting eye in the final two games of the series, collecting a pair of hits in each game.

Baker continued his return to better batting as the highly touted White Sox with Joe Jackson and Eddie Collins visited the Polo Grounds on May 9. He smashed the first pitch from Claude "Lefty" Williams over the right field fence for his first round-tripper as a Yankee. The crowd of 8,000 fans jumped to their feet and cheered as he touched each bag. This was the Frank Baker they hoped to see as the season progressed. Less than a week later, Frank walloped a solo homer off of right-hander Guy Morton of Cleveland. As usual, he started slow with the bat but raised his average to .268 by mid–May.

Injuries started to hit the Yankees as their sparkplug Maisel fractured his collarbone. Donovan moved Magee center field and started Hugh High in left field. Baker was sidelined from May 24 until June 3 with a bad left leg. When he returned to the lineup, he struggled at bat for nearly three weeks, hitting .163 over 15 games. By June 5, however, New York was 24–17 and one game behind first-place Cleveland.

Philadelphia *Evening Bulletin* cartoon of former Athletics shooting at Mack's dirigible.

Baker's bat ignited the Yankees when they won five out of six games against the Senators, including a sweep of back-to-back doubleheaders, June 23–26, at the Polo Grounds. He collected six hits in the doubleheaders, including his fourth homer of the season off of right-hander Doc Ayers, one of his favorite targets, in the second game of the second doubleheader. Baker thumped his second homer in two days the following day off lefty Harry Harper in a 9–8, 11-inning loss. He crushed his third home run in as many days off southpaw Joe Boehling in a 6–5 win. In six games, Baker went 10-for-23 with three home runs to help the Yankees move within a half-game of the first-place Indians.

Meanwhile, back on the Eastern Shore, fans of Home Run Baker were pointing with pride again at his batting heroics while reading game accounts in the *Baltimore Sun* or the *Philadelphia Evening Bulletin*. New York continued its run for the pennant when it defeated Philadelphia and moved into first place on June 28.

The Yankees suffered another setback, however, on July 3, when their leadoff hitter and right fielder Frank Gilhooley broke his leg while sliding into third base. He was expected to be out of the lineup for six weeks. With Maisel already out, the Yankees were minus two-thirds of the starting outfield.

On July 4, New York split a doubleheader with the Senators. In the fourth inning of the second game, Baker crushed a homer off right-hander Bert Gallia over the 328-foot right field fence, which was dominated by a 30-foot high concrete wall. It marked the first time in two years that anyone had accomplished the feat with the cork-centered ball and only the third time in the history of Griffith Stadium.

The Yankees reached their high water mark of the season on July 7 with a 4–3 win in 12 innings over the White Sox. The victory upped their season record to 43–27 and gave them a three and a half game lead over the Indians. New York had won 18 of 22 games.

Donovan's club was in first place midway through the season, an amazing accomplishment for a perennial second-division club. Fans were starting to believe the team was for real and crowds were getting larger each week. More than 25,000 fans rooted for the Yankees at the Polo Grounds as the White Sox earned a 2–1 victory behind Eddie Cicotte's four-hit pitching on July 8.

A July 14 doubleheader against the Detroit Tigers proved rather costly to the Yankees' pennant hopes. Donovan's men lost the opener 6–2 in 12 innings, as Cullop was saddled with his first loss. Baker was seriously injured in the fourth inning of the second game. Infielder Ralph Young lifted a high foul ball and Baker ran full speed after it toward the stands. Shortstop Peckinpaugh yelled at Baker, warning him to slow down as he rapidly approached the steel railing. In the midst of crowd noise, Baker didn't hear him and kept pursuing the ball. Unaware of where he was, Baker ran full speed into an iron gate that led to the left field section of the grandstand. The impact knocked him to the ground. The crowd fell silent and stared in shock as Frank lay still for several moments before his teammates began picking him up. He was assisted to the clubhouse, where

he was examined by a physician, who had been watching the game. The initial exam revealed severe lacerations and deep bruises on his left side but no broken bones. A couple days later club officials revealed that the hard-hitting third baseman had suffered three broken ribs. The slugger was out of action for nearly two months.

Baker had played 82 games and was batting .266 with eight home runs at the time he was injured. The Yankees were 48–34, held a two-game lead over the Indians and the Red Sox, and had perhaps the best balance of pitching and offense in the league. They had scored only seven fewer runs than the Indians and Tigers, who tied for the top honor, but had given up fewer runs than either of the two teams.

The Yankees' injury list continued to mount. Three days later, Cullop pulled a muscle below his lower rib while pitching against the Tigers and collapsed on the field. He was relieved by Ray Caldwell, who was hit in the kneecap with a line drive and had to leave the game. The following day, left fielder Hugh High strained his left leg trying to make a catch and was expected to miss several games.

The injuries were too much for the Yankees to survive. The club was in first place by one and a half games when it departed on an 18-game road trip on July 22. Donovan's club held onto first place until the end of the month when it lost six consecutive games to the

Baker advertisement for Coca-Cola from the June 1916 issue of *The American Boy.*

seventh-place Browns in St. Louis, knocking them into third place. New York's misery continued when it dropped three straight in Detroit.

At the end of July, centerfielder Lee Magee was sent back to New York with sore ankles to be treated by a club physician. Four months into the season, the club had lost its starting outfield and third baseman to injuries. By the time the team returned from its 4–14 road trip, it was in sixth place, six games behind Boston.

The low point of the season came on August 12 when the Yankees dropped a doubleheader at the Polo Grounds to the lowly 20–81 A's in front of 500 fans. Slightly more than a month earlier, they had played in front of 25,000 fans at home.

Baker returned to the lineup on September 5 and played out the rest of the meaningless season. The fractured ribs, however, had taken a great toll on him. Late in his career with the Yankees, he discussed the injury and said, "I have never since been able to swing as freely or with such force as I used to do."[8]

The Yankees finished 80–74 and in fourth place, 11 games behind the Red Sox. It marked the first time since 1910 that they finished above .500. Sidelined by injuries for the first time in his career, Baker couldn't help but be a disappointment as he hit .269 average, slugged 10 home runs and drove in 52 runs in 100 games. He finished second to teammate Wally Pipp in round-trippers in the American League. Wally smashed 12, but had 545 at bats compared to Frank's 360 at bats. Had it not been for the time missed from his injury, Frank probably would have led the American League in home runs.

Maisel and Gilhooley were also disappointments. Maisel was limited to 53 games and hit just .228 while Gihooley played in 58 games and batted .278. Pipp carried the offensive burden, driving in 93 runs while hitting .262. Shawkey led the pitching staff with a 24–14 record and nine saves and a 2.21 ERA. Cullop finished 13–6, after starting 9–0, and posted a 2.01 ERA.

A promising season had ended in disappointment for both Baker and the Yankees.

TEN

Wartime Baseball

As disappointing as 1916 was, the Yankees knew their fourth-place finish was due to an inordinate amount of injuries, not lack of talent. New York rewarded manager Bill Donovan with a one-year contract shortly following the World Series. Donovan was given credit for working effectively with a number of young players who filled in for the injured veterans.

Despite being hopelessly out of the pennant race by mid–August, the Yankees drew 469,000 fans, an increase of more than 200,000 over the previous season. They were one of the reasons baseball enjoyed a banner season. American League attendance was up more than a million from 1915 and National League attendance reached its highest level in its 40-year history.

Owners had hoped to reduce salaries, inflated by the Federal League war, but had been relatively unsuccessful. The 1917 season was going to be the most expensive in history. The 16 major league clubs were expected to pay an estimated $1.5 million for players' salaries. Brooklyn owner Charles Ebbets took a hard line stance in cutting salaries and 10 players were unsigned going into spring training. Meanwhile the Phillies signed 33-game winner Grover Alexander for $12,500 a season, proving owners realized it was often necessary to pay high salaries to the game's biggest stars.

Americans had been closely following the events in Europe since the start of World War I in 1914. The activity had increased in 1916 when battles broke out on all fronts as Germany attacked at Verdun and the Austro-Hungarians and Italians fought battles along the Isonzo River. The Allies (not including the United States yet) took the offensive along the Somme River in France and the Russians assaulted Polish Galicia. Great Britain and Germany clashed in the Battle of Jutland off the coast of Denmark, the greatest naval battle of the war. In January 1917, Germany declared that its submarines would sink any vessel bound into or out of any Allied port.

With the situation in Europe worsening, the American League adopted a resolution, offered by T.J. Huston, co-owner of the Yankees, to make baseball players into civilian soldiers. The plan called for baseball players to receive military training and ballparks to serve as military camps. Players would march from their hotels to the ballparks in military formation. Under the proposal, players would drill one hour every morning and a training camp would be established after the World Series for baseball players.

Manager Donovan was optimistic as spring training opened in Macon, Georgia. With basically the same team returning, he expected to be in the pennant race, if his club could avoid injuries and last year's injured players were recovered. The only position unsettled was second base, where Donovan planned to move Fritz Maisel.

One of the first questions reporters asked Baker when he reported to camp on March 5 along with Hugh High and Joe Gedeon was, "What kind of shape are you in?"

"Fifty percent better than last spring," he replied.[1]

The following day, the Yankees participated in their first military drill. Sergeant Gibson, a recruiting officer, led them through an hour drill. Dressed in their baseball uniforms, the players received a primer on how to stand at attention, military commands, and marching formations.

On April 2, President Woodrow Wilson read a war message to Congress. "The world must be made safe for democracy," he said. On April 6, America declared war on Germany. After discussing how the announcement affected the lives of thousands of young men, the conversation turned to what effect the war would have on baseball. Would it decrease or increase interest in the game? Would baseball be an appreciated distraction from a much more serious matter? John Tener, president of the National League, believed 1917 would be a great season for baseball, which was returning to normalcy after the Federal League war, talk of a possible players strike, and inferior play.

Both the Boston Red Sox and Chicago White Sox had talented returning veteran pitchers and solid lineups. They were expected to be the strongest contenders in the American League as the season prepared to open. The defending champion Red Sox were led, in part, by Baker's former teammate Jack Barry, who had taken over managerial duties from Bill Carrigan.

With high hopes, the Yankees opened their season against Boston at the Polo Grounds on April 11. It was a scene unlike anything baseball had ever witnessed as Major General Leonard Wood drilled the Yankees before 16,000 fans. A band played military tunes, dozens of flags and pennants waved from the stands to greet the Yankees, who marched out onto the field with their bats on their shoulders like rifles. They went through their military maneuvers and marching formations with impressive precision and style. The crowd gave the players a standing ovation.

The Yankees' Opening Day lineup featured Pipp at first base, Maisel at second, Peckinpaugh at shortstop, Baker at third, Les Nunamaker at catcher, High in left field, Magee in center, and Gilhooley in right. Pipp batted cleanup and Baker fifth. The Yankees faced the Red Sox left-hander Babe Ruth, who led the American League pitchers in ERA and shutouts in 1916 and won 23 games. Donovan tabbed Caldwell to start for the Yankees but Ruth led the Red Sox to a 10–3 victory.

It only took the third game of the season before a Yankee was injured. Baker suffered a broken thumb in his first at bat against former teammate southpaw Herb Pennock of the Red Sox. Surprisingly, he returned to the lineup the following game.

By early May, the Yankees were in third place and struggling on offense. The club was hitting .220, seventh in the American League and four starters—Gilhooley, Maisel, Magee and Nunamaker—were batting under .200. On May 7, right fielder and leadoff hitter Frank Gilhooley fractured his collarbone diving for a ball in Philadelphia and was expected to miss at least a month of the season.

As World War I completed its first month, baseball leaders started to realize the season might not hold the promise they once thought. A 10 percent war tax on the purchase of baseball tickets was to go into effect after June 1. The question of a possible draft and its impact on younger players loomed and the mood of the country was serious. The decision to complete the season, however, had already been made. Boston Braves catcher Hank Gowdy, hero of the 1914 World Series, became the first major leaguer to enlist when the draft was implemented.

The Yankees put together their best streak of the season from May 7 through May 18 when they won nine of 11 games on the road. The spurt pushed their record to 17–9 and they moved into first place for three days.

Baker's brilliance returned when he snapped out of a slump in the final three games of the streak. Frank clouted his first home run of the season on May 16 off right-hander Bob Groom to spark a 5–2 win over the Browns at Sportsman's Park. The following game, he rapped three singles and stole four bases. He swiped second after each single and stole home in the seventh inning as part of a double steal. As if that weren't enough, he made three brilliant defensive plays. He delivered a bases-loaded double in the ninth inning to score three runs and break a 3–3 tie against the Tigers on May 18. He had earlier collected a pair of singles and a walk.

As if World War I hadn't given baseball enough problems to deal with, the spring weather complicated the picture. The cold, rainy weather forced the New York clubs to postpone more than one-fourth of their games. In their first 41 scheduled games, the Dodgers had 13 postponements, the Giants 12 and the Yankees 10. That meant a slew of doubleheaders in the summer months, a significant loss at the ticket window, diminished interest early in the season, extra strain on pitching staffs and the prospect of players having to play back-to-back doubleheaders on occasion. The Yankees played 27 doubleheaders in 1917.

Baker's luck continued to go bad in a doubleheader against the Athletics on May 30. In the second game, he charged the plate for what he thought was going to be a bunt. But Philadelphia pitcher Russell "Jing" Johnson swung and connected with the ball and it hit him just below his right eye. He fell to the ground, but was able to walk off the field after the game had been held up a short time. Despite the injury, he missed only one game.

The Yankees entered July with a 35–29 record and in third place seven games behind the White Sox and Red Sox. Although Baker was hitting only .265, he was about to enjoy the hottest month of hitting in his career. Batting fifth in the New York lineup, he started the month with four hits against Red Sox pitchers Ernie Shore and Lore Bader as the two clubs played to a 4–4 tie in 11 innings. The Yankees lost a July 4 doubleheader to the Senators but it was no fault of Baker's, who went 3-for-4 in the opener and 2-for-4 in the second game. The following day, the clubs hooked up in another doubleheader. After the Yankees lost the first game, Baker smashed his second career inside-the-park home run off Walter Johnson in the bottom of the 13th inning to give the Yankees a 2–1 win and snap their seven-game losing streak. He collected a pair of hits in each game.

New York embarked on an 18-game road trip on July 7. After going 13-for-23 in his last five games, Baker was held hitless by St. Louis hurler Allen Sothoron, who tossed a 1–0 game. New York fell to fourth place as the Browns followed with another win, but Baker resumed his hitting ways with a pair of singles.

His hard hitting continued when his single in the 17th inning off Sothoron on July 10 gave the Yankees a 7–5 victory. It was his fifth hit of the day. Then, he went 6-for-17 as New York lost three out of four to first-place Chicago.

By mid–July, the Yankees had lost their starting outfield to injuries for the second consecutive year. Tim Hendryx, Paddy Baumann, and Elmer Miller replaced High, Magee and Gilhooley. New York traded Magee to the Browns for Armando Marsans on July 15. By mid–July, Baker had upped his batting average to .297, but the Yankees were seventh in the league in hitting.

On July 15, the streaking third baseman showed a record Cleveland crowd of nearly 28,000 fans his best batting form in a doubleheader. He collected five hits in eight at bats, raising his July average to .500 (32-for-64) as the Yankees swept the Indians.

American League President Ban Johnson detracted from Baker's performance on July 16 when he gave him 24 hours to answer charges that he had attempted to induce St. Louis Browns hurler Allen Sothoron to jump to the Delaware County League. Johnson had previously written Baker demanding an explanation, but he had not responded to the request.

Baker explained the matter simply. "Before we came West, one of the backers of the Delaware County League asked me about Sothoron and I told him he was a good pitcher. Last week, I attended a boxing show in St. Louis with Baumann and we met Sothoron. He asked me what money they paid in the Delaware County League and I told him he was foolish to think of jumping organized baseball. That's all there was to it."[2] Johnson exonerated Baker of alleged tampering charges the following day.

On July 18, Baker was able to put the recent incident with Ban Johnson behind him as he sparked the Yankees' 12–7 win over Cleveland with his all-round play. He went 4-for-5, accounted for six runs, stole second and home, and made a spectacular one-hand catch in the bottom of the tenth. New York lost three out of five in Detroit and fell into fifth place. By July 22, Baker had lifted his average to .313, fifth highest among starters in the American League. Only Cobb, Speaker, Sisler and McInnis had higher averages.

Donovan's club returned to the Polo Grounds on July 25 after going 8–10 on the road trip. They were 44–42 and in fifth place, 11.5 games behind the White Sox, who were in town for a six-game series. After the Yankees dropped a doubleheader, Baker delivered a win with a sacrifice fly in the bottom of the 14th inning. The New Yorkers swept a doubleheader from the White Sox on July 28 before 20,000 fans. Although Baker's bat cooled in the final week of July, he finished the month 50-for-122 for a .409 average.

In August, the Yankees fell out of any chance of finishing in the first division or having a respectable season. Starting with the second game of a doubleheader against Cleveland on August 8, the Yankees lost 17 of 20 games. They fell from 11 games behind to 23 and from fifth place to sixth.

Donovan's crew entered September hopelessly out of the pennant race once again. The team was weary and no rest was on the horizon. Yet, they won nine of their next 13 games. They started the month with back-to-back doubleheaders in Boston, winning three of the four games. After a single game in Washington and a day off, they played back-to-back doubleheaders against the Senators, splitting them both. Another day off and they played back-to-back doubleheaders against the Athletics, sweeping both of them. They played 13 games in nine days as Baker went 13-for-47 during the twin-bill frenzy.

The club returned to the Polo Grounds and lost two out of three games to the Red Sox. The Yankees were scheduled to play an exhibition game in Bridgeport, Connecticut on Sunday, September 16. Exhibition games during the season were frowned upon by players, who preferred to have a day off, particularly late in the season. Owners, however, saw it as an opportunity to make some money. Baker didn't accompany the team to Bridgeport. His absence disappointed Bridgeport fans as well as Yankees manager Donovan. It had been heavily advertised that he would play in the exhibition game.

The next day at the Polo Grounds, Donovan confronted Baker and told him, "If you can't play Sunday ball, you need not play any more this season. You may warm the bench the rest of the season."[3]

After being told that, an upset Baker refused to sit on the bench, went to the clubhouse without permission, removed his uniform and headed to his home in Trappe. Donovan immediately suspended his star player, saying it wasn't because he didn't play in the exhibition game but because of his actions on Monday. The suspension was indefinite.

In his book, *Baseball: The Golden Age*," historian Harold Seymour writes: "A few players like Branch Rickey, Christy Mathewson and Frank Baker, objected to participating in Sunday games for personal reasons. Rickey was fired for refusing to play on Sundays and Baker was suspended in 1917 for the same reason."[4] Sunday baseball had nothing to do with Baker not playing in Bridgeport. He had played in countless Sunday games in the American League. The point of contention was whether or not he was obligated to play in exhibition games. He maintained the Yankees had assured him he would not have to play in exhibition games when he signed with them. Donovan insisted Baker wasn't exempt from exhibition games.

The Yankees took a hard line approach with Baker, insisting that club discipline would be maintained even if it meant going without the services of their highest paid player. Baker responded quickly that the club owed him an apology and that if Col. Ruppert didn't revoke the suspension in the next couple days, he would retire.

"It is entirely up to Baker," said Donovan. "Baker had been ordered to report to Bridgeport with the other members of the team and he didn't show up. It is entirely up to him if he plays with the team again this season."[5]

Despite Frank's hot hitting in July and overall batting performance, Donovan launched into a personal attack. "I think I have given Baker every possible consideration this season. He has not been going well at all. In fact, his failure to hit in his old form has been one of the chief factors that militated against the success of the team this year. But we haven't held this against Baker. He has been getting a big salary and we thought it no more than right that he should play in an exhibition game."[6]

More than likely the New York manager was frustrated by the toll of another injury-riddled season and was unfair and off target in his criticism of Baker.

Baker showed he could be headstrong, too, as he had at other times during his career. He told reporters: "I told Donovan last Saturday that I wouldn't be at Bridgeport on Sunday and he said all right. Then I'm told on Monday that I'm to sit on the bench and Maisel would play third. As I wasn't to play I couldn't do any good on the bench, so I went to the clubhouse and took off my uniform. I'm willing to play, but I am still suspended and don't know that I shall play any more."[7]

The third baseman erred by not staying in the dugout to watch his team play in the heat of reacting to Donovan's ruling. He should not have headed for home without meeting with Donovan and the owners. Ruppert confirmed that he said Baker wouldn't have to play in exhibition games, but added he didn't mean to excuse him from exhibitions in which he was booked as the team's big attraction.

Baker insisted he had not broken any agreement with the Yankees, but the club had broken an agreement with him. He said it was immaterial if he ever played another game. He had always taken pride in his behavior, on and off the field. This was the first time he had been in trouble and it wasn't of his making, he maintained.

Baker contacted Ruppert, but the owner initially refused to get involved, saying the matter was entirely between Baker and Donovan. Ruppert promptly departed for Cincinnati to attend the annual draft meeting with the idea that any misunderstanding would be worked out between his star third baseman and manager by the time he returned.

But Ruppert was clearly in Donovan's corner. "Donovan told me of his plans (to bench Baker and play Maisel at third) and I told him anything he did was agreeable with me. After Baker's actions on Monday, there was nothing left for Donovan to do but suspend him," said the Yankees owner.[8]

The *New York Tribune* came down hard on the Yankee slugger, who it felt would be the big loser in the incident. "His play this year has been more indifferent. He has slowed to a walk. He could scarcely hope to do more than figure in a pinch-hitting role next season, the last year of his three-year contract." The newspaper termed his $10,000 a year salary as "ridiculously fabulous."[9]

Most fans, however, sided with Baker, believing Donovan had acted too hastily and harshly. Instead of seeing him as a star with declining ability, they pointed to his .291 average as a mark of consistency on a weak-hitting team. They understood his pride had been hurt and he deserved better treatment. Sooner or later, fans believed Donovan would be forced to admit he had made a mistake and reinstate Baker.

Baker met with Donovan in an attempt to resolve the issue, but was told the case was entirely up to Col. Ruppert. With that information, he headed back to Trappe for an indefinite stay. Unless the Yankees sent for him and were willing to reimburse him the money he had lost due to suspension, Baker said he would retire.

The slugger sat home while the Yankees lost five of six games. Donovan and Ruppert met on Sunday, September 23 while the Yankees played an exhibition game in Plattsburgh, New York. Ruppert decided to reinstate Baker without loss of pay, making Donovan the big loser in the showdown.

Baker returned to New York by train and was at his familiar position at third base when the Yankees played the Detroit Tigers at the Polo Grounds on September 25. He went hitless in five at bats. It's understandable if his mind and heart weren't in the final eight games of the season. After being reinstated, he collected just two hits in 29 at bats for a .068 average. Interestingly, he played in an exhibition game against the Brooklyn Robins on September 30. The game was played at Fort Hamilton before 3,000 soldiers and their friends. He played the entire game at third base and cracked one of seven home runs in the game.

It was another disappointing season for the Yankees, who finished in sixth place with a 71–82 record, 28.5 games behind the first-place White Sox. The club hit .239, the lowest in the league. Baker's .282 average was subpar by his standards, but it was 20 points higher than any other player on the team. His 71 runs batted in led the team and Wally Pipp was close behind with 70. No other Yankee, however, had more than 44 RBI. His six homers were second to Pipp's league-leading nine. Maisel, once highly touted, batted just .198 in 114 games. On the mound, Shawkey and Caldwell each won 13 games, but didn't have winning records.

ELEVEN

Huggins
Takes the Reins

The three-year effort to build the Yankees into a pennant contender hadn't been successful. The club appeared to have the potential on several occasions, but injuries always managed to sidetrack the progress. With two subpar seasons, Baker had been a major disappointment. He hadn't produced the way he had for the Athletics, but his supporting cast in New York wasn't nearly as talented as it had been in Philadelphia. Fritz Maisel, Frank Gilhooley, and Lee Magee were not Eddie Collins, Danny Murphy and Stuffy McInnis, even when they were healthy. The Yankees hadn't been able to utilize their speed on the bases or give Baker the RBI opportunities he had in Philadelphia.

Under Donovan, the Yankees had finished fifth, fourth and sixth. Attendance had increased from 1915 to 1916, but had declined in 1917. The Yankees drew 330,000, nearly a 140,000 less than in 1916. McGraw's Giants still overshadowed the Yankees. The competitive owners Ruppert and Huston were used to being highly successful in other ventures but they had little to show for their investments in the American League club.

Their first order of business after the World Series was to fire manager Bill Donovan. Huston preferred Wilbert Robinson, the 54-year-old manager of the Brooklyn Dodgers and former John McGraw disciple, to succeed Donovan. Ruppert thought Robinson was too old and sought out American League President Ban Johnson for his opinion. Johnson strongly recommended Miller Huggins, a former utility infielder who was the player/manager for the St. Louis Cardinals. The diminutive 39-year-old

Huggins had limited success with the Cardinals. In 1917, they were 82–70 and finished in third place. He was brainy, witty and a disciplinarian. Johnson considered him someone who would help the Yankees. Without conferring with Huston, who was in France helping to fight the war, Ruppert selected Huggins. The decision upset and enraged Huston, who fired off a series of blistering cables and letters. The two, who had never been very close, grew more distant and they eventually dissolved their partnership as Huston left Ruppert behind the Yankees' sole owner.

The Yankees signed Huggins to a two-year contract, but there was some doubt as to whether or not he would get to manage. Baseball was considering curtailing the 1918 season due to the war. Fewer games and no World Series were possibilities, if the war continued into the spring. Tighter economic conditions and attention to the war would definitely impact attendance even more than it had in 1917. There was talk of a 140-game schedule, starting later in April and finishing near the beginning of September, and decreasing player rosters to 18. Owners could save money by eliminating a month of the season and not having to pay players for that period.

As the season approached, Huggins looked to fill two needs—a second baseman and a hard-hitting outfielder. He and Detroit Tigers owner Frank Navin were rumored to be discussing a possible deal involving Ty Cobb. The outfielder was still one of the best players in the game and a star attraction, but he had alienated most of his teammates and was difficult to deal with. The Tigers hadn't won a pennant since 1909 and needed pitching. The Yankees were also rumored to be interested in Detroit's other two starting outfielders, Bobby Veach and Harry Heilmann. Another name that cropped up in trade rumors was Joe Jackson of the White Sox. Even though Chicago had won the pennant, Jackson had a second consecutive subpar year by his standards, batting just .301.

On March 8, the Yankees purchased the five-foot-eight, 195-pound Ping Bodie (born Francesco Stephano Pezzolo), a 30-year old outfielder from the Philadelphia Athletics. Bodie, a five-year veteran, had hit .291, slugged seven homers and drove in 74 runs for a woeful A's team that finished 40.5 games out of first place. Only Wally Pipp thumped more homers than Bodie in the American League. Bodie was available because he was a holdout with the Athletics. Mack wanted to cut his salary and offer him a share of the gross receipts, if the club made money. The risky proposition didn't appeal to the outfielder. According to Bodie, he and the Liberty Bell were the only attractions left in Philadelphia — now, it was only the Liberty Bell.

Huggins filled his other need with the acquisition of second baseman

Del Pratt from the St. Louis Browns. Pratt, 29, was a six-year veteran who was coming off the worst season in his career. In 1916, however, he had driven in 103 runs while hitting .267. He had a reputation as a team player and good influence in the clubhouse. With a lineup featuring Pratt, Pipp, Baker, and Bodie, Huggins was optimistic the Yankees would be a much better hitting club in 1918.

By the end of March with Opening Day two weeks away, players were beginning to be drafted for military service. Pitchers Bob Shawkey and Ray Fisher were drafted and four other Yankees—Wally Pipp, promising pitchers Bob McGraw and Ed Monroe, and rookie catcher Herold "Muddy" Ruel—were classified 1A and could be drafted any time. The uncertainty made it difficult for the players to focus and managers to plan their lineups.

The Yankees played the Boston Braves in a series of spring training games as they moved up the coast to New York. Baker, who reported to training camp 16 pounds lighter than the year before, was rounding into shape as he clouted a pair of doubles and a home run as the Yankees defeated the Braves, 7–3, in Greenville, South Carolina. In six games against the Braves, Baker hit .522 with six RBIs.

The Great War, as it was called, continued to cast a cloud of uncertainty over major league baseball as the 1918 season prepared to open. The war had had little impact on baseball in 1917, but now with the draft implemented and the escalation of fighting in Europe that was no longer the case. And, there was no telling what would happen once the season started. Certainly, interest and attendance would be affected.

The Giants and White Sox were favored to repeat as pennant winners, if the draft didn't deplete their rosters. Players under the draft age and older players were prepared to fill in roster spots as needed.

The Yankees opened their season in Washington as southpaw George Mogridge opposed Walter Johnson before 15,000 fans. The Yankees pounded 11 hits en route to a 6–3 as Baker and Pipp each collected a pair of hits. Huggins's Opening Day lineup featured Gilhooley in right field, Elmer Miller in center field, Bodie in left field, Pipp at first, Pratt at second, Peckinpaugh at short, Baker at third, and Pipp at first, and James "Truck" Hannah catching. Huggins was counting on a rotation that included three left-handers—Mogridge, Slim Love and 21-year-old Hank Thormahlen, and a pair of right-handers—Ray Caldwell and Alan Russell.

The Yankees beat Johnson again the following day as Baker refused to take an intentional walk in the 12th inning. With the game tied 7–7 and men on first and third, Johnson, who had come on in relief, decided to

intentionally walk Baker, his long-time nemesis. The veteran third baseman, however, had other ideas. He lashed at the third pitch, sending it to
deep center field to score Pratt from third base with the winning run.

Baker continued to stand out offensively as the Yankees traveled to
Boston. On April 22, he paced the club to a 11–4 win with a pair of singles, two long doubles and a sacrifice fly. He slugged his first homer of the
year on April 25 off right-hander Jim Shaw in a 7–5 win over Washington. It was the earliest he had homered since 1911. In the Yankees' first 10
games, Baker batted .417. The club was batting .290, third best in the league,
and averaging nearly 10 hits a game.

The Yankees continued their hitting and got good pitching for the first
six weeks of the season. They went 16–8 in May and trailed Boston by one
game on June 1. For the first time in a Yankee uniform, Baker looked like
the player he was in Philadelphia. He was hitting .355, third in the league
behind Babe Ruth of the Red Sox, who was pitching and hitting .365, and
Tilly Walker of the Athletics, hitting .360. With Huggins at the helm, the
New Yorkers were playing with enthusiasm, scoring runs, and attracting
attention.

The tone of the 1918 season changed on May 18 when General Enoch
Crowder, Provost Marshal in charge of the United States Selective Service,
issued his "work-or-fight" order. The order stated that anyone between the
ages of 21 and 31 in a "nonessential" occupation must enlist, get a war-
related job, or be reclassified with a lower draft number. By September,
the draft would be extended to include 18 to 45 age range.

By mid–June, the major leagues were marking time awaiting a definite
announcement from the Provost Marshal's office on his interpretation of
the fight or work order which was to go into effect July 1. The order
included all men of draft age participating in professional sports but
exempted actors from mandatory service. Professional baseball contended
it should be considered in the same class as actors as it was a form of entertainment. If baseball players weren't ruled exempt, the leagues would have
difficulty playing out the season. Many club owners believed the work or
fight order would mean both leagues would have to pool all their players
into one eight-team league. The majority of baseball owners preferred to
continue the season, if any way possible, even if the quality of play was
much inferior.

Although the major league season had been surprisingly successful
judging from attendance, the minor leagues were already feeling the pinch
of the draft. The Southern Association announced it would end its season
at the end of June and other minor leagues were wavering on the brink of
making the same decision.

The Yankees were in first place on July 4, when they traveled to Washington for a doubleheader. Baker made his own fireworks, pounding six hits in nine at bats. In the first game, he slugged a home run, a double, and two singles to drive in five of the Yankees' seven runs in a shutout effort. He rapped Walter Johnson for a pair of singles in the second game, a 4–3 Senators' win.

On July 7, Baker was hitting .345, second only to Ty Cobb's .351 and the third-place Yankees were the top hitting team in the American League with a .269 average. Pipp was hitting .314 and Pratt .298.

Cobb made a startling announcement on July 14, saying he would quit baseball for the duration of the war when the season ended and enlist. He said baseball was good for entertainment and morale of the people, but he wanted to shoulder a rifle and be in the thick of the action. A week later, Ban Johnson announced American League ballparks would close their gates for the duration of the war following the next day's games unless unexpected developments occurred. This was in response to General Crowder's ruling that baseball was nonessential. He said there would be no attempt to finish the season with players too young or too old for the draft. A league meeting was scheduled in Cleveland to take care of the details.

On the heels of that announcement, the Yankees drew their largest crowd of the season at the Polo Grounds the following day as 25,000 fans watched them split a doubleheader with the Browns.

In spite of Johnson's announcement, American League teams continued to play. Johnson seemed to be alone in his wish to close the baseball parks before an effort was made to fill up the ranks with other players.

If all the eligible Yankees were drafted, only Baker, 32, and reserve outfielder Ham Hyatt, 32, would be left. Teams were being depleted as many players were either drafted or took war-related jobs. The Yankees lost Wally Pipp, Bob Shawkey, Ray Fisher and Ernie Shore; The Red Sox lost Stuffy McInnis, Dick Hoblitzell, Duffy Lewis, Jack Barry, Emil "Dutch" Leonard, and Herb Pennock; the White Sox were decimated with the loss of Joe Jackson, Claude "Lefty" Williams, Urban "Red" Faber, Jim Scott, Eddie Collins, and Oscar "Happy" Felsch. In all, more than 220 players served in the military or war-related jobs during the 1917 and 1918 seasons.

The fate of professional baseball rested on Secretary of War Newton Baker's decision on the work-or-fight order. A committee of baseball men met with Provost Marshall Crowder in Washington. They said if regulations were enforced, fewer than 60 players would be left in the major leagues and there would be no time to recruit new players to enable clubs to complete the season. Baseball officials hoped Secretary of War Baker would not implement the order until the end of the season.

On July 26, Secretary Baker granted baseball a reprieve. He decided to allow baseball until September 1 to adjust to the work-or-fight order as applicable to baseball players of draft age. After that date, all players affected by the work-or-fight order had to seek some other type of essential employment or enter the military draft. More than 235 players were affected by the decision.

As July came to a close, the question of a World Series became an issue. National League president John Tener opposed a World Series, saying it would lose its prestige.

Ban Johnson said the World Series should be played in the last 10 days of August. Understandably, owners of teams in the pennant race tended to oppose Johnson's idea because it would give them less time to overtake the leaders. Additionally, it would cut into gate receipts. Owners feared that if the World Series were played after September 1 the makeup of the clubs would be drastically different and fans would be turned off. Chairman August Herrmann of the National Commission proposed asking an extension beyond September 1 for the players who would appear in the World Series.

The National League voted to end the baseball season on September 1. The following day, the American League voted to play their schedule through September 2 with the World Series beginning September 3 or 4.

As the discussion of baseball's future was unfolding, the Yankees were slumping. From July 7 through August 9, they went 8–21 and fell to fifth place. During that time, Baker hit .240, going 35-for-146 and his average plummeted 37 points to .308.

On August 22, Secretary of War Baker approved the World Series, based in part on the intense interest of American soldiers in France, and granted an extension of the work-or-fight order for the players involved. The World Series would begin on September 4 with three games in Chicago. The other games would be played in Boston or Cleveland, whichever team won the American League pennant. The schedule differed from past years because the commission was trying to save travel expenses. Harry Frazee, president of the Red Sox, objected to the schedule, calling it unfair to the Red Sox and an insult to their fans. He suggested the first two games be played in Chicago and the second two in Boston. He didn't believe the expense of an extra trip between the cities should be a factor.

The National Commission suggested 10 percent of the revenue from the series be donated to war charities, an amount estimated to be between

$30,000 and $40,000. The commission also recommended each league as well as the two clubs in the series, participating players, and officials contribute a similar percentage.

Because of demands made on the public for patriotic causes such as Liberty Bonds and thrift stamps, the Commission decided to reduce the prices of admission to make the series more affordable. Box seats, which sold for $5 in 1917, cost $3. Grandstand reserve seats sold for $1.50, pavilion seats for $1 and bleacher seats for 50 cents. Ban Johnson also announced that the National Commission would cable reports and features about each game to the troops overseas.

The Red Sox beat the Cubs four games to two in the World Series. The teams received little financial reward for their efforts as the winners collected $1,102.51 per man, the smallest ever, and the losers earned $671.09, the second lowest ever. The paltry shares were the result of lower admission prices, smaller crowds and a new plan devised by National League President John Tener to allow teams finishing in second, third, and fourth places to share in the World Series receipts. Additionally, players had pledged 10 percent of their World Series money to the American Red Cross.

The players wanted the new plan for having eight teams instead of two sharing the World Series receipts to be postponed until after the war. They approached the National Commission only to be told that decision would have to be made by the leagues. That was unacceptable to the players, who decided to force the issue prior to the start of Game 5 of the World Series. They were prepared not to play the rest of the games. Members of the Commission — John Heydler, Johnson and Herrmann — arrived shortly before game time only to see the field empty. The players were refusing to take the field until the issue was resolved. After calling extra police in case trouble broke out, the Commission met with the player representatives in the umpires' room under the stands. An inebriated Johnson addressed the players and pleaded for them to play the game. Considering Johnson's condition, negotiations were out of the question. The players decided to play the game for the fans and hoped to resolve the issue later. They received assurances from the Commission they would not be penalized for their actions and the game started one hour late. During the winter, however, the Boston players were informed they had been fined by not being given their World Series emblems, which were traditionally awarded to the winners.

After playing in all the Yankees' 126 games, batting .306 and finishing third in the American League in total bases, Baker returned to Trappe with the intention of retiring from baseball. His three-year contract had expired and he was tired of traveling and wanted to settle down on his farm. He owned three farms, a bank, and a jewelry store and was financially well off. He had been handsomely compensated with the Yankees.

The *Easton Star-Democrat,* the closest weekly newspaper to Trappe, offered this slightly off-base, end-of-the-season appraisal of the Eastern Shore's favorite son: "It is a strange thing that until this season, Baker was never fully appreciated by the public nor by baseball men in general. This year, due to a little batting spurt and the fact that he was with a club which received considerable attention, he finally received the credit for being a truly great player."[1]

Baseball officials were spared winter-long uncertainty about the 1919 season when World War I ended officially on Armistice Day, November 11, 1918. Although the war was over, ballplayers were not immediately released from their military obligations. By mid–February there was still concern players would not be discharged in time for spring training, which had been postponed until early April.

During the off-season, Huggins was busy trying to improve the Yankees. He acquired Duffy Lewis, an eight-year veteran of the famed Boston Red Sox outfield which included Harry Hooper and Tris Speaker and was generally considered to be the best of its day. Lewis was expected to improve the outfield, a long time weak spot. He was an excellent defensive player with valuable experience, had batted over .300 twice and played in three World Series.

Few Yankees had signed contracts by mid–March. After having suffered through the past two seasons which were heavily impacted by World War I, owners were not in a generous mood when it came to increasing salaries. Yankee co-owner Col. Huston was not worried about the limited number of players signed, maintaining the club would field a team, and a good one, on Opening Day, even if it meant filling out the roster with other players. "Baseball will have to be put on a strictly business basis and the sooner the better. It's about time the players learned something about the business end of the game,"[2] he said.

Although Baker had expressed his intention to retire, Huggins felt he could persuade Frank to play again. He had been the club's best hitter in 1918 and had led the league's third basemen in fielding and putouts. The Yankees felt he could still be productive. Huggins and Huston traveled to Trappe to visit Baker in mid–March to convince him to suit back up again. The Maryland farmer was flattered to see how much he was valued, particularly after two sub–par seasons. Despite his desire to retire, he consented to rejoin the club. His decision was out of a sense of duty to Huston and Ruppert, who he felt hadn't gotten a just reward for their investment in him. He made it clear that money wasn't a consideration. Frank had the long-term security of his farms, but he loved playing baseball. The constant travel and extensive time away from his family remained his main objections.

"I feel I owe the game of baseball a great deal, for it has done me a great deal of good physically, morally and financially," he said. "It is because of my sense of duty and devotion to the game that I feel it almost obligatory to return."[3]

Baker felt veteran stars like himself would help the game return to its former popularity. He believed he was performing a duty to the country because baseball would help normalize America. He was glad to return to New York, but not enough to attend spring training. He told Huston and Huggins he wasn't sure he could get his business affairs in order soon enough to make spring training in Jacksonville. It was later agreed that he could join the club shortly before Opening Day on April 24.

On April 8, Yankees business manager Harry Sparrow announced the club would play an exhibition game against Rochester of the International League at Cambridge, Maryland just seven miles from Baker's home in Trappe, on Friday, April 18. He would join the Yankees in Cambridge for the exhibition game and then go north with the club.

Baker used the game to make an impressive debut in front of 3,000 of his most loyal friends and fans. It was a rare opportunity for Eastern Shore fans to see their hero without traveling to New York or Philadelphia. The Trappe native helped the Yankees to an easy 11–7 win as he enjoyed a perfect day at the plate. He doubled into the crowd that ringed the outfield grass in his first at bat and added another double, two singles and walk before calling it a day. His only other action before Opening Day was in an exhibition game against the Brooklyn Dodgers on April 22 when he went hitless in three plate appearances. Frank, 33, risked being rusty at the season's outset not having faced much major league pitching yet.

The renewed interest in baseball following the war was evidenced when the Yankees hosted the Boston Red Sox in their home opener on April 23. The game attracted 30,000 enthusiastic fans, making it the largest Opening Day crowd in the Yankees' history at the time. Huggins' lineup featured Pipp at first, Pratt at second, Peckinpaugh at short, Baker at third, Sam Vick in right field, Lewis in center, Bodie in left and Truck Hannah behind the plate. While the infield was the same as in 1918, two-thirds of the outfield was new with Vick and Lewis joining Bodie.

The Red Sox, featuring Babe Ruth in left field and batting cleanup, overpowered the Yankees, 10–0, behind the pitching of Carl Mays. Ruth slugged a two-run homer in the first inning and it proved to be all the Red Sox needed.

Typically, Baker started slowly. He didn't snap out of the early season slump until May 23 when he touched Chicago's Eddie Cicotte, one of the league's best pitchers, for a double and three singles and followed with a three-hit effort against the Browns. He smacked his first home run of the season off the Browns's Allen Sothoron on May 26.

For Baker, there was no better way to snap out of a slump than facing Washington pitching in Griffith Stadium. In a four-game series, he went 12-for-18. He collected two hits, including a game-winning single in the 10th inning, in the opening game. He went 6-for-9 in a doubleheader and completed the series with a four-hit effort.

By June 12, the Yankees had moved into first place ahead of the Chicago White Sox. They were playing aggressively, relying on power and timely hitting, and strong pitching. Fans and the media were taking notice because they were creating excitement at home and on the road. They had played well against strong teams such as Boston, Detroit, Cleveland and Chicago and were considered to be a team to be reckoned with. Huggins had instilled a desire to win in his players. The *New York Times* observed that the Yankees had "developed a spirit of aggressiveness which has been missing in the past."[4] Instead of taking losses quietly and without much objection, they exhibited a never-say-die attitude.

Pitching and timely hitting were the Yankees' strength. Bob Shawkey, 21-year-old southpaw Herb Thormahlen and 35-year-old Jack Quinn carried the club's pitching burden and won the majority of the games. The trio couldn't continue to carry the load the rest of the way. The Yankees hoped Ernie Shore, George Mogridge and perhaps Pete Schneider could pick up the lack. The Yankees ranked fourth in the league in batting, but made most of their hits count. In the past, the New Yorkers had tried to build their club on speed. Now, the emphasis was on power and there was not as much emphasis placed on moving up runners a base with a sacrifice bunt or stealing bases.

The addition of Duffy Lewis (who Huggins batted cleanup in front of Baker) in left field, the improved performance of Pratt at second base and the exceptional play of Peckinpaugh at shortstop were prime reasons for the club's improvement.

The new spirit and talent made the New York team more popular than ever as it attracted the largest weekday crowd in the club's history and the largest crowd ever to see an American League game at the Polo Grounds.

Once again, the Yankees reached July 4 in first place. It was the third time in four years they had accomplished the feat. No other Yankee team, however, appeared as strong. Baker and his teammates celebrated by sweeping a doubleheader from the Senators as the third baseman turned in his traditional outstanding holiday performance. The doubleheader attracted 8,000 fans in the morning and 22,000 in the afternoon to Polo Grounds. In the first game, the Yankees pounded 15 hits to win 8–2 behind Shawkey, who earned his 10th consecutive victory. In the seventh inning, the Yankees expanded a 2–1 lead as Peckinpaugh homered to left and Baker followed with a circuit clout to right off right-hander Eric Erickson. With two outs, Bodie sent a low line drive into the left field bleachers. Three home runs in one inning were almost unheard of. In the eighth inning, lefty Charlie Whitehouse relieved Erickson and Baker greeted him with his second homer of the day. The Yankees scored a dramatic 6–5 win in the second game when Duffy Lewis delivered a two-run double with two outs in the bottom of the ninth. At the conclusion of the doubleheader, Peckinpaugh had stretched his consecutive hitting streak to 25 games, one of the longest in years.

After the Yankees' 3–2 victory against the Senators on July 7, fueled by Baker's two-run homer in the bottom of the ninth off of Erickson, the *New York Times* referred to the club as "Miller Huggins' famous Murderers' Row."[5] Robert Ripley, *New York Globe* editorial cartoonist, had coined the term in a cartoon he drew featuring the home run hitting exploits of Baker, Pipp, Peckinpaugh and Pratt.

The Yankees were in first place with a one-game lead over the Chicago White Sox when they embarked on a 21-game, three-week road trip on July 7 which virtually decided their season. The club suffered through a 6–15 spell, dropping from first place to fourth place, seven and a half games behind the White Sox as their dependable pitching, hitting and fielding seem to collapse all at once. The pitchers started showing signs of wear and tear and no one stepped in as the fourth and fifth starters. Shawkey, 13–5, and Quinn, 11–4, in mid–July, struggled in the second half of the season as Shawkey was barely a .500 pitcher and Quinn won just four of 15 decisions.

The Indians snapped Shawkey's 10-game winning streak on July 9 and knocked the Yankees out of first place the following day as they split a doubleheader as Elmer Myers halted Peckinpaugh's hit streak at 29 games in the first contest. The streak tied Zack Wheat's 1916 record but fell short of Cobb's 35-consecutive game streak of 1917. Wee Willie Keeler of the Baltimore Orioles held the major league record of consecutive games with a hit at 44.

By mid–July, with both leagues engaged in tight pennant races and pulling record attendance to major league parks, club owners regretted they had decided to scale back the schedule to 140 games as a precaution to protect their losses. There was a growing feeling among fans that the season should be lengthened to the regular 154 games to give every team in the pennant race an opportunity to prove its superiority. If the owners were going to add 14 games, however, they needed to do it soon.

On July 29, the third-place Yankees acquired disgruntled right-handed pitcher Carl Mays from the Boston Red Sox for pitchers Allan Russell and Bob McGraw and $40,000. American League President Ban Johnson intervened and ordered Mays back to Boston but the Yankees refused to comply. Johnson suspended Mays for leaving the Red Sox and ordered umpires to prevent Mays from playing. The Yankees announced they would go to court.

The Mays case dated back to early July when he left the Red Sox during a game in Chicago and turned up two days later in Boston. He told manager Ed Barrow he was disgusted with the conditions (he was unpopular with his teammates and the Red Sox were out of the pennant race) and was ready to quit baseball. Once it became known that Mays had quit the Red Sox, a number of clubs including Chicago, Detroit, and Cleveland, all in the pennant race, began bidding for his services. During the more than three weeks of negotiations, Johnson did not intimate that Mays would be suspended for the remainder of the season nor did he inform clubs that he would not allow any other team to use him.

Huston and Ruppert met with Johnson on August 2 to discuss the Mays case. They argued that if Johnson was going to suspend Mays he should have done it before the Yankees purchased him.

The Yankees needed Mays if they were to stay in the pennant race. Of course, other league contenders preferred the Yankees not be allowed to acquire him. Johnson refused to lift the suspension, saying five of the owners had requested him to suspend Mays. Huston and Ruppert maintained that three of the five were negotiating with Mays before the Yankees purchased him. Huston and Ruppert sought an injunction from New York City judge Robert Wagner against Johnson in the Mays case.

It promised to be a bitter fight. Johnson was accustomed to ruling with an iron fist, but the Yankees were not about to let Mays slip away. To add fuel to the fire, the club accused Johnson of having an interest in the Cleveland team, making him biased. The New York owners charged that Johnson suspended Mays only after Cleveland had failed in its bid to secure him.

On August 6, the Yankees received a temporary injunction restraining Johnson from interfering with any of their scheduled games or their contract with Mays. The right-hander made his first appearance for the

Yankees in the second game of a doubleheader against St. Louis on August 7. He displayed fine form as he struck out nine and surrendered just six hits in an 8–2 win before 16,000 curious fans.

Mays received one of the loudest receptions any player had received at Polo Grounds when he took the mound in the first inning. He responded by striking out the side in the first inning and received a standing ovation. Baker gave Mays some support with a solo home run off of Allen Sothoron in the third inning.

Baker unloaded his tenth homer of the season the following day off right-hander Bert Gallia as the Yankees beat the Browns, 6–1, and moved within a game of the second-place Detroit Tigers. He had lifted his average to .283 and slugged seven home runs since July 4. Peckinpaugh led the team with a .340 average while Bodie, Lewis, Pratt and Baker were making it difficult for opposing pitchers. The formidable lineup made the Yankees a constant threat and an exciting team to watch.

Pitching, however, was the problem. Shawkey, Quinn and Thormahlen were struggling and Huggins was fortunate to get some good performances out of George Mogridge, who had been the steadiest hurler since July 4. Huggins hoped to get the pitching straightened out before the start of a 12-game western road trip.

Mays continued to pitch well on the trip as the club avoided disaster, going 5–7. The team couldn't make up any ground and was in fifth place, 12.5 games behind Chicago on August 28. The Yankees played well the rest of the season, going 22–8, but the White Sox were uncatchable.

While the Yankees were relegated to playing for pride and trying to reach the first division, the Ban Johnson-Carl Mays case continued. In a hearing to make permanent the injunction restraining Johnson from suspending Mays, attorneys for the Yankees stressed the fact that Johnson was a big shareholder in the Cleveland club, thus giving him a vested interest in the Mays matter. The injunction hearing was delayed.

On September 8, the Red Sox swept a doubleheader from the Yankees as Babe Ruth clouted his 26th homer of the season, breaking Buck Freeman's old home run record of 25 set with the 1899 Washington Club. Ruth, of course, accomplished it in style. The *New York Times* reported, "His home run was not one of those fluke affairs which just manage to tumble into the stands. The ball kept rising as it traveled and when it banged into the seats in the farthest corner it was still going upward."[6]

The 24-year-old Ruth was revolutionizing the game. The distance and frequency of his home runs were unlike anything anyone had witnessed. Playing 111 games in the outfield, four games at first base and pitching in 17, Ruth clouted 29 home runs; the rest of the Red Sox hit 4. Baker and Tilly Walker of the Athletics were the only other American Leaguers to finish with double digit homers.

Although Ruth was individually captivating fans, the Yankees established a team home run standard. They walloped 45 homers, the most since the 1910 Red Sox had registered 44. Baker led the team with 10 homers while Pipp, Peckinpaugh, and Lewis added 7 each.

The White Sox clinched the pennant on September 24. Joe Jackson (.351) and Eddie Collins (.319) paced their offense while Eddie Cicotte and Lefty Williams won 29 and 23 games, respectively. Chicago faced Cincinnati in the World Series, which attracted the most fans since the 1912 matchup. The Reds easily defeated the White Sox, 5 games to 3, in an experimental best-of-9 series. The Series, however, was tainted as it turned out that seven Chicago players had agreed to throw the Series for $100,000 from gamblers.

The Yankees had made great strides in 1919, winning 20 more games than in 1918, even though it was a shortened season. Their collapse after July 4 still puzzled Huggins. But it was clear their pitching wasn't strong or deep enough. Mays went 9–3 for the Yankees and many fans wondered what would have happened if they had acquired him earlier. Would a longer season have helped Huggins's men overtake the White Sox?

Shawkey won 20 games while Quinn chipped in with 15. Thormahlen went 13–9 and Mogridge was 10–7. For the first time in several seasons the Yankees' starting lineup stayed intact for most of the season. Except for platooning catchers Muddy Ruel and Frank Hannah, all the other position players saw action in at least 100 games. A healthy Baker played in all 141 games, batted .293, second to Peckinpaugh's .305, and drove in 83 runs, second to Lewis' 89 RBIs.

The Yankees were riding high at the end of the season, optimistic they could win the pennant in 1920. The future held more than they could have ever imagined.

TWELVE

Babe Comes to New York

The Yankees drew 619,164 fans in 1919, more than twice as many as in 1918. Baseball's popularity had returned faster and stronger than anyone anticipated as attendance jumped from 3 million in 1918 to 6.5 million in 1919. Owners confidently restored the prewar schedule for the 1920 season.

Attendance figures and the fans' fascination with the home run exploits of Babe Ruth made an impression on the owners, who were still trying to recover from the effects of wartime baseball. They recalled the increased interest when the ball was made livelier with the introduction of the cork center in late 1910 and 1911 (a time when Baker's home run production increased from 2 to 11). They felt a livelier ball would definitely be good for business. Some people believe the owners agreed to make the ball livelier without telling the public, even though ball manufacturers insisted there had been no changes and no tests had proved otherwise. Author William Curran attributes the offensive explosion to the influence of Babe Ruth, who showed other players the value of an upper cut and going for the fences.

Others point to several other moves made to benefit hitters and increase offensive production. Umpires were instructed to keep a fresh ball in play at all times. For most of Baker's career, foul balls were required to be returned to the umpire and most games were played with one ball, even though it may have been tobacco-stained, lopsided and defaced. As late at 1916, an entire game was played using one ball.

In 1945, Baker recalled some of the challenges he faced during the Dead Ball Era. "I'd like to see them swinging against the spitters, shiners and emery balls we used to look at. About the worst of all was the 'dark' ball. Following a couple times around the infield, smacked into gloves, floating into tobacco juice, a new ball would be as black as a black hat. Such a ball, thrown by a pitcher like Walter Johnson, was also impossible to see."[1]

Trick pitches such as spitballs and practices of scuffing or nicking the ball's surface or applying any foreign substances were outlawed beginning in 1920. Doctoring baseballs made them react in an unpredictable fashion, making them often impossible to hit. Seventeen pitchers were granted permission to throw spitballs for the remainder of their careers. Whatever the reason, the Dead Ball Era was about to quickly vanish.

The Yankees knew they were competitive, but they needed another hard-hitting outfielder and a couple starting pitchers to win the pennant. The club's outlook was cloudy as Lewis, 31, and Baker, 34, were uncertain if they would return for 1920. The complexion of the upcoming season changed dramatically, however, when Huston and Ruppert announced the purchase of Babe Ruth for $125,000 on January 5 from the financially troubled Red Sox owner Harry Frazee, who planned to use the money to buy several players. It was the most money ever paid for a player. In fact, it was more than twice the price that had ever been paid for a player. Cleveland had purchased Tris Speaker from Boston for $50,000, plus several players while the White Sox had paid $50,000 for Eddie Collins. At 25, Ruth was in his prime and was clearly a phenomenal player, unlike any baseball had seen.

The Yankees assumed Ruth's contract, which called for $10,000 a year and had two more years remaining. Ruth, of course, was seeking a substantial raise, which Frazee had declined. Frazee sold Ruth to the Yankees because he thought the Red Sox were becoming a one-man team. In a statement issued several days after the sale, Frazee detailed his reasons for selling the superstar. "Ruth had become simply impossible and the Boston club could no longer put up with his eccentricities. While Ruth, without question, is the greatest hitter that the game has ever seen, he is likewise one of the most selfish and inconsiderate men that ever wore a baseball uniform. If he possessed the right disposition, had he been willing to take orders and work for the good of the club like the other men on the team, I would never had dared to let him go. Twice during the past two seasons Babe has jumped the club and revolted. He refused to obey orders of the manager."[2]

The Yankees had been considered Murderers' Row without Ruth. What would they be with him? The thought of him playing 77 games at Polo Grounds with its short right fence was tantalizing for New York fans. He had proven, however, that he could reach any fence, regardless of the distance. Certainly, his presence in the lineup would make every hitter better. Ruth led the American League in homers, RBI, runs, total bases and slugging percentage in 1919. His assets, however, weren't limited to offense. While playing left field for Boston, he led the league in fielding percentage and assists.

Pitcher Bob Shawkey's immediate response was that the acquisition of Ruth should make the Yankees a pennant winner in 1920. The possibility of a World Series at the Polo Grounds involving the Yankees and the Giants became a popular topic among New York baseball fans.

The sale of Ruth left Boston in turmoil and generally disgusted. Like many other fans, Johnny Keenan, leader of the Royal Rooters, wondered how the Red Sox were going to replace Ruth. Surely, the gate receipts would suffer dramatically.

The sale of Boston stars Cy Young and Tris Speaker had upset fans in the past, but nothing rivaled the sale of Ruth. The *Boston Post* observed: "Ruth is in a class of ball players that flashes across the firmament once in a great while and who along bring crowds to the park whether the team is winning or losing."[3]

Prominent Boston baseball men Fred Tenney and Hugh Duffy said the sale of Ruth was good for the team. They argued that two or three players willing to work with the team were more valuable than one star who created problems.

The *Boston Herald* asked fans to reserve judgment on the deal. "Frazee has carefully considered the Ruth angle and believes he has done the proper thing. Boston fans undoubtedly will be up in arms but they should reserve judgment until they see how it works out."[4]

The Yankees dispensed manager Huggins to Los Angeles to negotiate with Ruth. At the same time, he planned to visit with Duffy Lewis and persuade him to re-sign. In late January, Huggins traveled to Trappe to convince Baker to return to New York. Despite the addition of Ruth and the increased chances for a pennant, Baker told Huggins he did not plan on playing any more.

Baker's wife, Ottilie, took sick shortly after Huggins's visit and died on February 17 from scarlet fever at the age of 31. A large number of relatives and friends attended the funeral, which was held on Sunday, February 20. Due to scarlet fever in the home the only services were held in Easton's Spring Hill Cemetery.

The *Easton Star-Democrat* wrote, "Mrs. Baker possessed a wonderful personality, always bright and happy which drew to her a large number of friends and her death came as a shock to the community at large; but her influence was best felt in her home, where she made an excellent wife and

Frank Baker is shown here with his two daughters, Ottilie (right) and Janise, during spring training in 1921 in Shreveport, Louisiana. Baker's wife died in February 1920 and he sat out the season because he could not find anyone to take care of his daughters. He said, "My children are dearer to me than baseball and the Yankees will have to get along without my services this season." NATIONAL BASEBALL HALL OF FAME LIBRARY, COOPERSTOWN, NY.

mother. The keenest sympathy is felt for her bereaved husband and little girls, Ottilie, age 9, and Janise, 2."[5]

Following his wife's death, Baker said, "The death of Mrs. Baker killed all chances of me ever playing baseball again. There has been more or less talk throughout the country about my playing this year with the Yankees. But there is no possible chance of me wearing a uniform. Since the death of my wife, I have lost heart and interest in the game and I could not do justice to the club or myself under the circumstances."[6]

Christy Mathewson responded to Baker's announcement, saying, "It is a sad ending to a brilliant career. Baker was one of the coolest, steadiest men in the game. Like Eddie Collins, he always played better in a World Series than he did in any other games during the season."[7]

Babe Ruth was the center of attention on February 28 when he arrived 10 minutes before the Yankees train departed for spring training in Jacksonville. The Yankees had been in spring training for about two weeks when Col. Huston announced Baker very likely would rejoin the club. The two had met in Baltimore and Baker promised Huston he would return if he could obtain proper care for his two daughters.

On March 19, Ruth captured everyone's attention with an estimated 478-foot home run during batting practice. The blast cleared the 428-foot center field feet by an estimated 50 feet. It was the first time anyone had cleared the fence. Ruth said it was the second hardest ball he had hit in his career. His top drive was an estimated 550-foot homer he hit during a Giants-Red Sox spring game in Tampa in 1919.

Chick Fewster, a 24-year-old Baltimorean, who was expected to take over Baker's spot at third base, was seriously injured in a March 25 game against Brooklyn as pitcher Jeff Pfeffer hit him in the temple. The impact sounded like a coconut cracking and he fell to the ground and lay unconscious for 10 minutes before the trainer revived him and fellow players took him to the clubhouse. The injury was more serious than originally thought and he was transferred to Johns Hopkins Hospital in Baltimore. Fewster had lost his ability to speak and although he had no fractures, there were deep bruises and some crushed blood vessels. He was expected to be hospitalized for 10 days and be out of the lineup until June. He underwent an operation to remove a blood clot, put in a drainage tube, and relieve pressure on the damaged nerves.

Fewster's injury put more pressure on Baker to return to the Yankees' lineup. But Baker decided to hold to his original decision, saying it wouldn't be right to leave his daughters so soon after their mother's death. "My children are dearer to me than baseball and the Yankees will have to get along without my services this season," he said.[8]

Huggins tabbed newcomer Bob Meusel, a powerful six-foot-three, 23-year-old Californian who had been successful in the Pacific Coast League, to take over the hot corner. On April 1, Huggins said, "We take this as Baker's final word and will not try any further to get him to rejoin the club. Perhaps in a few months, Baker will see things differently. If he cares then to rejoin the club, he will be welcome."[9] Huggins told Meusel to consider himself the Yankees' permanent third baseman, not a temporary replacement. Huggins was high on Meusel, saying he didn't think there were any pitchers who could stop him and Ruth. He predicted Meusel would be one of the most talked about hitters in the upcoming season.

New York broke training camp the first week of April, Huggins was rightfully optimistic. He knew he had a mix of youth and veterans, a strong hitting club with power, a talented starting rotation and depth on the bench. The pitching staff of Carl Mays, Bob Shawkey, George Mogridge, Ernie Shore, Herb Thormahlen and Jack Quinn ranked with the league's best. The Yankees had been pennant contenders last season with Mays for only part of the season and without Ruth. Now, it was firmly expected the club would be the team to beat.

The Yankees opened the promising 1920 season with a 3–1 loss to the Athletics in Philadelphia before 12,000 fans as Ruth's fielding error in the eighth inning allowed the winning runs. The sounds of "Play Ball" must have stirred some previously dormant feelings in Baker, who called Huggins from his home in Trappe to set up a conference the following day in Philadelphia. Baker and several friends drove to Shibe Park to meet with Huggins after the game. After an hour's conversation, Huggins said he could not induce Baker to return.

Baker's solution to playing baseball without having to be frequently away from home was to approach the Upland team once again. Slightly more than a week after meeting with Huggins, Baker announced he would captain the Upland team for the 1920 season. He was back in uniform on May 2 as Upland hosted the Chester Athletic Club before a record-breaking crowd. The 7–4 loss was disastrous as he committed an error, fanned with two runners on and hit into a double play. A reporter for the *Chester Times* wrote, "Baker looked like a bush-leaguer compared to the youngsters picked up on the lots in the city."[10]

As Baker struggled with Upland, Ruth wowed 25,000 fans at the Polo Grounds with his second homer in two days against the Red Sox. The Bambino unloaded his first homer of the season on May 2, a colossal shot over the right field grandstand. He rocketed a line drive over the right field fence the following day.

The frequency of Babe Ruth's homers and the spectacular manner in which he hit them was capturing the attention of virtually every New York. Fans had to see his prodigious shots to believe them and they clamored for the opportunity.

On Sunday, May 16, the fourth-place Yankees, sporting a lackluster 12–11 record, hosted the Cleveland Indians and attracted a record crowd of 38,600. More than 10,000 chagrined fans were turned around. Police lines were formed to keep the disappointed throng away from the gates. Once the gates were closed, police didn't open them for anyone, fearing a mad rush to storm the gates and a mob scene. Newspapermen with credentials had to scale a fence between the old Manhattan Field and the Polo Grounds after getting the okay from club officials. Hundreds of other credentialed writers had to wait two innings until the crowd subsided before they were admitted through the gates. Ruth had attracted a World Series type crowd to an early season game. The record crowd unfortunately had little to cheer about as the Indians roughed up Yankee starter Carl Mays for five runs in the first inning en route to an 8–2 win.

Ruth reached May 18 with five homers, well ahead of his 1919 pace when he had only one at the same point. After he slammed his eighth homer against the Tigers on May 26, the *New York Times* wrote, "Not in many, many years has a player become such an idol as Ruth is in the right field grand stand. Every day the same ardent admirers inhabit this section and pay homage to the home run king. Ruthville is Babe's own kingdom and its population is growing every day."[11]

Ruth caught fire in the final week of May, blasting four homers to bring his monthly total to 11, just one shy of Baker's top seasonal mark. Unlike Baker, Ruth focused on the long ball. He swung from his heels, had a slight upward swing, and wasn't afraid to strike out. Baker was a line drive hitter who was well trained in the art of advancing a runner. He had shunned making changes to his swing in order to hit more home runs. During most of Baker's career, clearing the fence was a monumental achievement. Now, Ruth was making a mockery out of the distances that had once intimidated most players as his shots were traveling unbelievable distances.

The Yankees set a local one-day attendance record on May 31 when nearly 50,000 fans attended a Sunday doubleheader against the Senators (11,500 in the morning game and 38,600 witnessed the afternoon game). Ruth treated the fans to a homer in the second game.

The Yankees put together an incredible display of hitting and popularity during the first week of June. They played before 108,200 fans in five consecutive days and clouted 21 homers, almost half the team's 1919 total.

Ruth tied his 1919 home run mark of 29 on July 14. By this time, crowds of 15,000 to 20,000 Monday through Friday were common while Saturday and Sunday games regularly drew 30,000 or more. By the end of July, baseball attendance records had been shattered in five of the eight American League cities and the Yankees were involved in each game. The Yankees, led by Ruth, had established themselves as the greatest drawing card in baseball history.

By mid–August, the Yankees were in second place and had slugged 91 home runs. Ruth had 42 and the rest of the team had 49. Meusel had 11 while Pipp and Peckinpaugh had 8 and Bodie 7.

While the Yankees were battling for the American League pennant in impressive fashion, Baker was playing against teams such as Brooklyn Royal Giants and Lincoln Giants of Chicago, Sun Oil and Baltimore Dry Dock, Cuban All-Stars, House of David, and American Steel. The highlight of his rather unimpressive season came on July 11 when his grand slam in the bottom of the ninth gave Upland a 6–5 win over Viscose. In mid–July, the *Chester Times* wrote "Baker had not been keeping up his reputation as a home run king."[12]

Tragedy struck on August 16 as Yankees' starter Carl Mays, known for pitching inside, struck Cleveland shortstop Ray Chapman in the temple with one of his submarine pitches. Chapman died the following day at age 29 to become baseball's only fatality related to being hit by a pitch. Three days later, Baker traveled to New York as a guest of owner Col. Huston to watch the Yankees lose to Cleveland 3–2, before 18,000 people. He witnessed Ruth unloading his 43rd home run over the roof of the right field stands in the fourth inning. As usual, the crowd erupted, tossing hats in the air and applauding for several minutes. The loss kept New York in third place, just one and a half games behind first-place Cleveland.

Baker's teammates were glad to see him and said they would welcome him back any time. Huston believed there was a possibility the third baseman would return for the remaining weeks of the season.

On August 28, the Yankees found a way to squeeze a few more fans into the Polo Grounds and set an attendance record with 39,000 for a game against the White Sox. An additional 15,000 were turned away. New York won 3–0 without the services of Ruth, who was expected to be out of action for 10 days with an infected insect bite on his right wrist. He returned within a week and crashed home runs numbers 44 and 45 in a doubleheader at Boston.

Attention on the American League pennant race was diverted at the start of September when the grand jury of Cook County in Illinois convened to investigate gambling in baseball. An August 31 game between the Phillies and Cubs was the original subject of the investigation. Presiding judge Charles McDonald also recommended that the grand jury consider looking into the 1919 World Series involving the Chicago White Sox and Cincinnati Reds. Rumors had been circulating since last October that members of the White Sox had taken money to throw the series. White Sox owner Charles Comiskey was among the first to testify. He told the grand jury that he would fire any of his players who were not honest, regardless of who they were. And, if he couldn't replace them with honest players, he would close the ballpark. Pitcher Eddie Cicotte and outfield Joe Jackson also testified, implicating a number of their teammates. Comiskey responded by suspending eight players—Cicotte, Jackson, Happy Felsch, Buck Weaver, Lefty Williams, Chick Gandil, Swede Risberg, and Fred McMullin—for the final days of the season and until the investigation had been completed. The move likely cost the White Sox the pennant, but it would have been an embarrassment to baseball if they had won the pennant again.

The Yankees took over first place on September 14 with a 13–3 win over the Tigers. Their stay at the top was short-lived as they lost four consecutive games, three to Chicago and one to St. Louis, falling three games behind Cleveland

On September 19, the *Chester Times* reported that Baker would join the Yankees by the end of the week. At that point, Baker's role for Huggins' team would probably be limited to pinch hitting. A couple of days later, Baker emphatically denied the reports and finished out the season at Upland.

The Yankees could not make up any ground down the stretch, even though they won seven of the remaining nine games and Ruth pounded five homers. On the final day of the season, the Yankees swept a doubleheader from the Athletics and Ruth notched home run number 54. New York finished 95–59 and in third place, three games behind first-place Cleveland, 96–45. Chicago took second at 95–56, one and a half games out of first.

Would the Yankees have won the pennant if Baker had played a portion of the season with them? During the off-season, the *New York Evening Telegram*, irked by Baker's indecision, wrote, "If Ruppert or Huston had said to Baker last September, 'Frank, we'll give you $10,000 if you jump right into our lineup,' Baker would have made the last Western trip with the club and it might have won the pennant."[13]

The Yankees apparently didn't hold it against the slugger for not signing as the club agreed to play an exhibition game in Upland at the end of the season. On October 3, Upland defeated the Yankees, 4–3, as Baker rapped two hits off Ernie Shore. Ruth did not make the trip because he journeyed to Boston to fulfill a contract with a motion picture company.

The Yankees finished with 115 home runs, 65 more than the second closest team, the St. Louis Browns. Ruth's 54 were more than any other American League team. The Bambino had an incredible season. In 142 games, he scored 158 runs, drove in 172, drew 148 walks and batted .376. In addition to his record number of homers, he collected 36 doubles and nine triples to give him a slugging percentage of .847. As if that wasn't enough, he also led the team in stolen bases with 14.

Ruth wasn't a one-man show. Meusel, splitting his time between outfield and third base, hit .328 and drove in 83 runs. Pratt enjoyed a fine all-round year, batting a career high .314 and driving in 97 runs. Mays led the pitchers with a 26–11 mark while Shawkey won 20 games, despite missing a month of the season. At age 36, Quinn surprised everyone with 18 wins.

The Yankees had failed to win the pennant, but they had captured the imagination and hearts of New York baseball fans. They became the first team to draw more than 1 million fans in a season, attracting 1.2 million. For the first time, they outdrew the New York Giants, their Polo Grounds landlords. The Yankees were now the city's most popular baseball club and were earning fans all across the country.

THIRTEEN

Return to New York and the World Series

Baker met with Yankee scout Joe Kelley in Baltimore in February to discuss the possibility of returning to the club. The biggest stumbling block wasn't salary, but whether he could make sure his daughters were taken care of. His oldest daughter, Ottilie, was recovering from a serious bout of double pneumonia. After meeting with Kelley, Baker met with Yankee infielder Chick Fewster. He told Fewster he wanted to play with the Yankees, who he figured had a chance to go to the World Series, rather than to be traded to a third or fourth place team.

Approaching age 35, Baker did not figure into the Yankees' long-range plans. He was, however, the best third baseman they had. He still had some power, was a clutch hitter, and would make the Yankees' powerful lineup even more dangerous. If Baker returned to the club, Huggins would shift promising 24-year-old Aaron Ward from third base to second base. Ward played 114 games at third base in 1920 and hit 11 home runs, tied for second on the club. The New York skipper would move 25-year-old Fewster, who missed most of the 1920 season, to the outfield, which was still an unsettled problem.

New York made two major trades during the off-season in an attempt to improve. On December 15, they shipped catcher Muddy Ruel, second baseman Del Pratt, outfielder Sammy Vick, and pitcher Hank Thormahlen to the Boston Red Sox in exchange for pitchers Waite Hoyt and Harry Harper, catcher Wally Schang and infielder Mike McNally. A little more than two weeks later, they traded outfielder Duffy Lewis and pitcher George Mogridge to the Washington Senators for outfielder Robert "Braggo" Roth.

Despite the contract talks and speculation, Baker remained unsigned. On February 27, the New York papers reported that Huggins had accepted a $30,000 offer from Washington Senators owner Clark Griffith for the release of Baker, who had been on the voluntary retired list due to the death of his wife. Griffith had long sought the services of the former home run king, who excelled against Washington pitching and thrived in Griffith Stadium. Huggins was willing to part with Baker, but preferred to acquire several players, including a quality outfielder for him instead of money. Huggins had suggested Sam Rice (a future Hall of Famer), but Griffith refused to part with him. Griffith made a counteroffer of $30,000 plus a couple of mediocre players. But the players weren't of high enough quality to help the team, so the Yankees turned down the offer. As spring training approached, however, Huggins apparently was willing to accept cash.

The Yankees quickly denied that Baker had been sold to the Senators. Business manager Ed Barrow said there was absolutely no truth to the story. "Any deals that might have been pending for Baker have been declared off," he said. "Baker is expected to be in the lineup with Ruth. His presence will add great offensive strength to the club."[1]

Returning from Georgia, Yankees' co-owner Col. Huston met with Baker in Washington to discuss the possibilities of retaining his services for the 1921 season. By the end of the meeting only a few details needed to be worked out and Baker was expected to report to Shreveport, Louisiana, for training camp. On March 1, team officials announced Baker would sign a one-year contract. While Baker wouldn't enhance the team's speed or youth, he would add power and character. As the club's oldest player, he was expected to be a strong, positive influence on the younger players.

Plans called for Baker's sister, Mrs. Eugene Slaughter, and his two daughters to accompany him to spring training in Shreveport, Louisiana. Upon his return to New York, his housekeeper Mrs. Edith Terrell and his daughters would make their home in New York for the summer.

While Baker's signing was hailed by the team and fans, no one knew if he could regain his old form. He had sat out his second full season and this time he was five years older than when he made his first comeback. The *Sporting News* shared its doubts: "Here's a player well past his 30's, never a brilliant performer, though indeed a dangerous hitter, slipping from his top form when he retired, out of the game for a season, and expected to come back so strong or to be so much stronger than he was when at his best, that he will be his club's deciding factor in a pennant winning struggle. The season will tell. Its story will be bitter or sweet for the Trappe farmer."[2]

The Yankees opened spring training in Shreveport without Baker, who was confined to his farm in Trappe with an infected throat. Baker, however, was no longer the Yankees' main attraction. It was clearly Ruth who attracted record crowds wherever he went. In a March 13 exhibition game against Shreveport, Ruth clouted three prodigious homers and three singles in six at bats and stole two bases. The Yankees drew crowds of 8,000 and 12,000 for exhibition games in New Orleans several days later.

Baker, looking trim and fit, reported to spring training on March 21. One of his first actions was to apply to Commissioner Judge Kenesaw Mountain Landis for reinstatement into organized baseball. This step was necessary because he had gone on the voluntary retired list and played independent baseball with Upland.

In his first game back in a Yankees uniform, Baker drove in the winning run in an 8–7 victory over Shreveport with a double in the eighth inning. As the Yankees broke camp to head North, Aaron Ward played third base for a series of games against Brooklyn. Ward was listed at third base instead of Baker when Huggins announced his Opening Day lineup on April 7. Baker was still waiting to be reinstated by Landis.

New York made several improvements over the off season and was one of the obvious favorites. The addition of catcher Wally Schang, Baker's old teammate in Philadelphia, strengthened their weakest position. The club also added speed with the addition of Roth in the outfield, the return of Fewster, and the acquisition of infielder Mike McNally.

On April 13, a record Yankees' Opening Day crowd of 37,000 warmly greeted Baker, who was still ineligible to play. With Baker on the bench, Ruth delighted the crowd with two doubles and three singles in an 11–1 rout of the Philadelphia Athletics. A record 160,000 fans watched major league baseball openers in 1921.

Baker's reinstatement was delayed until April 21 because he had been accused of competing against players who had been banned from organized baseball while he was a member of the Upland team. The charges most likely centered around a game Upland had scheduled against the Heinie Zimmerman All-Stars in late September 1920. Zimmerman had been banned from baseball in 1919 along with teammate Hal Chase for attempting to entice their New York Giants teammates to throw games. The game against Zimmerman's All-Stars, however, was rained out. After an investigation, the charges against Baker were dropped.

Baker didn't make his 1921 debut until May 2 at Fenway Park and it marked his first time in the lineup with Ruth. Baker, batting sixth, doubled and Ruth crushed a solo home run, his sixth of the season, but the Yankees lost 2–1.

In the twilight of his career, the former home run king was clearly

playing in the shadow of the Bambino. Although Ruth had quickly dwarfed Baker's home-run hitting exploits, the two sluggers had respect for each other. Ruth had pitched against Baker when the Trappe star was in his prime and knew he was one of the league's most dangerous hitters. Although they were as different as day and night off the field, Baker respected Ruth for his hustle, teamwork, and desire to win.

The Yankees were in first place and drawing outstanding crowds at the Polo Grounds and on the road when owners Huston and Ruppert made their final payment of $500,000 on May 17 on the club's new home to be built in the Bronx. Plans called for a three-tiered stadium with a seating capacity of 75,000. The timing couldn't have been better as teams were playing to bigger crowds than they had in the record-setting 1920 season.

The public heavily favored baseball's new Babe Ruth–inspired era of home runs, high-scoring games and record attendance over Baker's era of pitching duels, advancing runners one base at a time, and occasional capacity crowds.

The *New York Times* observed, "Home runs and hitting are apparently what the fans want to see.... When fans stay away from the ballpark because of too much hitting, it will be time to act, but that day apparently is far way."[3]

Baker put together his two best games of the season on May 19 and 20 in Chicago when he collected 7 hits in 10 at bats. The following day, however, he injured his leg chasing a foul ball. A severe sprain kept him out of the lineup until June 3. He picked up a pair of hits and Ruth slammed home run No. 16 as the Yankees lost to the St. Louis Browns. Six days later, Baker walloped his first homer of the season, a three-run shot off of former New York teammate Ray Caldwell, in a 14–4 loss to the Indians.

Baker and Ruth homered for the first time in the same game on June 13 in a 13–8 victory over the Detroit Tigers at the Polo Grounds. Ruth crushed a solo shot in the third inning off right-hander Howard Ehmke and two batters later Baker sent a line drive into the stands. In the seventh inning, Ruth awed the crowd with a blast to the center field

Opposite: **The New York Yankees won their first American League pennant in 1921. Babe Ruth, fourth from the right, center row, turned in one of the greatest seasons ever as he clouted 59 home runs, drove in 171, batted .378 and finished with a slugging percentage of .846. At age 35, Baker (directly behind Ruth in the photograph) was in the twilight of his career. Baker, however, was still dangerous enough with the bat for Manager Miller Huggins to put him behind Ruth in the lineup. NATIONAL BASEBALL HALL OF FAME LIBRARY, COOPERS-TOWN, NY.**

bleachers, a spot where no ball had ever been hit. As if his home runs weren't enough, Ruth also started the game, pitching into the sixth inning.

The duo maintained their act the following day as Ruth once again slammed a pair of round-trippers and Baker notched one. Ruth cleared the left field fence in the first inning and sent another tape-measure shot into the center field bleachers, which traveled further than his homer to the same area the day before. Baker delivered a three-run, line drive wallop in the seventh inning off right-hander George "Hooks" Dauss.

Ruth had slugged a record 7 home runs in five days to give him 23 for the season, putting him ahead of his 1920 pace. The Yankees were on an incredible almost-a-home-run-per-game pace, launching 48 homers in their first 56 games. Although they were batting .291 as a team in mid–June, it was only fourth best in the league. The Tigers were batting .331, two points higher than the Indians, and the Browns were hitting .302.

The leagues started to take steps to bring hitting back to a more realistic level. American League umpires were instructed to rub baseballs in a new white powder introduced by a Philadelphia chemist. Without discoloring the ball, the powder was supposed to help pitchers gain a better grip on the balls. The balls had been tried in a few games and pitchers agreed they could get a better break on their curve balls. National League umpires were instructed to rub at least two dozen baseballs in moist dirt before each game. Officials mentioned nothing about making the ball less lively. National League President John Heydler believed the slowness of pitchers to round into shape due to a cold spring was a major cause for the outlandish offensive production. He thought the hitting exploits would soon end.

Baker's average hovered around .280 near the end of June when Huggins moved him into the cleanup spot, hitting behind Ruth. The move agreed with Baker, who went on a batting streak after missing a couple games with a mild leg injury.

Baker turned in his traditional July 4 explosive performance as the Yankees clouted five round-trippers in a doubleheader sweep of the A's. In the opener, he slammed home runs in the first and seventh innings off right-hander Dave Keefe, driving in Ruth both times. He also singled. In the second game, he went 2-for-4. He continued his stellar hitting from the cleanup position as New York started a Western road trip in Chicago. He had gone 15-for-32 and raised his average above .300 by the time Red Faber of the White Sox held him hitless on July 9.

The Yankees went on their longest winning streak of the season, reeling off nine consecutive victories from July 11 through July 20. The ninth win, a 7–1 decision over Cleveland, moved them briefly into first place past the Indians. The Yankees and Indians traded first place over the next couple weeks. On August 8, New York split a doubleheader with Chicago, their toughest opponent. In the third inning of the first game, Ruth and Baker clouted back-to-back home runs off southpaw Jack Wieneke in a 7–0 victory. Ruth added a second homer in the second game, lifting his total to 41 and keeping him ahead of his 1920 pace. Two days later, the duo teamed up again as the Trappe slugger unloaded his eighth homer in the second inning off right-hander Clarence "Shovel" Hodge and his ninth home run off right-hander Doug McWeeny in the sixth inning. Ruth smacked Number 42 off Hodge in the third inning.

On August 20, Baker strained a tendon in his right leg, trying to score from second base in the first inning of a game in St. Louis. He was hitting .297 and the Yankees were in second place, one game behind Cleveland. Baker missed the final six weeks of the season, making just one pinch hit appearance.

The Yankees entered September in second place, one-half game behind Cleveland. The schedule, however, heavily favored New York, who played 24 of 31 remaining games at home. The Indians had 27 of 32 games on the road. Despite the schedule disadvantage, the Indians refused to fold.

The clubs were in a virtual tie for first place as they prepared for a critical four-game series, September 23–26. More than 32,000 fans jammed the Polo Grounds on September 23 as Waite Hoyt and Stan Coveleski hooked up. The Yankees won 4–2 as Ruth, Meusel and Pipp broke the game open in the sixth inning.

The Indians evened the score the following day as 22-year-old right hander George Uhle limited the Yankees to four hits and tossed a 4–0 shutout. It was only the fourth time Huggins's crew had been shut out in 1921. The Yankees made up for their offensive silence the following game as they erupted for 21 runs and 20 hits to the delight of 38,000 fans. Meusel sparked the offense, hitting for the cycle. The grandstand was sold out two hours before game time and the bleachers were filled one hour before the start of the game.

The Yankees opened a two-game lead on the Indians with an 8–7 win to close the series. Ruth, who had been relatively quiet during the series, stepped into the spotlight with two titanic home runs and a double to drive in five runs.

New York clinched the pennant on October 1 with a 5–3 win over the Athletics in the opening game of a doubleheader. With the pennant wrapped up, Ruth made a brief pitching appearance in the second game. The New York Giants had secured the National League pennant two days earlier, edging out the Pittsburgh Pirates.

After one of the most outstanding seasons ever, it was only fitting for Ruth to be in the World Series spotlight. Besides clouting an unbelievable 59 home runs, the Yankees' star scored 177 runs and drove in 171. He tallied 204 hits, including 44 doubles and 16 triples, while batting .378, third highest in the league. His .846 slugging average was far ahead of Harry Heilmann's .606, which was the league's second best. Ruth walked 144 times and even stole 17 bases.

After the end of the season, Baker said, "Ruth can hit the ball farther than anyone I ever saw. There has never been anyone like him and I don't think there ever will be. I hope he lives long enough to hit 100 homers in a season. I wish him all the luck in the world. He has everybody hopelessly outclassed, including myself."[4]

Ruth got plenty of offensive help from Meusel, who knocked 24 homers and drove in 135 runs while hitting .318. Pipp drove in 97 runs and batted .298. Limited to 94 games, Baker finished with another productive season, slugging 9 home runs and 71 RBIs while hitting .294. As a team, the Yankees batted .300 and smashed an unheard of 134 home runs.

On the mound, Mays led the way with a league-best 27–9 record. Twenty-one-year-old Hoyt added 19 wins while veteran Shawkey chipped in with 18.

A Subway Series involving the Yankees and the Giants was a dream come true for New York baseball fans, the Yankee owners and American League officials who had worked to build the Yankees into a competitive club. It marked only the second time a World Series would be played in one city. Bragging rights for New York were at stake and the Series promised to be bitter and hard fought.

The Giants, like the Yankees, had been involved in an intense pennant race. McGraw's club trailed the Pittsburgh Pirates by seven and a half games on August 23. The Giants, however, won the pennant by four games as they won 24 of 33 games down the stretch. The Pirates faded, losing 22 of 36.

The Giants lacked a Babe Ruth, but were still a hard-hitting club. First baseman George Kelly led the club with 23 home runs and 122 RBI while hitting .308. Infielder Frankie Frisch, 22, and right fielder Ross Youngs, 24, each drove in 100 runs. Frisch was the Giants' sparkplug as he stole a league-high 49 bases while hitting .341. As a team, the Giants batted .298 and led the league in runs, walks and stolen bases.

The Giants' veteran pitching staff had no Mathewson or Marquard. McGraw relied on Art Nehf, his only 20-game winner, Fred Toney, Jesse Barnes and Phil Douglas. Toney won 18 games while Barnes and Douglas each won 15. The staff was at its best when it allowed just six runs in five games against the first-place Pirates in a crucial late-August series. The Giants won all five games and cut the deficit to two and a half games, demoralizing the Pirates and paving the way for their demise.

The excitement created by the first Subway World Series in New York was unmatched. *New York Tribune* sportswriter Grantland Rice described Manhattan as being "in the convulsive throes of a baseball fit."[5] Hotel rooms were booked solid and the demand for tickets was overwhelming. The Yankees had drawn 1.2 million fans and the Giants had attracted 973,000. There was hardly anyone in New York City who wasn't interested in the series or willing to place a bet. In fact, the entire country was interested. Fans as far away as California, Washington, Maine, Canada and Mexico headed to New York for the series. More than 600 reporters requested press credentials, assuring the most intense coverage in series history.

The Yankees and Giants were rated fairly even. Most observers expected the best-of-nine-game series to possibly go the distance since neither club had dominant pitching. Pitching, however, was expected to be the key. The Giants had the clear advantage in speed and pitching but the Yankees had power. The Giants' speed didn't faze Ruth. "The Yankees will win the World Series because we have the punch to do it. American League pitching is better than National League pitching and the Giants pitching is not the best in the National League by far. They say the Giants will show us up on the bases. Well, we do not have to be good base runners. We knock the ball out of the park and simply jog around," he said.[6]

Huggins said, "I think I have the very strongest baseball team in the world."[7]

McGraw countered, "I think the Giants have one of the strongest pitching staffs seen in baseball this year. "The Giants are going to rely on their pitching, speed and their ability to take advantage of opportunities to win the series, and I am confident they are equal to the task."[8]

Asked about Ruth, McGraw declared he would take no liberties with the dangerous slugger, saying it would be foolish to give him a chance to win a game by pitching to him.

Prior to the opener, a rumor circulated that Huggins would start Baker at third base instead of Mike McNally. While Baker hadn't played in six weeks, Huggins wanted to get his left-handed bat into the lineup and take advantage of his World Series experience. And the veteran Baker knew how to handle the pressure of playing in the World Series more so than any of his teammates. The 28-year-old McNally, however, had played well filling in for Baker and he had become popular with fans.

The *New York Times* wrote that benching McNally would be an unpopular move. "McNally has played the position brilliantly for a number of weeks. Baker has slowed down considerably in the past two months and his hitting has been spasmodic and uncertain. On the other hand, McNally's speed has steadily increased and his batting has shown vast improvement and he has delivered a number of timely hits. He's a dangerous batter when a hit means one or more runs."[9]

McNally also had World Series experience, playing with the Red Sox in the 1916. Other Yankees with World Series experience included Ruth, Mays, Shawkey, and Schang. The Giants with World Series experience included George Burns, Dave Bancroft, Phil Douglas, Casey Stengel, and Harry "Slim" Sallee.

Baseball fever in New York reached a crescendo on Wednesday, October 5 when 30,203 fans attended the opening game of the World Series at the Polo Grounds. Although a record crowd was expected, many fans stayed away thinking they would not be able to purchase tickets. As a result, there were thousands of empty seats and hordes of fans second-guessing their decision to stay away. While empty seats existed at the Polo Grounds, 13,000 fans packed Times Square to watch the game being reproduced on the *New York Times* Star Ball Player board, which mechanically informed the crowd of every pitch and action. It was the largest crowd ever to assemble in Times Square.

Carl Mays, with his submarine-style delivery, faced off against right handed spitballer Shufflin' Phil Douglas. Baker found himself in an unusual position for a World Series—sitting on the bench—as McNally started at third base. The Yankees opened the scoring in the first on Ruth's RBI-single and added single runs in the fifth and sixth innings as Mays' unique delivery baffled the Giants as he posted a 3–0 victory. Frankie Frisch collected four of the Giants' five hits and Douglas limited the Yankees to five hits despite the loss. Much to the delight of Giants fans, he struck Ruth out twice.

Good pitching continued to dominate the series in Game 2 on Thursday, October 6 as Waite Hoyt of the Yankees battled Art Nehf of the Giants in front of 34,939 fans. The Yankees snapped a 0–0 tie in the fourth inning on a bases-loaded infield out. The Yankees added two runs in the eighth as they won 3–0.

The Yankees were up two games to none and they had not hit a home run. They had gotten superb pitching, made the most of their opportunities and played tight defense.

McGraw had been through too much during his career to concede anything to the Yankees. "The Giants are never licked until they have taken the full count. A lot of people had us counted out of the National League race when we were seven and a half games behind the Pirates. But we came back, didn't we?"[10]

McGraw didn't have to wait long for his club to turn the tide. They erupted for 20 hits and an eight-run seventh inning to win Game 3, 13–5, before 36,509 fans on Friday, October 7. The Yankees looked like they were headed for their third consecutive win when they scored four times in the third inning off Fred Toney. McGraw made a key move when he tabbed Jesse Barnes to relieve Toney after five batters in the third inning. Barnes held the Yankees to one run the rest of the way. The Giants bounced back with four runs in the bottom of the inning before turning the game into a route. With the game out of reach, Baker batted for pitcher Tom Rogers with one out in the ninth inning and flied out to Irish Meusel.

In three games, Frisch had stolen the spotlight from Ruth with seven hits in 10 at bats, three walks and two stolen bases. The Bambino had inflicted little damage with two hits in seven at bats, five walks and four strike outs.

Game 4 was postponed by rain and it gave the Yankees a break, providing Mays and Hoyt with another day of rest. It also gave Ruth a chance to recuperate from a swollen elbow, the result of opening an old wound caused by sliding into third base in the second game. He had arrived for Game 4 with his left arm in a sling after having the infected wound lanced. The doctor had to make an inch-long incision along the elbow in addition to lancing the wound. Ruth said his doctor had advised him against playing. The loss of Ruth would be a blow to the Yankees, but the slugger suggested his absence might actually aid the club. "The Giant pitchers may have the nerve to pitch to the man who replaces me," said he. "They wouldn't put a ball near my bat."[11]

Huggins announced Ruth would miss the rescheduled Game 4 on Sunday, October 9 at the Polo Grounds and perhaps the series. After the Yankees had taken fielding practice with Chick Fewster in left field, Ruth surprised the crowd of 36,372 as he trotted out to left field with a bandage on his left arm. The crowd gave him a standing ovation. Mays and Douglas matched up again as they had in the opener. Wally Schang's RBI-triple in the fifth inning staked the Yankees to a 1–0 lead through seven innings as Mays held the Giants to two singles. After 16 scoreless innings against Mays, the Giants figured him out in the eighth inning, tallying three runs. McGraw's club added an insurance run in the ninth. Ruth homered with one out in the bottom of the ninth as the Yankees dropped the game 4–2.

After the game, Ruth said, "I have realized one of my great ambitions—hitting a home run in the World Series. But I'm sorry it didn't come with men on the bases. It might have meant winning of the game."[12]

The Yankees rode Hoyt's right arm to the series lead in Game 5 on Monday, October 10 at the Polo Grounds. The Giants touched Hoyt for a run in the bottom of the first, but it would be their lone tally of the day. The Yankees tied the game in the third inning and went ahead in the fourth inning. Ruth, visibly limping from a charley horse in his leg, started the rally as he barely beat out a surprise bunt. Ruth, who should have been in the hospital, was playing on spirit and courage. He had both of his legs bandaged up to his hips, his left wrist which had been badly bruised by sliding into bases was bandaged, his knees ached, and the elbow incision was still open with a tube to drain the infection. Bob Meusel doubled to left and Ruth called on all of his speed to score. Grantland Rice described him as a "pachyderm running on greyhound legs."[13] Breathless, he slid across home plate with the go-ahead run, went into the dugout and collapsed. He insisted upon staying in the game, despite his condition. Meusel took third on an infield out and scored on Aaron Ward's sacrifice fly.

The Yankees' 3–1 win in front of a crowd of 35,758 was tempered as Ruth's physicians ordered him not to play in Game 6, and perhaps the rest of the Series, because of the threat of permanent injury to his arm. The doctors warned that playing could possibly spread the infection and necessitate another incision. It took a lot of convincing for Ruth, who had ignored doctors' advice many times in the past, to accept the decision.

Reflecting on Ruth's performance, Huggins said, "It was an exhibition of gameness that will go down through baseball history."[14] The Yankees' manager took Ruth's absence from the lineup philosophically, saying injuries were part of the game. He figured the Yankees would play even harder without Ruth in the lineup.

Harry Harper of the Yankees and Fred Toney of the Giants started Game 6 on Tuesday, October 11, but neither was around very long. The Yankees scored three runs in the first inning before Barnes relieved Toney with two outs. The Giants tied it in the second inning on Irish Meusel's two-run homer and Frank Snyder's solo shot. In the bottom of the inning, Fewster picked on one of Barnes's few fastballs of the day and deposited it over the left field fence following Shawkey's single to give the Yankees a 5–3 lead. It marked the first time three home runs had been hit in a Series game. The Giants, however, weren't finished. They rallied for four runs in the top of the fourth inning. Barnes, considered a fading veteran, was in control the rest of the way as he fanned 10 Yankees with a baffling curve in the final seven innings and limited them to two hits.

With two outs in the eighth inning and a runner on first, Baker came in to pinch hit for Shawkey. The crowd of 34,283 held little hope that the veteran could send one out of the park to close the gap. An "almost stony silence"[15] greeted him as the crowd gave him only scattered applause when he stepped to the plate. Baker had no more luck than the rest of the Yankees in figuring out Barnes as he grounded weakly to Johnny Rawlings at second base. The Giants won 8–5, marking the third time in the Series they had come from behind. Ruth watched from the stands with his swollen arm in a sling.

With the series tied, 3–3, McGraw held the advantage, particularly if Ruth could not play. The Giants believed they would beat Mays in Game 7 and Hoyt, who would have to pitch on two days rest, in Game 8.

Mays and Douglas matched up for the third time in Game 7 on Wednesday, October 12 as 36,503 fans looked on and another 15,000 were turned away. The Yankees got on the board first in the second inning and the Giants tied it in the fourth.

The Giants notched the winning run in the seventh as Johnny Rawlings reached first on Ward's error with two outs. Ward, whose error in the second inning set up the Giants' first run, muffed a routine grounder, setting the stage for Snyder's RBI double to left.

Douglas shackled the Yankees to earn the 2–1 win. After Peckinpaugh singled with one out in the third inning, he retired 13 consecutive hitters until Baker singled in the seventh inning. Baker entered the game in the third inning after McNally hurt his right arm sliding into second base in the second inning. He walked toward the bench with his right arm hanging limply by his side. His shoulder ligaments had been torn. McNally tested his arm in practice before the inning started and it was apparent he was in pain. He signaled to Huggins, however, that he was okay to play. In the bottom of the second with one out, McNally made a low and wild throw to Pipp at first base on Emil Meusel's sharp shot between shortstop and third base. Pipp managed to get the throw with a one-hand stab to beat the runner by a step. On the next play, he painfully threw out Rawlings.

With Ruth out of the lineup, the rest of the Yankee hitters had been ineffective. In the ninth, Baker came to the plate as the club's last hope with two outs. He singled sharply past Kelly at first and drew loud applause on his way to first base, but was stranded as Schang grounded out.

"If the Giants aren't world champions by sundown tomorrow, I'll be disappointed,"[16] said McGraw, who had watched his club come back for the fourth time in the series.

All of the Yankees hopes now fell on 22-year-old Hoyt, who had held the Giants to one unearned run in 18 innings. Mays opposed Nehf for the third time in Game 8 on Thursday, October 13. It turned out to be one of the closest, hardest fought and most dramatic Series-deciding games ever.

Baker started at third base in place of McNally. In the first inning, Bancroft and Youngs walked. With two outs, Kelly's hard grounder rolled through Peckinpaugh's legs, allowing Bancroft to score.

Trailing 1–0 in the bottom of the ninth, the beaten and battered Ruth pinch hit for Pipp. His physical ailments were well documented and every fan knew that each swing of the bat was painful to the slugger. They knew he was playing on heart and they cheered his courage. Ruth swung at the first pitch and missed. The second pitch was called a strike and the third a ball. He swung at the next inside pitch and hit it on the handle of the bat sending a slow roller to Kelly, who easily stepped on first for the out. Ruth drew another warm ovation for his effort as he disappointedly headed toward the dugout.

Ward coaxed a base on balls from Nehf. Baker walked slowly to the plate and Nehf worked him carefully. Catcher Frank Snyder turned frequently to McGraw in the dugout to make sure they were handling Baker properly. Nehf and Baker battled each other to a 2–1 count before Baker fouled off a pitch to even the count 2–2. Nehf was willing to walk Baker, throwing the next couple pitches way inside. But, the seasoned veteran refused to accept the generosity. He wanted to capitalize on the chance to tie or win the game. Swinging with all of his might, he fouled off the next pitch and the following pitch was ball three. With a full count, Ward dashed for second but had to come back as Baker fouled off the pitch. Again, Ward darted for second as Nehf released the pitch. This time Baker connected solidly, sending a rocket shot to toward second base that looked like a sure hit. W.J. Macbeth from the *New York Tribune* described the play: "(Second baseman) Rawlings rushed over and threw himself at the grounder after the fashion of a football tackle. He smothered the ball in his glove, clutched it, rolled over a couple of times and came up in time to make a saving play at first." Macbeth called Rawlings' play "one in a million."[17]

Kelly saw Ward racing to third and threw a strong, perfect strike to Frisch. Ward slid, sending up a cloud of dust, and Frisch threw himself into Ward's path, blocking the bag. With both players sprawled on the ground, Frisch raised his hand to show a glistening white ball. Umpire Ernie Quigley signaled Ward out and the Series was over in dramatic fashion. Nehf had pitched a four-hit, 1–0 shutout.

It was undoubtedly the play of the Series. If Rawlings had missed the ball, runners would have been on first and third with one out and the dangerous Schang at bat. Rawlings was the unsung hero of the Series, fielding 47 chances flawlessly and collecting 10 hits in 30 at bats.

Thousands of Giants fans swarmed the field, hoping to get to McGraw

Frank "Home Run" Baker, home run king of the Dead Ball era, and Babe Ruth, who revolutionized the game in the early 1920s, teamed up on the 1921 and 1922 New York Yankees. Baker and Ruth walloped home runs in the same game on four occasions in 1921. Baker said, "Ruth can hit the ball farther than anyone I ever saw. He has everybody hopelessly outclassed, including myself." In their two seasons as teammates, Ruth smashed 94 home runs and the often-injured Baker clubbed 16. Baker earned $16,000 a year in 1922, second highest on the club to Ruth's $52,000 a year. NATIONAL BASEBALL HALL OF FAME LIBRARY, COOPERSTOWN, NY.

before he entered the clubhouse. McGraw was escorted through the crowd as fans tried to touch him, shake his hand, or offer congratulations. The "Little Napoleon" couldn't suppress his joy and satisfaction after 16 years between World Championships. The Giants wildly celebrated a hard-fought series victory.

There was no joy, however, in the Yankees' locker room. Jack Lawrence of the *New York Tribune* described the scene: "In the Yankees' stuffy little locker room, Ruth, Peckinpaugh and Baker approached Hoyt, who was sitting on a little bench dressing. They extended their hands to congratulate him on one of the most glorious defeats. Hoyt took it with a smile, but when Col. Huston, half owner of the club, strode through the sweating group of players and, looking over his glasses, offered a silent hand, the defeated pitcher broke down. The two men clasped hands and tears flowed down Hoyt's cheeks while Huston's eyes moistened. Huston didn't say anything. It wasn't necessary. The words in his eyes and handclasp were probably worth a winner's share of the series money to Hoyt."[18]

"Everything considered, this was the greatest world series of all-time," beamed McGraw. "We won because we were the better team."[19]

"This is one of the happiest moments of my life and I am indeed proud to be the manager of the new champions," he added. "We won the Series by outplaying the Yankees. We outhit, outpitched, and outshone them in the field."[20]

Huggins said, "It was a wonderful Series and it would have been a great one to win, but we lost it and have no alibi to offer. When teams are even after six games and the final two games end 2–1 and 1–0, there is no need for excuses."[21]

It was indeed one of the hardest fought Series ever. Of course, Yankee fans could only wonder what the outcome would have been if Ruth hadn't missed the final three games. Without Ruth to worry about, Giant pitchers handled Murderers' Row like a Sunday school class. They drove in just one run in the final 25 innings.

"Leading the series at the time Ruth left the lineup, the Yankees became a slow, heavy-footed club with its morale in the dust,"[22] wrote the *New York Tribune*.

The Yankees, who had played outstanding defense the first five games, were victims of crucial errors in the final two games. Unfortunately, Huggins only had two dependable pitchers in Mays and Hoyt, who limited the Giants to 38 hits in 52 hits. The rest of the Yankee hurlers gave up 33 hits in 19 innings. Hoyt pitched 27 innings without giving up an earned run. With a break here or there, Hoyt and Mays each had a chance to win three games, but they didn't get any support the final two games. The Giants got off to a slow start, but never gave up. Nehf and Douglas turned in three impressive outings while Barnes was the surprise of the series.

The Giants held the Yankees to 22 runs and a .207 batting average. Ruth batted .313 with five hits in 16 at bats while Wally Schang hit .286 with six hits in 21 at bats. Baker finished two for eight for a .250 average. Despite the efforts of Mays and Hoyt, the Giants batted .269 with five starters batting over .300: Snyder (.364), Meusel (.345), Burns (.333), Rawlings (.333) and Frisch (.300). Nehf, Barnes, and Douglas surrendered just 13 earned runs in 68 innings.

The 1921 Series was the last of the best-of-nine format. It set new financial and attendance records, despite the final game attracting the smallest crowd of the series (25,410). The eight games drew more than 269,900 fans. With more than $900,000 in revenue, the players shared a record purse. The Giants each received $5,200 while the Yankees collected $3,400 each.

FOURTEEN

The Final Season

Frank Baker signed his final contract with the Yankees on February 9, 1922, for an estimated $16,000. At age 36, he was by far the oldest player on the team but Huggins still had great confidence in him. He planned to start him at third base, despite critics who felt he was well beyond his prime.

A number of other Yankees remained unsigned, including Babe Ruth, Carl Mays, Waite Hoyt, Wally Pipp, Bob Meusel, Mike McNally and Aaron Ward. The Yankees' first World Series appearance had fueled higher salary demands and possible holdouts. Yankees co-owner Col. Ruppert termed some of the salary requests as "fabulous, almost beyond belief."[1] After some negotiating, Ruth signed to a five-year contract calling for $52,000 a year, an unheard of amount. But, of course, Ruth was worth it. Eventually, the other Yankees were signed, too.

The Yankees would be without the services of Ruth and Meusel for the first six weeks of the 1922 season because the pair had been suspended by baseball commissioner Judge Landis for participating in a barnstorming tour following the 1921 World Series. They had also been fined $3,362, the equivalent of their World Series share and they would lose their salary during their suspension.

Landis had warned Ruth there would be a severe penalty if he violated the 1912 rule prohibiting members of the World Series teams from playing postseason exhibition games. Ruth, who had made a lucrative income in past years from barnstorming, ignored Landis's warning and played games in Buffalo, Jamestown and Elmira before cutting short his tour at the request of Yankees owner Col. Huston.

Although the Yankees undoubtedly had the talent to repeat as American League champions, the big question was: Could they stay in the race for the first six weeks without Ruth and Meusel? They had lost two-thirds of their outfield and their top power hitters. One of Huggins's challenges in spring training was to try to find replacements for the suspended duo. Chick Fewster was expected to play left field while newcomers Norm McMillan and Camp Skinner were right field possibilities.

The Yankees had strengthened their pitching staff in the off-season by acquiring Sad Sam Jones, a 23-game winner, Bullet Joe Bush, a 16-game winner, and shortstop Everett Scott from the Boston Red Sox. In exchange, New York sent shortstop Roger Peckinpaugh and pitchers Jack Quinn, Rip Collins, and Bill Piercy to the Red Sox.

Ruth and Meusel were allowed to practice with the club in spring training, participate in exhibition games, and attend morning practices during the regular season. But they had to be out of uniform by the afternoon.

Huggins had more problems than just figuring out who would start. Success was taking its toll as players resisted authority and discipline. In April, the little manager fined Mays $200 for throwing the ball over the grandstand in an exhibition game at Little Rock, Arkansas, after Huggins had taken him out in the middle of an inning. Huggins and Mays got into a heated argument later on the train ride from Memphis to Bristol, Tennessee. Huggins and Hoyt also battled over discipline.

The *New York Times* wrote, "Huggins is suffering from an oversupply of high-salaried and temperamental stars who have a bump of ego too big to be reduced in a few weeks. They take authority lightly, do their playing as they think best and refuse to take seriously the exhibition games with Brooklyn."[2]

Baker, however, was one player Huggins didn't have to worry about. He went about his business professionally and enjoyed one of his best springs ever with the bat. In the field, however, he appeared slow and rumor was that his legs were shot. Two days before the season opener against Washington, however, he put on an impressive show against Brooklyn in the final exhibition game. He handled several difficult chances at third base, homered, rapped two singles, stole a base and scored a couple of runs.

The Yankees lost the season opener 6–5 to the Senators in Washington, with President Warren Harding and Babe Ruth as spectators. Ruth sat in the stands with Col. Huston and American League President Ban Johnson, just behind the Yankees' bench.

Baker got off to his customary slow start, batting under .200 for the first two weeks of the season and Huggins considered taking him out of the lineup, but the wise manager knew from experience that the slugger was seldom impressive early in the season. The Yankees raced out to first place, fashioning an 11–3 record. Baker blasted his first home run of the season, a two-run shot off right-hander Rollie Naylor of the Athletics, on April 25 and unloaded his second, a solo effort off former teammate Jack Quinn, a 38-year-old Red Sox right-hander, on April 29. His second homer, however, was overshadowed as Hoyt and Huggins came to blows after the 5–2 loss to the Red Sox in 14 innings. With two runners on and one out in the fourteenth inning, Huggins ordered Hoyt to walk Elmer Smith, a dangerous hitter. Hoyt preferred to pitch to him, but was over-ruled. Before the inning was finished, Hoyt had surrendered three runs.

Baker drilled five singles against Boston on May 2 en route to put-ting together a 12-game hit streak and Huggins moved him from third to fourth in the lineup. His bat stayed hot as he belted home runs on succes-sive days, May 8 and 9, against White Sox hurlers Dixie Leverett and Jose Acosta, a pair of right-handers, at the Polo Grounds.

Huggins served a two-game suspension on May 5 and 6 for contest-ing calls of umpire Ed Walsh. The veteran Baker, who was respected by his teammates, took over running the team. New York beat the Athletics both games with the third baseman at the helm.

By mid–May, Baker had lifted his average over .300 and was in the midst of one of the hottest home run streaks of his career. He pounded number 5 on May 17 against Cleveland's Dave Keefe and added number 6 against the Indians' Jim Bagby two days later.

His long-distance hitting was entertaining fans in Ruth's absence. Ruth's return was just days away and fans were clamoring for tickets to his first game on Saturday, May 20. Only World Series tickets were more sought after and a capacity crowd was expected to greet Ruth and Meusel. In their absence, the Yankees had gone 22–11 and were in first place, two games ahead of the St. Louis Browns.

Ruth's return was disappointing as he failed to get the ball out of the infield in four at bats and the Yankees managed just three hits off the Browns' Urban Shocker in an 8–2 loss before 38,000 fans. The Browns scored seven runs with two outs in the ninth inning, including Baby Doll Jacobson's grand slam. The following day, 40,000 fans cheered Ruth as he slashed his first hit, a double in the fifth inning of a 6–5 win over the Browns.

Fans grew impatient quickly with the Babe as he went hitless in his first three at bats in his third game. He was booed for his failures at the plate and cheered derisively twice when he made routine catches in the outfield. Ruth responded with a sarcastic tip of the hat. The Yankees slugger, however, turned the tide of fan sentiment in the eighth inning when he blasted an Elam Van Gilder pitch between the upper tier and the roof. Despite the enthusiastic applause, Babe refused to tip his hat or acknowledge the crowd. The Yankees went on to win the game 4–3, in 13 innings.

Baker slammed his fifth home run of the month off right-hander Urban Shocker on May 23 in an 11–3 loss to the Browns. He also registered a triple and a single. It marked the first time he had walloped five homers in a month since June 1912. With seven home runs in 37 games, he was on pace to hit 28. He had never hit so many home runs so early and only one of them had come batting behind Ruth. He had never tallied more than four home runs by the end of May. In 1921, when he slugged nine, he didn't register his first one until June 9. He attributed part of his increased home run production to the livelier ball.

The fans were still riding Ruth, who was batting .093, when he was involved with an ugly incident with an umpire and a fan on May 25. In the third inning of a game against Washington at the Polo Grounds, Babe tried to stretch a single into a double and was thrown out at second base by Sam Rice. When umpire George Hildebrand signaled him out, the incensed Ruth jumped up, grabbed a handful of dirt and threw it in Hildebrand's direction. The umpire immediately ejected him. As he walked back to the dugout, the crowd jeered and booed the star. Babe responded with his now typical sarcastic tip of the hat. One of the fans sitting behind the dugout yelled something at Ruth that he took offense to. He quickly bounded onto the dugout and went into the stands, chasing the heckler, who fortunately escaped. He later apologized for his actions toward the umpire, but refused to say he was sorry for going after the fan.

Ban Johnson went easy on the Babe, suspending him for a game and fining him $200. Ruth was also demoted from captain of the Yankees, a position he had held for just six games. The leniency, however, didn't change his behavior. The slugger was suspended again in June and September for his behavior and abusive language.

The Yankees were leading the second-place St. Louis Browns by two and a half games when they arrived in St. Louis for a crucial four-game series on June 10. The Browns had the hardest-hitting team in the American League, finishing the season with a .313 mark and a .455 slugging average. First baseman George Sisler won the batting title with a .420 average and stole a league-high 51 bases. Outfielder Ken Williams led the league in home runs (39) and runs batted in (155). Second baseman Marty McManus and outfielder William "Baby Doll" Jacobson joined Sisler and Williams with 100-plus RBIs. The Yankees, in contrast, had no player drive in 100 runs. Former Yankee Urban Shocker, a 24-game winner, led the underrated Browns' pitching staff that produced the lowest ERA in the league.

St. Louis fans, unaccustomed to a talented Browns team, turned out in force for the opening game of the series at Sportsman's Park. The grandstands were packed an hour before game time and two rows of temporary seats were installed in front of each pavilion. More than 22,000 fans were on hand for what promised to be an exciting game between bitter rivals. The challenge of stopping the potent batting lineups went to Shocker and Mays.

The Browns plated two runs in the bottom of the first, but the Yankees tied it in the top of the second on Wally Pipp's two-run homer. Things turned ugly in the third inning when New York erupted for six runs. Babe snapped the tie with a long, two-run homer over the right field fence. This upset Shocker, who retaliated against Baker, hitting him on the right side of his ribs with the next pitch. Baker, obviously in pain, slowly made his way to first base. Meusel followed with a double and Baker scored as Jacobson mishandled the ball in the outfield and Meusel sauntered into third. Pipp singled home the fourth run of the inning. Everett Scott grounded to Wally Gerber at shortstop who threw wildly to second and Marty McManus committed another throwing error when he recovered the ball, allowing Pipp to score and Scott to reach third. Al Devormer's long sacrifice fly chased home the sixth run of the inning.

Mays, always a subject of heckling by fans and hated by many opposing players, taunted the Browns' hurler as he stepped into the batter's box. Shocker's first pitch was high and inside, forcing Mays to duck to avoid being hit in the head. The second pitch was almost a duplicate of the first, knocking Mays to the ground. He got up, dusted off his uniform and yelled at Shocker, who stood on the mound and nodded his head. Shocker wound up slowly for the third pitch. Again the ball sailed toward Mays, high and inside. It curved in and down at the last moment, barely missing Mays's jaw. The third time was too much for the fiery Mays. He charged to the mound with his bat behind him as he and Shocker yelled at each other. It appeared as if a fight was ready to break out, but umpire Billy Evans stepped between them and shoved them apart. By that time, the ballpark police had arrived. With the matter quelled, Mays stepped back into the box and drew a walk on the fourth pitch, which was a slow ball, high and inside.

Tension was still in the air when Whitey Witt stepped in to the batter's box. Shocker's first pitch was again high and inside, sending Witt to the dirt. The New York outfielder scrambled to his feet and rushed toward Shocker. Again, umpire Evans and the police intervened to prevent a fight.

McNally replaced Baker at third base to start the bottom of the third inning with the Yankees holding a commanding 8–2 lead. Bill Bayne relieved Shocker in the fourth inning and Huggins's men went on to win 14–5. Later that night, Baker was taken to a St. Louis hospital, where he was examined and X rays initially revealed no fractured ribs. He was expected to miss several games.

Baker, however, was back in the lineup the following day as the Browns started Shocker again. Shocker had pleaded with Manager Lee Fohl for another shot at the Yankees after his abbreviated start. More than 25,000 fans packed the ballpark and flowed onto the field. Baker played four and a half innings before being replaced by McNally. Despite his injury, he doubled in three at bats, scored a run and threw out two runners. This time, Shocker lasted seven innings, but the Yankees won 8–4.

The Browns rebounded to take the next two games from the Yankees 7–1 and 13–4 as Baker remained out of the lineup. He returned to third base June 14 as New York opened a four-game series at Detroit. The Tigers swept the Yankees as Baker singled in each of the first three games, but sat out the fourth game on June 17 as Huggins moved Ward to third base and McNally to second.

The *New York Tribune* wrote, "The move has been expected for some time. Baker is hitting well enough, but his fielding has been so poor during the last five days that Huggins had no alternative. Baker was letting more balls go through him than he could hope to hit through the enemy."[3]

Baker missed the next 26 games until he pinch hit against the Tigers on July 20. The Yankees suffered through their worst losing streak of the season, losing 13 of 16 games from June 12 through June 28 with Baker, Ruth, and Schang out of the lineup at times and their pitching staff faltering. New York fell out of first place and trailed St. Louis by three games on June 28.

The Yankees got back on the winning track in July, but couldn't close the gap between them and the Browns. Looking for help, New York pulled off a controversial trade with the Boston Red Sox, their favorite patsies. New York acquired third baseman Jumping Joe Dugan and outfielder Elmer Smith for outfielder Chick Fewster, outfielder Elmer Miller, seldom used shortstop Johnny Mitchell, a player to be named later, and $50,000. It was a lopsided deal that outraged the Yankees' opponents.

Boston had acquired both 25-year-old Dugan and 29-year-old Smith at the start of the 1922 season. Dugan, hitting .287, was considered the best third baseman in the American League. His acquisition pushed McNally off of third base and into a reserve role. It also sent the message that Baker's career as a starter for the Yankees was finished.

Ban Johnson called the trade regrettable and said midseason trades must be discouraged. He said the public viewed any deal between the Red Sox and Yankees with aversion and apprehension. The St. Louis Browns protested the trade of Dugan and the impact it would have on the pennant race. In response, Commissioner Judge Landis established a June 15 deadline for future trades.

Indians manager Tris Speaker said, "It's a crime. Dugan and Smith are each worth $10,000 or more and the entire bunch of New York players traded is not worth $10,000."[4] Speaker said the Indians had twice tried to get Smith back, but each time Red Sox owner Harry Frazee had imposed exorbitant terms.

White Sox manager Kid Gleason wasn't any happier. "I tried to make a deal for Dugan, but was told there was nothing doing."[5] The *Boston Post* reported that the White Sox had supposedly made an offer for Dugan in spring training, an offer that Frazee had said was more than he had gotten for Ruth. The paper wondered how Frazee could now trade Dugan and Smith even up for three or four Yankees without any money considerations. Frazee denied he received $50,000 to $75,000 from the Yankees as part of the trade.

The *Boston Herald* termed the deal "another disgusting trade between the Red Sox and Yankees. It added that "Frazee has tightened his grip on the title 'The Champion Wrecker of the Baseball Age.'"[6]

Despite being in the thick of the pennant race, the Yankees were still an undisciplined team. Two days before they acquired Dugan, the *New York Times* reported an incident where Huggins, coaching at third base, signaled to the bullpen for an inning to have someone start to warm up. His signals were ignored as the players had other things on their minds.

The Yankees beat the Browns three out of four games in St. Louis in late July and trailed the Browns by one-half game when the Midwesterners came to the Polo Grounds for a four-game series in late August. Ken Williams was riding a 28-game hit streak and George Sisler had a 22-game hit streak.

More than 38,000 fans attended a doubleheader on August 25 as the Browns won the opener 3–1 behind Shocker, and the Yankees took the second game 6–5, as Bush won his 21st game. Hoyt ended Williams's streak at 28 games in the opener, but Sisler extended his streak to 24. The Yankees took over the American League lead with a 9–2 win behind Carl Mays and they stretched it to one and a half games when Shawkey topped Shocker 2–1 in 11 innings on Bob Meusel's sacrifice fly in the eleventh inning.

The Yankees carried a slim one-half game lead when they traveled to St. Louis for the biggest series of the year, September 16–18. A record 30,000 fans from nearly every part of the Midwest filled every available space in Sportsman's Park for the opener. The Yankees opened a 2–0 lead on Scott's RBI-single in the second and Pipp drove in the second run with a sacrifice fly. Eddie Foster's RBI-single in the sixth plated the Browns' only run. George Sisler doubled in the fourth inning to tie Cobb's record of hitting in 40 consecutive games. In the ninth, Meusel and Witt were racing toward a fly ball when a fan threw a soda bottle and hit Witt in the forehead, knocking him unconscious.

It was all Browns the following day as 21-year-old rookie southpaw Hubert "Hub" Pruett scattered five New York hits, including a solo homer to Ruth, en route to a 5–1 win before 31,000 fans. Pruett fanned seven, including Babe, who he had struck out 10 times in 14 at bats before allowing the home run. Browns highlights included Sisler's single in the sixth inning, stretching his hitting streak to 41 games, which stood until Joe DiMaggio broke it in 1941, and Ken Williams's 38th home run in the eighth inning.

The third game on September 18 was probably the biggest of the year since it was the last time the two clubs faced each other and first place was still at stake. Fittingly, another attendance record was broken as 32,000 frenzied fans witnessed the game pitting Frank "Dixie" Davis against Joe Bush. St. Louis staked a 2–0 lead going into the eighth inning when the Yankees scored their first run.

In the ninth, Schang singled off Davis's glove and went to second on a passed ball. Pruett relieved Davis and McNally pinch hit for Ward. McNally bunted and catcher Hank Severeid threw too late to third to get Schang. Scott walked to load the bases and Browns' manager Lee Fohl signaled for Shocker out of the bullpen. Bush grounded to McManus at second, who threw home to force Schang. Witt delivered in the clutch, lacing a sharp single to center to score two runs.

Trailing 3–2, the Browns had their top hitters due to the plate — Sisler, Williams, and Jacobson. Bush retired them easily as neither one got a ball out of the infield. New York left St. Louis with a one and a half game lead. The Browns lost the next three games to Washington as Sisler was sidelined with an injured shoulder. New York faltered down the stretch, however, losing four of its last five games. With two games remaining, the club faced the possibility of ending the season in a tie with the Browns. The Yankees clinched the pennant with a 3–1 win over Boston on September 30, edging out St. Louis by one game.

Despite playing only 110 games, Ruth pounded 35 home runs, third best in the league, drove in 99 runs and batted .315. His slugging average

of .672 was tops in the league. Pipp drove in 90 runs and batted .329 while
Meusel and Schang also hit over .300. Baker, limited to eight unsuccessful pinch hitting appearances after June 16, appeared in just 69 games and
hit .276. His sensational start to the season had long been forgotten and
1922 was a "what might have been" year.

Bush paced the pitchers with a 26–7 mark, Shawkey went 20–12 and
Hoyt added 19 wins. Sam Jones and Mays were disappointments with 13–13
and 12–14 records.

For the second year in a row, the Yankees faced the New York Giants
in the World Series. McGraw's club had dominated the National League
and won the pennant by seven games over the Cincinnati Reds. The Giants
batted .304, second to the Pittsburgh Pirates, and every starter with the
exception of third baseman Heinie Groh hit over .300. Irish Meusel and
George Kelly drove in 132 and 107 runs while hitting .331 and .328, respectively. Thirty-one-year-old Casey Stengel, platooning in the outfield with
Bill Cunningham, batted 368. Frankie Frisch (.327), Dave Bancroft (.321)
and Frank Snyder (.343) rounded out the most balanced hitting attack in
the majors.

The Giants pitching staff, led by Art Nehf (19–13), compiled the lowest ERA in the league. McGraw got a surprising 17 wins from 24-year-old
rookie Wilfred "Rosy" Ryan and double figure wins from Phil Douglas
and Jesse Barnes. Douglas, however, had been released in mid–August
after the hard drinker wrote a letter to a former teammate saying he didn't
want to see McGraw win the pennant and that with some inducement he
could be a factor in preventing it. Jack Scott, signed in midseason after he
had been released by the Reds, went 8–2 down the stretch, and Hugh
McQuillan was 6–5.

The Yankees entered the World Series as 7–5 favorites. Based on the
closeness of the 1921 World Series, many observers felt the Yankees, with
the addition of Bullet Joe Bush, Sad Sam Jones, Whitey Witt, Everett Scott
and Joe Dugan, were more improved than the Giants. Plus, the Yankees
wouldn't have to play without Ruth as they had in 1921. This time around,
it seemed Huggins' crew had the clear advantage in pitching as they had a
number of dependable starters.

New York Tribune sportswriter Grantland Rice rated winning the 1922
World Series "the hardest assignment of McGraw's long and conquering
career."[7] Never had McGraw, winner of eight pennants, faced a Series with
so much uncertain pitching nor with finer pitching to beat, pointed out
Rice. The 1922 World Series also was the first to be broadcast on radio.
Rice announced Game 1 to an estimated audience of 1.5 million in a
300-mile radius from New York City and to ships at sea.

Both managers went with their aces in the opener on Wednesday, October 4, as Bullet Joe Bush opposed Art Nehf in front of 36,514 at the Polo Grounds. The Yankees missed a chance to score in the fifth when center field Ross Youngs made a sliding, somersault catch of Everett Scott's sinking liner with runners on first and second. Youngs threw to second to complete the double play.

The Yankees initiated the scoring in the sixth as Ruth poked a two-strike slow curve ball into right field for a solo homer. The Yankees added one more run in the seventh for a 2–0 lead. Bush, who had been fooling the Giants on fork balls and change of pace pitches, lost his effectiveness in the bottom of the eighth inning. The Giants loaded the bases with three consecutive singles and Irish Meusel tied the game with a two-run single. That was the cue for Huggins to lift Bush and bring in Hoyt. Youngs greeted Hoyt with a sacrifice fly to center to score the winning run. The come-from-behind 3–2 effort in the opener increased the Giants' confidence.

Game 2 on Thursday, October 5, ended in a 3–3 tie after 10 innings and was controversial because the umpires called it on the account of darkness at 4:40 p.m. while there was still at least a half hour of daylight remaining. The Yankees ran out on the field to start the top of the eleventh inning, but umpire-in-chief George Hildebrand surprisingly announced that the game had been called. The bewildered and upset crowd of 37,020 responded with boos and catcalls. Five thousand fans surrounded Landis's field box and besieged him with cries of protest and outrage. Some fans suggested the game had been called to give the owners another big payday. Landis, who had no say in calling the game, and his wife had to be escorted from the Polo Grounds by police as fans threw folded newspapers at him. Angry and perturbed by these charges, Landis declared that night that all receipts from Game 2, more than $120,000, would be donated to New York-area charities.

The tie game wasted strong efforts by Shawkey and Barnes, presenting a bigger problem for McGraw, who now had to go with his unproven pitchers. McGraw tabbed Jack Scott to go against Waite Hoyt on Friday, October 6. Not many people gave Scott much of a chance against Hoyt, the Yankees' pitching hero of the 1921 Series. The six-foot-two, North Carolinian had been cast off by the Reds because of a sore shoulder after doctors declared he would never pitch again. Looking for work, he sought out McGraw and asked for a chance to practice with the team. McGraw, figuring he had nothing to lose, gave him a uniform and $50 to hold him over. Scott's arm returned to its old form and he proved valuable down the stretch. The 30-year-old completed his rags-to-riches story as he shut the Yankees down on four scattered hits en route to a 3–0 victory. With the Yankees trailing by three runs in the eighth inning, Baker batted for Hoyt to lead off the inning and grounded to first base.

McGraw was forced to go with McQuillan, a six-game winner, on Saturday, October 7, as the Yankees countered with Mays, one of the toughest pitchers in the American League. The Yankees looked like they were about to reverse their losing trend with two runs in the first inning on singles by Witt, Dugan, Pipp, and Bob Meusel. But a series of base-running blunders by Bob Meusel and Wally Schang proved to be the Yankees' downfall as the Giants' rookie settled down, surrendering just four hits and one run the rest of the way to post a 4–3 victory.

The *New York Times* wrote that the Yankees had reached their lowest ebb and critiqued their play as "the sorriest spectacle in recent World Series history. They went misfortune one better and dug their own grave with as stupid baseball any ball field will ever see."[8]

Few teams had ever been as heavily favored as the Yankees to win the World Series. And few had ever been in a direr situation, down three games to none. Huggins called on Bush to stop the surging Giants while McGraw tabbed Nehf to try and wrap up the series on Sunday, October 8.

The Yankees got on the board early, touching Nehf for a run in the first inning, but the Giants answered with two in the bottom of the second. The Yankees tied the game in the fifth and grabbed a 3–2 lead in the seventh. With two outs in the bottom of the eighth inning and Giant runners on second and third, Ross Youngs stepped to the plate. Huggins signaled from the Yankees' dugout for Bush to walk the left-handed hitter to get to George Kelly, a right-handed hitter. Bush violently disagreed, throwing his hands in the air in disgust and yelling, "Let's play baseball." After 11 years in the majors, Bush felt he should be able to make the decision who he wanted to pitch to. Huggins was going with the percentages of having the right-handed Bush face the right-handed Kelly. Plus, Kelly had been in a slump and Youngs hadn't. Bush, however, had handled Youngs easily in the opening game while Kelly had gotten two hits off of him. He preferred to pitch to Youngs with first base open, hoping to get him to chase a bad ball. And, if his strategy failed and he walked Youngs, he would pitch to Kelly with bases loaded. Kelly foiled Huggins' strategy, drilling Bush's second pitch for a two-run single. Lee King followed with a RBI-single, making it 5–3.

As the Giants took the field in the top of the ninth inning, the fans gave them an appreciative applause, recognizing their gameness. For the third time in the Series, the Giants had come from behind, making it seven come-from-behind wins in nine World Series triumphs against their city rivals. The Yankees went quickly and quietly in the ninth as Nehf retired them in order.

Against great odds, McGraw had not only beaten the heavily favored Yankees, he had embarrassed them with four straight victories despite incredibly weak pitching. It was the greatest feat of his career. Thousands of fans swarmed onto the field, all seemingly wanting to congratulate McGraw, shake his hand, pat his back or give him a kiss. It was a reception the likes of which New York had never seen.

McGraw's pitchers had once again turned the Yankees' Murderers' Row into a bunch of choirboys, this time with Ruth in the lineup at every game. The Yankees hit just .203 while the Giants batted .309. Babe was the biggest embarrassment, batting just .118 with two hits, a single and a double, one RBI, in 17 at bats.

Recounting Ruth's effort in the final game, the *New York Times* wrote, "Ruth plumbed the depths of ineptness. He swung at pitches he couldn't have reached with an oar."[9] McGraw had instructed his hurlers to feed Babe a steady diet of low, slow curve balls throughout the five games. The series was the Bambino's lowest point of his career. Despite his past achievements, his critics wondered if the Yankees had been wise to give him such a lucrative three-year contract.

"The nightmare is over," wrote Waite Hoyt in his syndicated column. "The Giants are a better club."[10]

After the game, Col. Huston and his partner Ruppert argued over Huggins's fate. Huston insisted that Huggins had managed his last game. Ruppert thought it was unfair to fire him after he had won two consecutive pennants. Meanwhile rumors circulated about Huggins's fate and that of many of the Yankees. Reports had Eddie Collins of the White Sox, among others, in line to manage the club. Many argued the Yankees needed a manager who could bring discipline to the club. Former Yankees manager Frank Chance suggested the team needed a bruising manager who could convey his ideas with his fists as well as his tongue. Speculation was that players who had given Huggins a lot of trouble would be traded. Ruppert said the Yankees would trade any man on the team, if they would improve the club — and that went for Babe Ruth. Others rumored to be on the trading block were Carl Mays, Aaron Ward, Waite Hoyt, and Bob Meusel. Huston and Ruppert squelched the speculation about Huggins by signing him to a one-year contract within a week after the series. During the winter, Ruppert bought out Huston and became the team's sole owner.

The Yankees had hoped to move into their new home, Yankee Stadium, in 1923 with a World Championship, but they would start empty handed. They were ready to embark on a new era, one that would produce many World Series titles and soon make fans forget about their embarrassing loss to the Giants in 1922.

FIFTEEN

Retirement

Baker returned home to Trappe following the World Series to manage his farms and hunt ducks and geese with his longtime friends and neighbors. The Yankees sent him a contract in the winter for the 1923 season and he was flattered Huggins wanted him back for another season. If he returned, he would probably be used mainly as a pinchhitter and occasional replacement for Joe Dugan at third base. The thought of playing in another World Series and in the new Yankee Stadium was appealing, but he was convinced this was the right time to retire. A series of injuries during the past two seasons had kept him on the sidelines for nearly 50 percent of the games. He had married Margaret Mitchell on August 16, 1922, and they were expecting a baby. After years of traveling on trains, staying in hotels, being separated from his family, and battling the day-to-day grind of the major league season, he was eager to stay home.

He informed the Yankees of his decision in February after expressing an interest in possibly playing for one of the teams in the fledging Class D Eastern Shore Baseball League, which was formed in 1922. The *Easton Star-Democrat* quickly encouraged Eastern Shore League club owners to rush to Trappe and sign Baker for the 1923 season. "Baker would be an attraction all over the Peninsula; his presence on any club would strengthen the circuit and draw fans through the turnstiles."[1]

Baker couldn't play for any team, however, until he received his official release from the Yankees, who wanted to make sure he wouldn't play for another major league team. In June, it was rumored that he sought to purchase controlling interest in the Cambridge club of the Eastern Shore League and would do so only if he could manage the team. If he received his release from the Yankees, he would possibly play for Cambridge, which would allow him to stay close to his home.

In the meantime, Baker played for Trappe in the Talbot County League, where practically all the players were farmers. Other towns in the league included St. Michaels, Easton, Oxford, Tilghman's Island and Neavitt. The teams played a 13-game schedule and Baker helped lead Trappe to the title with an 11–2 record after a hard battle with St. Michaels. Understandably, his involvement upset Trappe's opponents. After all, he was batting behind Babe Ruth less than a year ago. Before a June 27 game between St. Michaels and Trappe, the St. Michaels manager protested Baker's presence. The famed slugger didn't do much to help matters as he arrived on the field dressed in his old Yankees road uniform, a reminder of his legendary status. Trappe posted a lopsided victory that day, but the former major leaguer was barely a factor as he went hitless in four trips, drew two walks and scored a pair of runs. He appeared in six of the team's games and batted .400.

"The rivalry between St. Michaels and Trappe is almost unbelievable," he said. "It is, on a very small scale, what the rivalry between the New York Yankees and the New York Giants is. Everything is at a standstill when we play St. Michaels. I mean that literally. The women drop their work as well as the men."[2]

At the time, Trappe, with a population of 300, regularly drew crowds of 500 to 600 while Easton with a population of 2,000 frequently attracted crowds of 2,000.

"Some people wonder why I'm content to play on a farm team," he said. "The game of baseball itself, and not the particular setting, is what interests me. Baseball is baseball anywhere and I love it. I get far more out of the game by spending most of my time farming and playing baseball for recreation. I work two farms that net me a comfortable income and when I knock off of work to join the boys at the field I approach the game of baseball with a zest I never knew as a big-league player, as much as I enjoyed my American League career."[3]

By September, Easton officials had a strong interest in joining the Eastern Shore League with Baker as a player/manager. A meeting was held in the Easton courthouse to discuss if the town wanted to pursue a team. Rev. Thomas Donaldson, president of the Talbot County League, was chosen chairman of the group, which enthusiastically voted to pursue a franchise. The support extended beyond Easton as fans from Chestertown, Centreville, St. Michaels, Trappe, Oxford, and Tilghman vowed to back the team.

Easton gained entrance to the already shaky and financially troubled

Eastern Shore League in March. Three of the eight franchises, Milford and Dover in Delaware, and Pocomoke in Maryland, had failed to finish the 1923 season. Baker, who had been granted his unconditional release by the Yankees in January 1924, was named player/manager shortly after Easton entered the league. His first challenge was to recruit players, who were not only talented, but also of upstanding character. Of the first 15 players he signed, five were from Chester, three from Baltimore, two from Philadelphia, one from Brooklyn, one from Virginia. Pitchers Mildred Slaughter of Trappe and Alton Scott of Centreville were local players he recruited. When Marcus Chaconas read that Baker was to manage the Easton team, he walked and hitchhiked about 100 miles from Washington, DC to Trappe. He knocked on Baker's door and asked for a chance to play. He said he would play for free. Baker found it hard to say no to the ambitious youngster and agreed to give him a tryout. Chaconas played infield, outfield and pitcher for the Easton Farmers and became one of the club's most popular players.

Sixteen-year-old Jimmie Foxx of Sudlersville was one of Baker's top recruits. There are several versions of how it happened. This is the version Baker told the *Sporting News* in 1955:

"One evening in the summer of 1924, a man walked into the living room at my home in Trappe and asked if the could talk to me for a few minutes. It was Dell Foxx, who had his son, Jimmie, with him.

"'Frank,' he asked, 'will you give my boy a chance with your ball club?' A quick glance at the big, 16-year-old youngster (Foxx was about five-foot-eleven and a muscular 170 pounds) told me all I needed to know. If this kid can play baseball, I thought, he's got to be good. I told Mr. Foxx to have Jimmie at Federal Park in Easton the next day.

"At 16, Jimmie was big and strong, could hit to all fields, and could throw well. He was given an immediate contract with Easton. It wasn't long before he was one of the best catchers in the league. Jimmie experienced trouble in getting his throws away to second base. It took a little work to correct, but once he mastered it, the runners stopped running."[4]

Foxx recalled the incident in a *Sport Magazine* article many years later: "One morning I walked down to the mail box and found a penny post card, written in pencil, addressed to me. It was from Frank 'Home Run' Baker, who was starting out as manager of the Easton Club of the Eastern Shore League. He invited me to come see him for a tryout. I'd never given much thought that I might be able to play pro ball, but I was excited."[5]

Mark Millikin, author of *Jimmie Foxx: The Pride of Sudlersville*, writes that if the account is true, then Baker probably sent the note to Foxx as a

Baker (center of the second row) managed the Easton Farmers in the Eastern Shore Baseball League in 1924 and part of 1925. Although the team wasn't very successful in the standings, Baker did discover future Hall of Famer Jimmie Foxx (center, back row) from nearby Sudlersville. Foxx went on to become one of the game's most prolific home run sluggers. TALBOT COUNTY HISTORICAL SOCIETY.

formality after already having talked with his father and mother at his home in Trappe.

Baker's challenge of pulling together a winning team was complicated by having less than two months to sign players and one of the rainiest springs in 35 years, which made it difficult to practice or play exhibition games. Despite a shortage of talent, optimism ran high when the Easton Farmers opened the 1924 season.

An early season assessment of Foxx appeared in the May 24 issue of the *Easton Star Democrat*. "Fox (sic) is a young man in his teens, but he is good behind the bat, his arm is strong, he is fast, and besides he can play infield. Many predict that he will be in the big leagues in two or three years time. He is said to be a hard hitter."[6]

Foxx (referred to as Fox for the entire season by the *Easton Star-Democrat*) made his professional debut on May 30 at Dover, Delaware, in front of an estimated crowd of 3,000 fans. Batting eighth, the muscular teen was intentionally walked in the second inning and doubled in the eighth. Behind the plate, he was charged with two passed balls and threw out a runner trying to go from second to third on a sacrifice bunt.

The following day, the two clubs played the first Eastern Shore League game in Easton, attracting a crowd of more than 2,000 spectators. Although Easton lost, the highlight of the game was Foxx's two-run homer over the left field fence in the seventh inning.

Easton quickly settled into last place with a 2–11 record. Things got worse as the club plummeted to 2–21. Despite the losses, Foxx remained a bright spot. By mid–July he was leading the team in hitting with a .322 average. He was prospering and learning under Baker's watchful and patient eye. Baker proved to be an excellent teacher, showing Foxx the finer points of playing third base, lecturing him on his approach to the game, and serving as an excellent role model. Foxx studied the home run king's batting style and said years later, "I tried to stride and swing at the same time the way Baker did."[7]

Foxx said Baker taught him the basic rules of hitting that season. Baker told him, "Keep your eye on the ball," and "you don't realize it, but you make a pitcher's job just 50 percent easier than it would be if you forced him to pitch the way you want him to…. If you wait for the balls you want to hit instead of taking any old thing the pitchers want to give you, you would be batting .350."[8]

Baker knew he had a bona fide major league prospect on his hands. Years later, he recollected how he placed Foxx with the Athletics. "Easton didn't want to lose Jimmie for the $500 draft, so I waited for the New York Yankees to play the Athletics at Shibe Park," said Baker. "I offered the Yankees first crack at Foxx, who I knew was destined to be a great player. On the Yankee bench, Manager Miller Huggins and Babe Ruth both laughed at me when I told them about this kid who could knock the cover off the ball, play any position, run like a deer, and throw golf balls.

"'Frank, this beats anything we ever heard. What are you trying to pull over?' Somewhat taken back by their attitude and complete disinterest in a real prospect, I decided to talk with Connie Mack. When leaving, I pointed to the diamond and told Babe and Huggins, 'You'll see him out there.'

"Once more, I started with my story only to have Mack stop me. 'Frank, if he's all you say he is, I'll take him and I don't even want to see him first.' Mack later told me, 'He's all you said he was and a lot more.'"[9]

Mack followed up and sent his scout Mike Drennan to Easton to observe Foxx, who Baker termed, "the best prospect I ever saw." Drennan was the same scout who had discovered Baker, according to the *Centreville Record*. The young slugger also had attracted the attention of the New York Giants. Easton sold Foxx to the Athletics for approximately $2,000 on July 30. The deal was closed the day before Giants scout Howard Berry called Baker offering to purchase his prospect. Foxx, batting .309 with five home runs in 46 games at the time, was expected to join the Athletics at the conclusion of the Eastern Shore League season.

The news of Foxx signing with the A's assured continual interest in the Easton club, despite their losing ways. The highlight of Easton's season came on August 15 when it hosted Crisfield with Baseball Commissioner Judge Landis, Eastern Shore League President Harry Rew, and Blue Ridge League President J. Vincent Jamison, Jr. in attendance. The powerful Sudlersville teen stole the show as he singled and crashed a home run in the fifth inning as Easton defeated Crisfield 4–1.

Easton finished last with a dismal 23–57 record. Foxx played in 76 of 80 games, batting .297 with 11 doubles, two triples and 10 home runs. He overshadowed his 38-year-old mentor who chose to play part-time while managing. Baker occasionally played third base and often was a pinch hitter. Frank batted .293 with five homers in just 92 at bats.

Although Foxx was originally to report to the Athletics at the end of the season, Mack permitted him to play in a couple of postseason exhibitions with Parksley in the Five State Series between the Eastern Shore League and the Blue Ridge Mountain League pennant winners. Each team was permitted to select two players from other teams in their league. Parksley's manager Poke Whalen wisely selected Foxx. Parksley captured the best-of-seven series, winning four of six games. Foxx delighted his followers with nine hits, including four home runs and a .391 average for the series.

He headed to Philadelphia to join the A's shortly after the conclusion of the Five State Series on September 10. Baker was confident Foxx would succeed and knew he was in good hands with Mack, known for his ability to develop young players. Foxx sat on the A's bench the remainder of the season. Mack did, however, let him play in a couple exhibition games.

Foxx made his major league debut on May 1, 1925, as a 17-year-old. He went on to play for 20 years in the major leagues, clout 534 home runs, drive in 1,922 runs and bat .325. He won four home run crowns, three RBI titles, three batting titles, and three Most Valuable Player awards. He is considered one of the greatest right-handed batters of all-time.

Foxx's success was always a source of pleasure for Baker, who had the last laugh on the Yankees. "The following season when the A's had Foxx for a short time, I paid Miller and the Babe another visit in the dugout," he recalled. "Pointing to the infield where Foxx was, I asked, 'Who is that fellow out there catching? Is it Foxx? 'Bake, you didn't tell us he was that kind of player,' was their only reply."[10]

Despite the last place finish, Easton's board of directors considered the 1924 season a success as its attendance was among the best in the league. Easton was reported to be financially better off than any other team in the league. Demand for seats and boxes was so great that the board of directors voted to enlarge the grandstand and add more boxes, and install club rooms with showers for both the home and visiting teams under the grandstand.

Team officials pointed proudly to their adherence to a policy advocating "clean and honest baseball" and following league rules. The two main rules, designed to keep teams competitive, were a $1,750 monthly payroll limit and a class player rule, which stated that no team could have more than three players who had played more than 25 games in a higher division league. The class player rule was frequently violated. Milford, Delaware joined the league in 1923, but dropped out on July 5 rather than forfeit all the games it had won using an ineligible player. Violations such as these wreaked havoc on the stability of the league and the standings.

The *Easton Star Democrat* reported, "Visiting managers tried to impress upon Baker the importance of winning no matter what methods were resorted to. This did not appeal to Baker, who insisted on clean sport from start to finish."[11]

According to the *Star Democrat*, Baker had managed the team in a "very businesslike manner." Despite being hopelessly in last place all season, he was not tempted to violate league rules. The newspaper reported, "This was not true of the other clubs. Reports were heard almost daily about other managers exceeding the limit and players who tried to play in Easton were turned down on account of the money they wanted. Afterwards, they were seen in the lineup of other clubs."[12]

Baker spent the spring of 1925 scouting and recruiting players for Easton. As the best-known manager in the Eastern Shore League, many players were anxious to join his club. His experience and eye for talent were helpful, but the limited talent, particularly within the confines of the salary limit and the class player rules, was difficult to overcome.

Fans' hopes for a better season in 1925 were crushed as Easton was outclassed and outplayed in the beginning of the season. Nearly 2,000 fans attended the home opener against Cambridge and the crowd was larger the following day. The euphoria of having a team in the Eastern Shore League, however, quickly faded in the second season. Fans and the board of directors were now demanding a winning team, or at least a team that played .500. Fans took a stand, saying they would refuse to attend games as long as Easton was losing.

The season was barely two weeks old when Baker unexpectedly announced his resignation through a statement to the *Star-Democrat*. When asked for an explanation, he replied that when the directors of the club asked him to lay off a player without any cause it was time for him to step down and let someone else take charge.

The newspaper reported Baker stated the directors did not take kindly to his judgment and for this reason he believed his services were of little use to the club. The directors were disappointed with the recent slim crowds at the games and were determined to strengthen the team. While Baker was at the helm, the directors voted money for a new pitcher, reduced the club's roster, and ordered a player to be put on the bench without pay for two weeks until he got in condition. After he resigned, the order was rescinded. Farmers' catcher Charles Gault was named to replace Baker as manager and given a one-month trial.

Rev. Thomas Donaldson, former president of the club, recalled the 1925 season 30 years later. "When the 1925 season came around there were signs that a lot of uptown managers were yapping at the heels of those in charge of the club. We weren't winning enough games, we had sold Jimmy Foxx to the Philadelphia Athletics, where he had wanted to go, for what some people thought was too little money. A general spirit of criticism and undercutting was rampant. Frank and I were asked, if that's the proper term, to resign so that another manager and president could be installed."[13]

Within a month, Gault was released and Buck Herzog of Baltimore was hired to manage the team. Herzog had managed Baker in Ridgely in 1905 and been his teammate on several occasions. He had played 13 years in the major leagues and had opposed Baker in the World Series in 1911 and 1913 with the New York Giants.

Herzog was counted upon to bring more talented players from Baltimore and breathe new life into the struggling Easton club. He brought an aggressive, hard-nosed approach to Easton in contrast to Baker's quiet, laid-back style. The *Star-Democrat* observed, "Former managers have been men of high type, with characters above reproach. Possibly they were not aggressive enough on the field. Players must be keyed up to the highest point of enthusiasm, and if the manager does not show it he can't expect the players to get it."[14]

SIXTEEN

Life After Baseball

Baker's experience managing the Easton club was enough to convince him that he didn't need those kinds of headaches. A farmer at heart, Baker devoted his energies over the next nearly 40 years to managing his farms, raising wheat, corn, asparagus, tomatoes, and peas. He was also actively involved in the community. He served several terms on the Trappe Town Board and served as president from 1932 to 1933; he filled the office of tax collector for a while; served as a director of the State Bank of Trappe; he was a booster and worker for the Trappe Volunteer Fire Company. He also enjoyed attending baseball functions such as Old Timers' Day at Yankee Stadium, the Baseball Hall of Fame ceremonies, Little League banquets and working with youngsters. He enjoyed raising and training hunting dogs, fishing and hunting. He was consulted on many baseball matters and served as president of the Easton team in the Eastern Shore League in 1941, when the club was affiliated with the New York Yankees. Frank and Margaret lived on Main Street in Trappe for nearly 40 years. They had two children, Margaret Elizabeth, born March 10, 1923, and John Franklin, Jr., born March 27, 1924.

In 1940, the *Baltimore Sun* wrote, "Home Run Baker ... is as fine a citizen as any town could have. You can see something in the way the eyes of the people here twinkle when they talk about him that indicates a deep respect as well as a wholesome admiration for this special citizen of their community."[1]

For most of Baker's life, the Eastern Shore was geographically separated by the Chesapeake Bay from the main part of Maryland. It was a barrier of social significance. Traveling to cities such as Baltimore or

Philadelphia was a major undertaking because transportation was poor on the Eastern Shore. It required four hours to drive from Easton to Baltimore by going around the bay. The alternative was to take the Matapeake-Annapolis ferry across the Chesapeake Bay. This was expensive and the service was slow. It was much easier to travel to Wilmington, Delaware or Philadelphia and many Eastern Shoremen were more oriented to those cities than Baltimore.

As a result of the geographic barrier, Eastern Shoremen felt alienated from the rest of Maryland. Life was slower, the standard of living was lower and progress was regarded by some residents as a dirty word. Most, however, couldn't figure out a good reason why they might want to travel to a city. A 1944 study of life on the Eastern Shore by University of Pennsylvania sociologist Frank Goodwin revealed little evidence of crime, gangs, slums, poverty, begging and other maladjustments. Goodwin described the Eastern Shore as "proudly self-conscious. There is a long history, fine tradition and no very sharp break with the past. The Eastern Shoreman does not envy, but pities the city dweller. The Shoreman knows his land is the world's garden spot and his people are God's people. His is the good life."[2]

Life on the Eastern Shore changed forever on July 30, 1952, when the 4.35-mile Chesapeake Bay Bridge opened, connecting the Eastern Shore to the main part of Maryland. The presence of the bridge and new highways meant potential problems for the long-sheltered region. Some local leaders feared it would lead to the influx of city dwellers, over commercialization, increased crime and declining property values.

From time to time, reporters would seek the Trappe slugger out for his thoughts on the changing nature of baseball. The changes wrought by the livelier ball, the lighter bat and the continuous quest for the home run drew this observation from Baker in 1955: "The ball goes about 100 feet further than the old ball when hit with the same force," he said. "I hit 12 home runs for the Philadelphia Athletics in 1913. And, in that year, I hit the right field fence at Shibe Park 38 times. You've got to figure just about every one of those as a homer with the lively ball."[3]

He recalled being astonished to see Joe DiMaggio of the New York Yankees effortlessly slug a home run over the fence in right center at Shibe Park. The fence was unchanged from the days Baker played with the Athletics.

"I don't like to cast aspersions but a Little Leaguer today can hit the modern ball as far as grown men could hit the ball we played with,"[4] he added in a 1958 interview.

"I'd sure loved to have swung against today's lively ball. Yes, with my 52-ounce bat. I received a letter from Sam Crawford (former Detroit outfielder and Hall of Famer) the other day and he described the baseball used today as an overstuffed golf ball."[5]

The former home run king believed the emphasis on hitting homers in the 1950s and early 1960s was ruining many fine young batters.

"Many hitters are swinging for the fences instead of choking up (on the bat). Of course, homers are nice. But I'll take a good .300 hitter who can get on base often. You can't drive in many runs batting .225 no matter how many homers you hit," he said.[6]

Baker also lamented the decline on the emphasis on "inside baseball," the art of advancing a runner. He believed players in the 1950s didn't have as much skill as players in his era when it came to bunting, sliding, executing the hit-and-run, and general baseball knowledge.

Although Baker was the game's first famed home run slugger, he didn't gain membership into the National Baseball Hall of Fame until nearly 20 years after the first group of players was elected. Ty Cobb, Babe Ruth, Walter Johnson, Christy Mathewson and Honus Wagner were the first players elected, in 1936. Fifty-one players received votes in the initial balloting. The baseball writers were tough critics—none of the five greatest players was a unanimous selection. Four writers didn't vote for Cobb and 11 didn't vote for Ruth or Wagner. Cy Young and his 511 victories garnered less than 50 percent of the vote. Baker was one of 13 players who received one vote.

Young, Larry Lajoie and Tris Speaker were elected in 1937. This time, Baker received 13 votes. His vote total increased to 32 in 1938 and reached a peak in 1947 when he received 49 votes (30.4 percent). Players need 75 percent of the votes to be elected to the Hall of Fame. After that, his name fell to the background as he received less than 10 votes a year until 1952 when his name was dropped from the ballot and into the hands of the Veterans Selection Committee.

While many baseball writers had forgotten about Baker, Sherwood Yates of Cambridge, a lifelong fan, had not. In early 1951, Yates walked into the Cambridge *Daily Banner* office and made the case to 21-year-old sports editor Bobby Layton that Baker had been unfairly passed over in the Hall of Fame voting. Layton joined Yates in a letter-writing campaign to get the Eastern Shore slugger inducted. The two wrote hundreds of letters to sports editors and columnists across the country. Layton wrote a series of articles advocating Baker's election to the Hall of Fame and he recruited other writers and columnists to further the cause. Ed Nichols of the *Salisbury Times*, Bill Perry of the *Easton Star Democrat*, Rodger Pippen of the *Baltimore News Post* and Jesse Linthicum of the *Baltimore Sun* were enthusiastic supporters.

The Associated Press joined the campaign in November of 1954 when reporter Gayle Talbot wrote a piece advocating Baker for the Hall of Fame. Talbot admitted that he was surprised to learn that Baker, "the first king of distance hitters in the era of the 'dead ball,'" had not been elected to the Hall of Fame. He considered it a serious oversight. Others who got behind Baker included Maryland Governor Theodore McKeldin, Senators owner Clark Griffith and J.G. Taylor Spink, editor of the *Sporting News*.

Tom Kibler, former president of the Eastern Shore League and teammate of Baker's, strongly advocated for the Trappe slugger's induction into the Baseball Hall of Fame. He said, "If this fella (Baker) played today with the lively ball, he'd kill somebody; he'd knock the fences down. He was the greatest hitter I ever saw. He hit the ball on the line, none of these long bloopers. He was a fella who would go over and knock down balls that other third basemen couldn't get — and he'd still throw them out. He had a great arm."[7]

Spink headed the Veterans Selection Committee, which voted on players who had been inactive for 25 years or more. Other members were Warren Giles, president, National League; Will Harridge, president, American League; Frank Shaughnessy, baseball's secretary-treasurer; Charles Segar, Charles Gehringer, Paul Kerr, Frank Graham, Jack Malaney, Branch Rickey and Warren Brown. Baker received word he had been elected to the Baseball Hall of Fame in late January 1955 when Spink called him with the good news.

"I heard a fella say once he'd rather have a rose bud when he's alive than to have a whole rose garden thrown his way after he's gone," he said. "It looks like they've thrown the roses my way while I'm still here. This is something you can't find words to express what's in your heart. I'm very pleased. I never gave up hope when they kept passing me up every year."[8]

"It really means something when your friends at home and away work so hard for an honor they think you deserve," he said.[9]

Baker along with catcher Ray Schalk, pitcher Dazzy Vance, outfielder Joe DiMaggio, pitcher Ted Lyons, catcher Leo "Gabby" Harnett were scheduled to be formally inducted on July 25. Baker and Schalk were voted in by the Veterans Selection Committee while the latter four were selected by the Baseball Writers Association. The six players brought Hall of Fame membership to 79.

On April 6, 1955, more than 225 people attended a testimonial dinner for Baker at Easton's Tidewater Inn. William P. Chaffinch of Easton presented the guest of honor with a gold-framed parchment marking the occasion and an oil portrait by Easton photographer Laird Wise. Former major leaguer Bill Werber was the master of ceremonies. Those delivering tributes included Harry Russell, Dallas Culver and Fred Lucas, past presidents of the Eastern Shore Baseball League; Jackie Farrell, chief of the New York Yankees speakers' bureau and former sportswriter for the *New York Daily News*; James Tatum, University of Maryland athletic director; Herb Armstrong, Orioles business manager; former major leaguers Bill Nicholson and Dick Porter; and Burton Shipley, University of Maryland baseball coach.

The famed third baseman was honored again on June 26 at Baltimore's Memorial Stadium with "Home Run Baker Day." The Orioles, who had moved to Baltimore from St. Louis prior to the 1954 season, hosted the Kansas City Athletics for a Sunday doubleheader before 16,439 fans, many of them from the Eastern Shore. It was an exciting time for many baseball fans from towns such as Easton, Trappe, Cambridge, Centreville and Salisbury. They had an opportunity to travel to see the Orioles play and celebrate one of their greatest players. Cambridge chartered buses and took 240 Little League and Pony League players to the game. Hundreds of fans from Easton and Trappe also made the trip.

Fans almost witnessed baseball history in the opener as Kansas City's Alex Kellner tossed a one-hit, 1–0 shutout. Afterwards, Baker was recognized for his election to the Baseball Hall of Fame. Those on hand for the ceremonies included former Philadelphia A's Jimmie Foxx, Lefty Grove, Max Bishop, and 92-year-old Connie Mack, as well as former major leaguers Rube Marquard, Jack Ogden, Fritz Maisel, George Maisel, Dave Danforth, and Bill Nicholson. Merwyn Jacobson, former International League Baltimore Oriole, and former Eastern Shore League officials Gene Corbett and Tom Kibler also were on hand.

Baker had been a World Series hero, ignited standing ovations and been idolized by thousands, but nothing quite prepared him for being inducted into the Baseball Hall of Fame. It was baseball's highest honor, one that assured everlasting fame. He would be forever considered among the game's greatest players.

More than 10,000 visitors, including several dozen of Baker's closest friends and relatives, descended on the tiny village of Cooperstown, New York, for the Hall of Fame inductions on July 25, 1955. Other Hall of Famers in attendance included Cy Young, Ty Cobb, Frankie Frisch, and Bill Terry.

The 69-year-old Baker was the first inductee introduced. He received mild applause from the crowd, most of whom had never seen him play. In keeping with his character, his speech was short. As he said, "This is a great honor," he choked up. It was an emotional moment.

The 1955 inductees were overshadowed by New York Yankee great Joe DiMaggio, who had played his final season in 1951. DiMaggio, estranged from his movie star wife Marilyn Monroe, attracted the most atten-

tion from the media as well as fans. The Yankee Clipper was the final inductee introduced and the crowd erupted when he approached the podium.

After being only the third third baseman inducted into the Baseball Hall of Fame (Jimmy Collins and Harold "Pie" Traynor preceded him), Baker and his long-time nemesis Ty Cobb were seen shaking hands and conversing about their playing days.

Playing in the Dead Ball Era and finishing with 96 career home runs, Baker can easily be underrated by modern writers and fans. How good was he?

In 1977, Fred Lieb, who covered Baker in the 1911 World Series, wrote an assessment of the Hall of Famer. "If playing today, he would, in my opinion, hit 40 home runs a year and be one of the most feared left-handed hitters in the game."[10] In 1977, Boston's Jim Rice led the American League with 39 home runs and Cincinnati's George Foster paced the National League with 52. Atlanta's Jeff Burroughs was second in the National League with 41.

Hall of Fame umpire Billy Evans, whose American League career spanned from 1906 to 1927, said, "I doubt if there was ever a more sensational batter than Baker. To dismiss him as a slugger, however, would be an injustice. He was a genuine player. He accepted fantastic fielding chances.

"Baker was a far better fielder than he ever received credit for being. Because he was awkward in his style, many people thought he was only fair on defense. But Mack and pitchers didn't have this opinion. Official averages show that season in and season out, Baker accepted more chances than any other third baseman in the two leagues."[11]

Interestingly, Hall of Fame third baseman Harold "Pie" Traynor, who compiled a lifetime batting average of .320 while playing for the Pittsburgh Pirates from 1920 to 1937, is generally regarded as a better fielder. His lifetime fielding average is .946 compared to Baker's .943, but gloves were much better in Traynor's era than Baker's. During their careers, Baker averaged more chances per game (3.6 to 3.3), more put outs per game (1.39 to 1.2) and more assists per game (2.0 to 1.88).

From a purely statistical analysis, Baker rates among the top 100 players of all time. Cyril Morong, a member of the Society for American

Opposite: **Some of the greatest Philadelphia Athletics appeared on this 1939 score card celebrating baseball's centennial anniversay. Players are, top row, left to right, Baker, Chief Bender and Eddie Collins; bottom row, left to right, Mickey Cochrane, Jimmie Foxx, and Lefty Grove.**

In 1951, Frank "Home Run" Baker showed off his glove, bats, trophies, and some of his key game baseballs to the photographer. *SPORTING NEWS*.

Baseball Research (SABR), employed sabermetrics, the mathematical and statistical analysis of baseball, to assess Baker's career. Win Shares, a statistic created by Bill James, is a way of quantifying individual performance and equalizing offensive and defensive contributions of players. It takes into account era and ballpark effects. Based on Win Shares, Baker ranks 28th best among all players, according to Morong. Using Peter Palmer's Linear Weights method of "Total Player Rating," Baker rates 46th among all players with at least 5,000 plate appearances. James ranks Baker 70th among baseball's greatest players of all time in his 2001 book "*The New Bill James Historical Baseball Abstract.*"

Life was a little more hectic for Frank and his wife Margaret for the next eight years after he was inducted into the Baseball Hall of Fame. He received more invitations to attend baseball-related functions, more requests for interviews, and more letters from fans, often seeking an autograph. He seldom turned down an invitation as long as his health was good. He was happy to know that fans hadn't forgotten him. The baseball

Frank "Home Run" Baker was inducted into the Baseball Hall of Fame on July 25, 1955. Baseball Commissioner Ford Frick, left, listens as Baker delivers his brief acceptance speech. Baker was the third third baseman inducted into the Hall of Fame. Other players entering the Hall of Fame that year were Ray Schalk, Ted Lyons, Gabby Hartness, Dazzy Vance and Joe DiMaggio. NATIONAL BASEBALL HALL OF FAME LIBRARY, COOPERSTOWN, NY.

star never lost his modesty, but his shyness faded considerably as he became older, when he talked interestingly and with authority to reporters.

Baker's health started to fail in August of 1961 when he was taken ill while attending the Baseball Hall of Fame ceremonies at Cooperstown. The 75-year-old gentleman farmer described the illness as "flu — almost pneumonia." He seemed to improve but suffered a slight stroke in September and a sharp relapse in October. He was rushed to Easton Memorial Hospital in serious condition on December 21 with an undetermined illness. He was discharged on January 1, 1962, after being treated for an ulcer, according to his physicians. His indomitable will to live pulled him through and he said he could hardly wait for the next baseball season to begin.

He sat watching television and waited impatiently for the first game to be televised. It was about this time, Baker said, "Baseball is a great game. The older I get the nuttier I get about it." Mrs. Baker added, "With Frank, baseball and life are the same."[12]

He suffered his second stroke in two years in June of 1963 and died on June 28 at the age of 77. Funeral services were conducted from the Trappe Methodist Church by Rev. Donald Knight, pastor of the church. Interment was in Spring Hill Cemetery in Easton. Two of his former Eastern Shore League players, Capt. George Klemmick of the Baltimore City Police Force, and Tony Chaconas of Washington, DC, attended the funeral. Others present were Lee Allen, historian from the Baseball Hall of Fame; Merwyn Jacobson of Baltimore, a former major leaguer; Jack Dunn III and Herb Armstrong of the Baltimore Orioles; Tom Kibler, athletic director, Washington College; Fred Lucas, former president of the Eastern Shore Baseball League from Cambridge; and John Steadman, sports editor, *Baltimore News-Post*.

"A full, rich life came to an end," wrote the *Easton Star-Democrat* upon Baker's death. "Mr. Baker, often referred to as the Maryland strong boy, swung a 52-ounce bat as though it were a fishing pole and his powerful arms often controlled belligerent players in fighting moods."[13]

John Steadman, sports editor of the *Baltimore News-Post*, described Baker as a "humble, conservative man who never lost his simplicity." He added, "The important and unforgettable characteristic of Frank (Home Run) Baker was that he was a model man. This, more than his baseball ability, will forever remain as the legacy he left in the hearts of those who knew and admired him."[14]

Chapter Notes

ONE

1. *Baseball Digest*, May 1955.
2. *Dorchester Democrat News*, August 27, 1887.
3. Dickson Preston, *Trappe: The Story of an Old-Fashioned Town* (Easton, MD: Economy Press, 1976), p. 100.
4. Ibid., p. 100.
5. Dickson Preston, *Talbot County: A History* (Centreville, MD: Tidewater, 1983), p. 18.
6. Ibid., p. 14.
7. James Michener, *Chesapeake* (New York: Random House, 1978), p. 649.
8. *Philadelphia Evening Bulletin*, October 11, 1913.
9. Copy of an International News Service article dated October 13, 1914, National Baseball Library, Cooperstown, NY.
10. *Baltimore Sun*, September 17, 1907.
11. Ibid., September 19, 1907.
12. *Reading Eagle*, April 14, 1908.
13. Ibid., June 28, 1908.
14. Henry Grayson, "Home Run Baker Could also Run, Field — and Fight," *Baseball Digest*, February 1945.
15. *Reading Eagle*, September 13, 1908.
16. Ibid., September 20, 1908
17. *Baltimore News-Post*, June 30, 1963.
18. David Anderson, *More Than Merkle* (Lincoln, NB: University of Nebraska Press, 2000) p. 9.
19. *New York Evening Telegram*, June 8, 1918.

TWO

1. Robert F. Burk, *Never Just a Game* (Chapel Hill, NC: University of North Carolina Press, 1994), pp. 160–161.
2. Benjamin Rader, *Baseball: A History of America's Game* (Chicago: University of Illinois Press, 1992), p. 92.
3. Larry Mansch, *Rube Marquard: The Life and Times of a Baseball Hall of Famer* (Jefferson, NC: McFarland, 1998), p. 15.
4. Lawrence Ritter, *The Glory of Their Times: The Story of the Early Days of Baseball Told by the Men Who Played It* (New York: Macmillan, 1966), p. 38.
5. *Philadelphia Evening Bulletin*, March 8, 1909.
6. *Philadelphia Public Ledger*, March 24, 1909.
7. Ibid., April 12, 1909.
8. Ibid., April 13, 1909.
9. Ibid.
10. *Philadelphia Evening Bulletin*, May 15, 1955.
11. *Philadelphia Public Ledger*, April 13, 1909.
12. *New York Sun* quoted in the *Philadelphia Public Ledger*, July 8, 1909.
13. Unidentified newspaper clipping from the collection of Norman Macht.
14. *Philadelphia Public Ledger*, August 27, 1909.
15. Copy of a letter written by Ty Cobb to J. Taylor Spink, editor, *The Sporting News*, February 15, 1955, provided by Marty Payne.

16. *Philadelphia Public Ledger*, August 27, 1909.

17. Joe S. Jackson quoted in the *Philadelphia Public Ledger*, August 28, 1909.

18. *Philadelphia Public Ledger*, August 27, 1909.

19. Ibid., September 16, 1909.

20. Ibid.

THREE

1. *Philadelphia Evening Bulletin*, April 14, 1910.

2. *Sporting News*, February 9, 1955.

3. *Philadelphia Evening Bulletin*, April 14, 1910.

4. Ibid.

5. Ibid., September 22, 1910.

6. *Chicago Tribune*, October 3, 1910.

7. *Philadelphia Evening Bulletin*, September 26, 1910.

8. *Chicago Tribune*, October 2, 1910.

9. *Philadelphia Evening Bulletin*, October 17, 1910.

10. Ibid., October 18, 1910.

11. *Baltimore Sun*, October 18, 1910.

12. *Washington Post*, October 18, 1910.

13. *Chicago Tribune*, October 18, 1910.

14. Ibid.

15. Ibid., October 20, 1910.

16. Ibid., October 19, 1910.

17. *Philadelphia Evening Bulletin*, October 22, 1910.

18. *Chicago Tribune*, October 22, 1910.

19. *Washington Post*, October 24, 1910.

20. *Chicago Tribune*, October 24, 1910.

21. *Philadelphia Evening Bulletin*, October 24, 1910.

FOUR

1. *Philadelphia Evening Bulletin*, March 9, 1911.

2. Ibid., July 16, 1911.

3. *Philadelphia Public Ledger*, July 29, 1911.

4. *Philadelphia Evening Bulletin*, September 30, 1911.

5. Ibid., October 16, 1911.

6. *Washington Post*, October 8, 1911.

7. Ibid., October 1, 1911.

8. Ibid.

9. Baltimore Sun, October 15, 1911.

10. Philadelphia Evening Bulletin, October 16, 1911.

11. Lawrence Ritter, *The Glory of Their Times: The Story of the Early Days of Baseball Told by the Men Who Played It* (New York: Macmillan, 1967), p. 173.

12. *Philadelphia Public Ledger*, October 17, 1911.

13. *Richmond Times Dispatch*, March 6, 1941.

14. *Philadelphia Public Ledger*, October 17, 1911.

15. Ibid.

16. *New York Times*, October 17, 1911.

17. Michael Gershman, "The 100 Greatest Players," in *Total Baseball*, 3rd ed. (New York: HarperPerennial, 1991), p. 159.

18. *New York Times*, October 17, 1911.

19. *Baltimore Sun*, October 17, 1911.

20. *New York Times*, October 18, 1911.

21. Fred Lieb, *Baseball As I Have Known It* (New York: Coward, McCann & Geoghegan, 1977), p. 80.

22. Philadelphia Public Ledger, October 18, 1911.

23. Ibid.

24. Baltimore Sun, October 18, 1911.

25. Larry Mansch, *Rube Marquard: The Life and Times of a Baseball Hall of Famer* (Jefferson, NC: McFarland, 1998), p. 91.

26. *Philadelphia Evening Bulletin*, October 18, 1911.

27. Ibid.

28. *Baltimore Sun*, October 18, 1911.

29. *Philadelphia Evening Bulletin*, October 18, 1911.

30. Ibid., October 23, 1911.

31. *Washington Post*, October 19, 1911.

32. *Philadelphia Evening Bulletin*, October 18, 1911.

33. *Baltimore Sun*, October 18, 1911.

34. Dickson Preston, *Trappe: The Story of an Old-Fashioned Town* (Easton, MD: Economy Press, 1976), p. 3.

35. *Philadelphia Public Ledger*, October 18, 1911.

36. *Philadelphia Evening Bulletin*, October 20, 1911.

37. Ibid., October 19, 1911.

38. Ibid., October 24, 1911.

39. Ibid., October 25, 1911.

40. *Baltimore Sun*, October 25, 1911.

41. *Philadelphia Evening Bulletin*, October 25, 1911.

42. Lieb, *Baseball As I Have Known It*, p. 83

43. Mansch, *Rube Marquard: The Life and Times of a Baseball Hall of Famer*, p. 93.

44. *New York Times*, October 27, 1911.

45. *Washington Post*, October 27, 1911.

46. *Philadelphia Evening Bulletin*, October 27, 1911.

FIVE

1. F.C. Lane, *Batting* (Lincoln, NB: University of Nebraska Press, 2001), p. 6.
2. Ibid.
3. Frank Yuetter, "Baker Homered with a 52-Ouncer," *Baseball Digest*, May 1955.
4. Fred Lieb, "Frank Baker: The Home-run Slugger of the World's Series, *Baseball*, December 1911.
5. *Baltimore Sun*, October 28, 1911.
6. *Philadelphia Evening Bulletin*, March 4, 1912.
7. Ibid.
8. Ibid., March 11, 1912.
9. *Philadelphia Public Ledger*, May 19, 1912.
10. *Philadelphia Evening Bulletin*, May 20, 1912.
11. Ibid.
12. Ed Grillo quoted in the *Philadelphia Evening Bulletin*, June 4, 1912.
13. Ibid., June 18, 1912.
14. Ibid., June 20, 1912.
15. Ibid., July 10, 1912.
16. Ibid., July 23, 1912.
17. Ibid.
18. Ibid., August 24, 1912.
19. *Philadelphia Public Ledger*, September 7, 1912.
20. Ibid.
21. Fred Lieb, *Connie Mack* (New York: G.P. Putnam's Sons, 1945), p. 161,
22. Ibid., p. 162.
23. *The Sporting News*, February 9, 1955.
24. *Philadelphia Evening Bulletin*, September 24, 1912.

SIX

1. *Philadelphia Public Ledger*, May 16, 1913.
2. Ibid., June 23, 1913.
3. *Philadelphia Evening Bulletin*, July 18, 1913.
4. *New York Times*, September 27, 1913.
5. Unidentified newspaper clipping from Norman Macht's collection.
6. *Baseball* magazine, August 1913.
7. Ibid.
8. *Cambridge Daily Banner*, April 7, 1955.

9. *Philadelphia Evening Bulletin*, August 30, 1913.
10. Ibid., September 29, 1913.
11. Ibid.
12. *Baltimore Sun*, October 8, 1913.
13. *Philadelphia Evening Bulletin*, October 8, 1913.
14. *Baltimore Sun*, October 8, 1913.
15. *Philadelphia Evening Bulletin*, October 8, 1913.
16. *Baltimore Sun*, October 8, 1913.
17. *Philadelphia Public Ledger*, October 9, 1913.
18. *Philadelphia Evening Bulletin*, October 10, 1913.
19. *Washington Post*, October 9, 1913.
20. *New York Times*, October 9, 1913.
21. *Philadelphia Evening Bulletin*, October 9, 1913.
22. *Baltimore Sun*, October 9, 1913.
23. *Washington Post*, October 9, 1913.
24. *Philadelphia Evening Bulletin*, October 9, 1913.
25. Ibid., October 10, 1913.
26. Ibid., October 9, 1913.
27. Ibid., October 10, 1913.
28. *Baltimore Sun*, October 10, 1913.
29. Ibid.
30. Ibid., October 11, 1913.
31. Ibid.
32. *Philadelphia Public Ledger*, October 11, 1913.
33. *Philadelphia Evening Bulletin*, October 11, 1913.
34. Ibid.
35. *Philadelphia Public Ledger*, October 12, 1913.
36. *Baltimore Sun*, October 12, 1913.
37. *Philadelphia Evening Bulletin*, October 12, 1913.
38. *Washington Post*, October 12, 1913.
39. Ibid.
40. *Baltimore Sun*, October 12, 1913.

SEVEN

1. *Washington Post*, June 5, 1914.
2. *Philadelphia Evening Bulletin*, October 28, 1911.
3. *Easton Star-Democrat*, January 23, 1914.
4. *Philadelphia Evening Bulletin*, March 6, 1914.
5. David Voigt, *American Baseball*, Vol. 2 (State College, PA: Pennsylvania State University, 1983), p. 122.

6. *Philadelphia Public Ledger*, March 15, 1914.
7. George Gipe, *The Great American Sports Book* (Garden City, NY: Doubleday, 1978), p. 98.
8. Henry Thomas, *Walter Johnson: Baseball's Big Train* (Washington, DC: Phenom Press, 1995), p. 125.
9. Ibid.
10. *Baseball Digest*, September 1958.
11. *Walter Johnson: Baseball's Big Train*, p. 125.
12. Ibid., p. 391.
13. *Philadelphia Evening Bulletin*, May 18, 1914.
14. *Washington Post*, May 25, 1914.
15. Ibid., June 5, 1914.
16. *Philadelphia Evening Bulletin*, May 13, 1914.
17. *Philadelphia Public Ledger*, June 17, 1914.
18. *Philadelphia Evening Bulletin*, July 20, 1914.
19. *The Sporting News*, February 9, 1955.
20. *Philadelphia Public Ledger*, September 2, 1914.
21. Fred Lieb, *Connie Mack*, p. 177.
22. *Philadelphia Evening Bulletin*, October 5, 1914.
23. *Washington Post*, October 1, 1914.
24. *New York Times*, October 9, 1914.
25. *Washington Post*, October 8, 1914.
26. *Philadelphia Evening Bulletin*, October 2, 1914.
27. *Philadelphia Public Ledger*, October 9, 1914.
28. *Washington Post*, October 1, 1914.
29. *New York Times*, October 7, 1914.
30. *Philadelphia Public Ledger*, October 9, 1914.
31. *Washington Post*, October 6, 1914.
32. Ibid., October 7, 1914.
33. *New York Times*, October 10, 1914.
34. Fred Lieb, *Connie Mack*, p. 177.
35. *Boston Globe*, October 10, 1914.
36. *Philadelphia Evening Bulletin*, October 10, 1914.
37. *Boston Globe*, October 11, 1914.
38. *Philadelphia Evening Bulletin*, October 10, 1914.
39. *New York Times*, October 10, 1914.
40. *Boston Globe*, October 11, 1914.
41. *Philadelphia Evening Bulletin*, October 13, 1914.
42. *New York Times*, October 13, 1914.
43. *Washington Post*, October 13, 1914.
44. *Philadelphia Public Ledger*, October 13, 1914.
45. Ibid.
46. *Philadelphia Evening Bulletin*, October 13, 1914.
47. *Baseball* magazine, February 1915.
48. *New York Times*, October 14, 1914.
49. *Boston Globe*, October 14, 1914.
50. *Easton Star-Democrat*, October 14, 1914.
51. *Philadelphia Evening Bulletin*, October 14, 1914.
52. *New York Times*, October 14, 1914.
53. *Philadelphia Ledger*, October 14, 1914.

EIGHT

1. Dennis and Jeanne DeValeria. *Honus Wagner: A Biography* (New York: Henry Holt, 1995), p. 263.
2. Connie Mack. *My 66 Years in Baseball* (New York: John C. Winston, 1950), p. 36.
3. Ibid.
4. *New York Times*, December 3, 1914.
5. *Sporting Life*, November 16, 1915.
6. *Philadelphia Evening Bulletin*, December 8, 1914.
7. *Sporting Life*, December 19, 1915.
8. *Easton Star-Democrat*, December 12, 1914.
9. *Baltimore Sun*, February 17, 1915.
10. *Philadelphia Evening Bulletin*, February 17, 1915.
11. Ibid., February 18, 1915.
12. *Philadelphia Public Ledger*, February 21, 1915.
13. Ibid., February 22, 1915.
14. Ibid., February 23, 1915.
15. Ibid., April 15, 1915.
16. *Chester Times*, April 22, 1915.
17. *Philadelphia Public Ledger*, April 27, 1915.
18. *Philadelphia Evening Bulletin*, April 27, 1915.
19. Ibid.
20. *Philadelphia Public Ledger*, April 27, 1915.
21. *Easton Star-Democrat*, May 1, 1915.
22. *Chester Times*, May 10, 1915.
23. Ibid., June 1, 1915.
24. *Philadelphia Public Ledger*, July 3, 1915.
25. Mack, *My 66 Years in Baseball*, p. 36.
26. *Chester Times*, August 23, 1915.
27. *Easton Star-Democrat*, October 23, 1915.
28. Ibid., November 15, 1915.

29. *Philadelphia Public Ledger*, December 16, 1915.
30. *Baltimore Sun*, December 30, 1915.
31. *Sporting News*, February 9, 1955.
32. *Philadelphia Public Ledger*, January 30, 1916.
33. Ibid.
34. *Philadelphia Evening Bulletin*, January 31, 1916.
35. Ibid., February 9, 1916.
36. *Philadelphia Public Ledger*, February 16, 1916.
37. *New York Tribune*, February 22, 1916.

NINE

1. Article reprinted in the *Easton Star-Democrat*, March 4, 1916.
2. Ibid.
3. *Philadelphia Evening Bulletin*, March 13, 1916.
4. *New York Tribune*, March 9, 1916.
5. *New York Sun*, March 15, 1916.
6. *New York Tribune*, March 25, 1916.
7. *New York Times*, April 19, 1916.
8. *Baseball* magazine, November 1921.

TEN

1. *New York Times*, March 6, 1917.
2. *New York Herald*, July 17, 1917.
3. *New York Tribune*, September 18, 1917.
4. Harold Seymour. *Baseball: The Golden Age* (New York, Oxford University Press, 1971), p. 361.
5. *New York Evening Telegram*, September 19, 1917.
6. Ibid.
7. *New York Herald*, September 19, 1917.
8. *New York Evening Mail*, September 20, 1917.
9. *New York Tribune*, September 18, 1917.

ELEVEN

1. *Easton Star-Democrat*, September 7, 1918.
2. *New York Times*, March 5, 1919.
3. Ibid., March 16, 1919.
4. Ibid., June 22, 1919.
5. Ibid., July 8, 1919.
6. Ibid., September 9, 1919.

TWELVE

1. *Baseball Digest*, February 1945.
2. *New York Times*, January 7, 1920.
3. *Boston Post* quoted in the *New York Times*, January 7, 1920.
4. *Boston Herald* quoted in the *New York Times*, January 7, 1920.
5. *Easton Star-Democrat*, February 21, 1920.
6. Ibid.
7. *New York Times*, February 22, 1920.
8. Ibid., March 31, 1920.
9. Ibid., April 1, 1920.
10. *Chester Times*, May 4, 1920.
11. *New York Times*, May 27, 1920.
12. *Chester Times*, July 15, 1920.
13. *New York Evening Telegram*, February 21, 1921.

THIRTEEN

1. *New York Times*, February 28, 1921.
2. *Sporting News* quoted in the *Shreveport Journal*, March 12, 1921.
3. *New York Times*, May 23, 1921.
4. *Baseball* magazine, November 1921.
5. *New York Tribune*, October 2, 1921.
6. Ibid.
7. *New York Times*, October 5, 1921.
8. Ibid.
9. Ibid.
10. Ibid., October 7, 1921.
11. *New York Tribune*, October 9, 1921.
12. *New York Times*, October 10, 1921.
13. *New York Tribune*, October 11, 1921.
14. *New York Times*, October 11, 1921.
15. Ibid., October 12, 1921.
16. Ibid., October 13, 1921.
17. *New York Tribune*, October 13, 1921.
18. Ibid., October 14, 1921.
19. *New York Times*, October 14, 1921.
20. *New York Tribune*, October 14, 1921.
21. *New York Times*, October 14, 1921.
22. *New York Tribune*, October 14, 1921.

FOURTEEN

1. *New York Times*, February 14, 1922.
2. Ibid., April 6, 1922.
3. *New York Tribune*, June 18, 1922.
4. *New York Times*, June 24, 1922.
5. Ibid.
6. *Boston Herald* quoted in the *New York Times*, July 25, 1922.

7. *New York Tribune*, October 3, 1922.
8. *New York Times*, October 8, 1922.
9. Ibid.
10. *Washington Post*, October 9, 1922.

FIFTEEN

1. *Easton Star Democrat*, February 3, 1923.
2. Ibid., April 26, 1923.
3. Ibid.
4. *The Sporting News*, February 9, 1955.
5. Mark Millikin. *Jimmie Foxx: The Pride of Sudlersville* (Lanham, MD: Scarecrow Press, 1998), p. 23.
6. *Easton Star Democrat*, May 24, 1924.
7. Millikin, *Jimmie Foxx: The Pride of Sudlersville*, p. 27.
8. Ibid.
9. *The Sporting News*, February 9, 1955.
10. Ibid.
11. *Easton Star Democrat*, December 20, 1924.
12. Ibid., April 4, 1925.
13. Ibid., March 25, 1955.
14. Ibid., July 11, 1925.

SIXTEEN

1. Dickson Preston. *Trappe: The Story of an Old-Fashioned Town* (Easton, MD: Economy Press, 1976), p. 103.
2. Dickson Preston. "Eastern Shore Life Before the Bay Bridge," *Tidewater Times*, June 1979.
3. *Cambridge Daily Banner*, February 1, 1955.
4. *Baseball Digest*, December 1958.
5. Unidentified newspaper clipping from the Norman Macht collection.
6. *Reading Eagle*, June 13, 1955.
7. *Cambridge Daily Banner*, December 23, 1954.
8. Ibid., January 31, 1955.
9. *Easton Star Democrat*, January 31, 1955.
10. Fred Lieb. *Baseball As I Have Known It* (New York: Coward, McCann & Geoghegan, 1977), p. 85.
11. Unidentified newspaper clipping from the Norman Macht collection.
12. *Cambridge Daily Banner*, June 21, 1962.
13. *Easton Star Democrat*, July 2, 1963.
14. *Baltimore News-Post*, July 1, 1963.

Bibliography

Books

Alexander, Charles. *John McGraw*. New York: Viking, 1988.
_____. *Ty Cobb*. New York: Oxford University Press, 1984.
Allen, Lee. *The World Series*. New York: Putnam, 1969.
Anderson, David. *More Than Merkle*. Lincoln: University of Nebraska Press, 2000.
Appel, Martin, and Burt Goldblatt. *Baseball's Best*. New York: McGraw-Hill, 1977.
Astor, Gerald. *Baseball's Hall of Fame 50th Anniversary Book*. New York: Prentice Hall, 1988.
Burk, Robert. *Never Just a Game*. Chapel Hill, NC: University of North Carolina Press, 1994.
Caruso, Gary. *The Braves Encyclopedia*. Philadelphia: Temple University Press, 1995.
Cobb, Ty, with Al Stump. *My Life in Baseball*, Lincoln: University of Nebraska Press, 1993.
Cohen, Jonathan, and Arleen Keylin (editors). *The New York Times Sports Hall of Fame*. New York: Arno Press, 1981.
Cohen, Richard, Roland Johnson, and David Neft. *World Series*, New York, The Dial Press, 1976.
Creamer, Robert W. *Babe: The Legend Comes to Life*. New York: Simon & Schuster, 1974.
Curran, William. *Big Sticks*. New York: HarperPerennial, 1991.
_____. *Mitts*. New York: Morrow, 1985.
_____. *Strikeout: A Celebration of the Art of Pitching*. New York: Crown, 1995.
Danzig, Allison, and Reichler, Joe. *The History of Baseball*. Englewood Cliffs, NJ: Prentice Hall, 1969.
David, Jay. *The New York Yankees*. New York: Morrow, 1997.
Davids, L. Robert (editor). *Insider's Baseball*. New York: Scribner, 1983.
DeValeria, Dennis, and Jeanne DeValeria. *Honus Wagner: A Biography*. New York: Henry Holt, 1995.
Durant, John. *The Story of Baseball*. New York: Hastings House, 1973.
Durso, Joseph. *The Days of Mr. McGraw*. Englewood Cliffs, N.J.: Prentice Hall, 1969.
Fimrite, Ron. *The World Series: A History of Baseball's Fall Classic*. New York: Bishop Books, 1997.

Fleitz, David. *Shoeless: The Life and Times of Joe Jackson*. Jefferson, NC: McFarland, 2001.

Gallagher, Mark. *The Yankees Encyclopedia*, Vol. 3. Champaign, IL: Sagamore, 1997.

Gipe, George. *The Great American Sports Book*. Garden City, NY: Doubleday, 1978.

Gorman, Bob. *Double X*. Camden, NJ: Holy Name Society, 1990.

Graham, Frank. *The New York Yankees: An Informal History*. New York: Putnam, 1943.

Harwell, Ernie. *The Babe Signed My Shoe*. Dallas, TX: Diamond Communications, 1993.

Honig, Donald. *The New York Yankees: An Illustrated History*. New York: Crown, 1981.

_____, and Lawrence Ritter. *The 100 Greatest Baseball Players of All Time*. New York: Crown, 1981.

James, Bill. *The Bill James Guide to Baseball Managers from 1870 to Today*. New York: Scribner, 1997.

_____. *Whatever Happened to the Hall of Fame?* New York: Simon & Schuster, 1997.

Jordan, David. *The Athletics of Philadelphia*. Jefferson, NC: McFarland, 1999.

Kaese, Harold. *The Boston Braves, 1871–1953*. Boston: Northeastern University Press, 2004.

Kavanagh, Jack. *Walter Johnson: A Life*. South Bend, IN: Diamond Communications, 1995.

Kohout, Martin. *Hal Chase: The Defiant Life and Turbulent Times of Baseball's Biggest Crook*. Jefferson, NC: McFarland, 2001.

Koppett, Leonard. *Koppett's Concise History of Major League Baseball*. New York: Carroll & Graf, 2004.

_____. *The Man in the Dugout*. New York: Crown, 1993.

Kuklick, Bruce. *To Every Thing a Season: Shibe Park and Urban Philadelphia, 1909–1970*. Princeton, NJ: Princeton University Press, 1991.

Lane, F.C. *Batting*. Lincoln: University of Nebraska Press, 2001.

Lieb, Fred. *Baseball As I Have Known It*. New York: Coward, McCann and Geoghegan, 1977.

_____. *Connie Mack*. New York: Putnam, 1945.

Longert, Scott. *Addie Joss: King of the Pitchers*. Cleveland: Society for American Baseball Research, 1998.

Mack, Connie. *My 66 Years in the Big Leagues*. New York: John C. Winston, 1950.

Mansch, Larry. *Rube Marquard: The Life and Times of a Baseball Hall of Famer*. Jefferson NC: McFarland, 1998.

McCarty, John, Jr. *Baseball's All-Time Dream Team*. Cincinnati: Betterway, 1994.

Michener, James. *Chesapeake*. New York: Random House, 1978.

Millikin, Mark. *Jimmie Foxx: The Pride of Sudlersville*. Lanham, MD: Scarecrow, 1998.

Mowbray, William. *The Eastern Shore Baseball League*. Centreville, MD: Tidewater, 1989.

Neyer, Rob, and Eddie Epstein. *Baseball Dynasties*. New York: Norton, 2000.

Pepe, Phil. *The Yankees: An Authorized History of the New York Yankees*. Dallas, TX: Taylor, 1995.

Pietrusza, David, Matthew Silverman, and Michael Gershman (editors). *Baseball: The Biographical Encyclopedia*. New York: Total Sports Illustrated, 2000.

Preston, Dickson. *Talbot County: A History*. Centreville, MD: Tidewater, 1983.

_____. *Trappe: The Story of an Old-Fashioned Town*. Easton, MD: Economy, 1976.

Rader, Benjamin. *Baseball: A History of America's Game*. Chicago: University of Illinois Press, 1992.

Ritter, Lawrence. *The Glory of Their Times: The Early Days of Baseball Told by the Men Who Played It*. New York: Macmillan, 1966.

_____. *Lost Ballparks.* New York: Penguin, 1994.

Robinson, Ray. *Matty: An American Hero.* New York: Oxford University Press, 1993.

_____, and Christopher Jennison. *Pennants & Pinstripes: The New York Yankees, 1903–2002.* New York: Viking Studio, 2002.

Romanowski, Jerome. *The Mackmen.* Camden, NJ: Graphic, 1979.

Robinson, George, and Charles Salzberg. *On a Clear Day They Could See Seventh Place: Baseball's Worst Teams.* New York: Dell, 1991.

Seymour, Harold. *Baseball: The Golden Age.* New York: Oxford University Press, 1971.

Shaughnessy, Dan. *Curse of the Bambino.* New York: Penguin, 1991.

Smith, Robert. *Baseball's Hall of Fame.* New York: Bantam, 1973.

_____. *World Series.* Garden City, NY: Doubleday, 1967.

Solomon, Burt. *The Baseball Timeline.* New York: Avon, 1997.

Stump, Al. *Cobb: A Biography.* Chapel Hill, NC: Algonquin, 1996.

Sullivan, George, and John Powers. *The Yankees.* Philadelphia: Temple University Press, 1997.

Thomas, Henry. *Walter Johnson: Baseball's Big Train.* Washington, D.C.: Phenom Press, 1995.

Thorn, John, and Peter Palmer. *Total Baseball.* New York: HarperPerennial, 1993.

Townsend, Doris (editor). *This Great Game.* New York: Rutledge, 1971.

Voigt, David. *American Baseball,* Vol. 11. State College: Pennsylvania State University Press, 1983.

Westcott, Rich. *Philadelphia's Old Ballparks.* Philadelphia: Temple University Press, 1996.

White, Edward. *Creating the National Pastime: Baseball Transforms Itself, 1903–1953.* Princeton, NJ: Princeton University Press, 1996.

Zingg, Paul. *Harry Hooper: An American Baseball Life.* Urbana: University of Illinois Press, 1993.

Unpublished Manuscript

Payne, Marty. *On Forgotten Grounds: Independent Baseball on the Eastern Shore of Maryland, 1867–1921.*

Newspapers

Baltimore News-Post
Baltimore Sun
Boston Globe
Cambridge (MD) *Daily Banner*
Caroline (MD) *Record*
Charleston (SC) *Courier*
Chester (PA) *Times*
Chicago Tribune
Easton (MD) *Star-Democrat*
Lancaster (PA) *Intelligencer*
Macon (GA) *Telegraph*
New York Evening Mail
New York Evening Telegram
New York Herald

New York Sun
New York Times
New York Tribune
Philadelphia Evening Bulletin
Philadelphia Public Ledger
Reading (PA) *Eagle*
St. Louis Post-Dispatch
Salisbury (MD) *Times*
Savannah (GA) *Morning News*
Shreveport (LA) *Times*
Sporting Life
Sporting News
Washington Post

Articles

Anthony, Edward. "Home Run Baker and His Farmer Baseball League." *Farm and Fireside,* May 1924.

Baker, J. Franklin. "Home Run Baker's Own Story." *Baseball,* April 1915.

Crusinberry, James. "Secret Factors in the Winning of a World's Championship." *Baseball,* April 1914.

Grayson, Harry. "Home Run Baker Could also Run, Field — and Fight." *Baseball Digest,* February 1945.

Johnson, Ban. "The Inside of the Collins Deal." *Baseball,* March 1915.

Kofoed, J.C. "The World Series from the Bench." *Baseball,* December 1914.

_____. "The Greatest Infield in the History of Baseball." *Baseball,* July 1913.

Lane, F.C. "Who is the Greatest Third Baseman and Why?" *Baseball,* August 1913.

_____. "Sidelights on the Famous Baker Case." *Baseball,* May 1916.

Leib, Frederic. "Frank Baker: The Home-run Slugger of the World's Series." *Baseball,* December 1911.

Mathewson, Christy. "Why We Lost Three World's Championships." *Everybody's Magazine,* October 1914.

Payne, Marty. "Frank 'Home Run' Baker." *Baseball Research Journal,* 2000.

Phelon, William. "How the World Series Was Lost and Won." *Baseball,* December 1911.

_____. "Why the Braves Won and the Athletics Lost the Championship of the World." *Baseball,* December 1914.

Steadman, John. "They Called Him Home Run Baker." *Baseball Digest,* December 1958.

Yeutter, Frank. "Baker Homered with 52-Ouncer." *Baseball Digest,* May 1955.

"'Home Run' Baker's Rise." *The Literary Digest,* April 6, 1912.

Index